You Can Thrive After Narcissistic Abuse

The #1 System For Recovering From Toxic Relationships

Melanie Tonia Evans

16pt

Copyright Page from the Original Book

This edition first published in the UK and USA 2018 by
Watkins, an imprint of Watkins Media Limited

Unit 11, Shepperton House
89–93 Shepperton Road
London
N1 3DF
enquiries@watkinspublishing.com

Design and typography copyright © Watkins Media Limited 2018

Text copyright © Melanie Tonia Evans 2018

1 3 5 7 9 10 8 6 4 2

Typeset by JCS Publishing Services Ltd

Printed and bound in the United Kingdom

A CIP record for this book is available from the British Library

www.watkinspublishing.com

The author and publisher are grateful to the following for permission to include
copyright material: Coleman Barks and HarperCollins for permission to use
lines from *The Essential Rumi* (New Expanded Edition), HarperCollins, 2004,
edited and translated by Coleman Barks.

Note/Disclaimer: The material in this book is set out in good faith for general
guidance and no liability can be accepted for loss or expense incurred in
following the information given. In particular this book is not intended to
replace expert medical or psychiatric advice. It is intended for informational
purposes only and for your own personal use and guidance. It is not intended to
diagnose, treat or act as a substitute for professional medical advice. The author
is not a medical practitioner nor a counsellor, and professional advice should be
sought if desired before embarking on any health-related programme.

TABLE OF CONTENTS

'In *You Can Thrive After Narcissistic Abuse,* Melanie Tonia Evans offers a healing and transformative pathway for the people who need it most. Suffused with her personal experience, deep wisdom, and powerful insights, Evans' writing provides all the tools you need to validate the effects of narcissistic abuse, and ultimately to release and heal the pain and claim a new life, not merely as a survivor, but as a thriver. Narcissistic personality disorder is a far more common problem than most people realize, and whether your romantic partner, parent, or child has this disorder, you would be well served to use Melanie's book as a map to help you navigate your journey toward liberation and personal empowerment.' **Arielle Ford, bestselling author, *The Soulmate Secret: Manifest the Love Of Your Life with the Law of Attraction***

'*You Can Thrive After Narcissistic Abuse* isn't just for women in recovery – it should be required reading for every woman who wants to have thriving relationships. In fact, in coaching and mentoring tens of thousands of women I haven't met one who isn't vulnerable to narcissistic abuse. Without the knowledge that Melanie brilliantly shares, our tendency towards empathy, forgiveness and unconditional love can make us a target for relationships with people who drain our power and leave us feeling empty and depleted. Learn to recognize the patterns, how to respond and when and how to disengage and heal. Melanie's book can save you years, if not decades of your life. She is the expert I most deeply trust, respect and refer all the women in my community to for support on this topic.' **Claire Zammit, PhD, founder,** Feminine Power.com

Melanie Tonia Evans is an internationally acclaimed narcissistic abuse recovery expert and the founder of Quanta Freedom Healing and the Narcissistic Abuse Recovery Program. Her leading-edge healing methods have helped thousands of people from over eighty countries make astounding full recoveries from narcissistic abuse. Her passion is bringing the Thriver Model to the world, a Model that saved her own life and granted her the life of her dreams, despite being told she would never recover from her symptoms of abuse.

Melanie's Narcissistic Abuse Recovery Program contains her pioneering super-tool, Quanta Freedom Healing, which enables people to heal from trauma in timeframes and ways they have never previously experienced – even when every other healing method has failed. Her work is revolutionising the old model of survivor recovery into one of Thriver status, whereby people become more confident, happy and successful after the Program than they ever were before it. The Thriver Model has gained attention and recognition worldwide, with psychologists, counsellors, domestic violence workers and relationship experts globally referring their clients to Melanie's Model as the way to heal for real from narcissistic abuse.

For more information, visit Melanie's website: www.m elanietoniaevans.com

By the same author

Breaking the Chains of Painful Love

Take Back Your Power

FOREWORD

Several years ago, a colleague called me with the shocking news that she and her handsome, successful husband – a pillar of the community – were divorcing after thirty years of marriage. She had found out that he was having an affair. But that was just the beginning. As the scales began to fall from her eyes, she discovered that her marriage and their relationship had all been an illusion. An illusion she had fed and watered with every bit of her energy for decades. He was never the man she had thought he was. The man whose attention she craved but could never quite attract. She always blamed her own shortcomings for this. No. He was far worse. Not only had he sexually abused their daughter, she also discovered that he was, in essence, living a double life: on the surface he was a dutiful father and spouse – respected by his entire community and extended family – but underneath, the story was far different. As is so often the case, no one believed her side of the story. But that didn't matter. She got out.

Because I had had so much experience with narcissistic personality disorder by this time, I was able to assist her in not only identifying what she was dealing with ... but more importantly, was able to steer her in the direction necessary to not just get out – but to thrive.

My colleague's healing, and that of thousands of others, has been greatly speeded up through the incredibly effective work of Melanie Tonia Evans which I discovered several years ago. I have another friend who, during her divorce, went through Melanie's Narcissistic Abuse Recovery Program. She would call me every day with her insights, her emotional breakdowns to breakthroughs, and her progress. She too is now Thriving on every level. And all of us listen to Melanie's *Thriver TV* regularly – to keep us from falling back into old empathic (but ineffective) patterns.

Our Thrivership is in sharp contrast to what goes on for most people who are in relationships with clever narcissists – master manipulators who often pull the wool over the eyes of so many – including the therapists to whom their victims go for help. Our culture has only just begun to understand that personality disorders, most of which include narcissism, are an enormous public health problem – an epidemic really – that has gone unrecognized for centuries. Only recently has the mental health profession even acknowledged the fact that conventional talk therapy doesn't do anything to help narcissists. Neither does 'anger management'. In fact, conventional therapy makes them worse. Why? Because they take what they learn in 'therapy' and turn it on their longsuffering partners or family members. Narcissists run for the victim position. And no matter what is going on, they play the victim role with a skill level worthy of an Academy Award. Their victims, meanwhile, do everything in their power to help the narcissist, not understanding that these energy vampires do not think and act like those of us with normal empathy. They don't have any. For many, that is simply hard to believe. We've grown up with the mistaken belief that our love and energy can heal anything and anyone. And in most areas of our lives, there is truth in this. But when it comes to a narcissist, that belief is downright dangerous.

Sandra Brown, author of *Women who Love Pyschopaths,* says that 'it seems like the world is strangely tilted in their favour.' Another colleague of mine – a clinical psychologist with thirty-five years of experience counselling men who have been sexually abused by priests – told me that these individuals are chameleons who can charm the pants off you. He said, 'Even after thirty-five years in this field, I realize that I can still be conned by a narcissist if he or she is charming and good looking enough.' Sobering, isn't it?

I wrote *Dodging Energy Vampires* because, after thirty-five years on the frontlines of women's health, I came to see that the vast majority of women who had so-called autoimmune or mystery illnesses like chronic fatique, adrenal exhaustion, fibromyalgia, rheumatoid arthritis, Hashimoto's thyroiditis, or lupus were living with an energy vampire. These individuals get well only when they finally see what they're dealing with and get out. As an expert on holistic women's health, I was compelled to sound the alarm on this phenomenon to help people remove themselves from this kind of toxicity before their health and their lives were ruined. And of course, like Melanie, I've also had my own personal experience with these characters. I know what it takes to turn this around. And I strongly believe that we are finally at a time in history when our culture is starting to wake up to the damage caused by narcissists. There is no question that the post-Harvey Weinstein #metoo movement has helped. It's a step in a long journey.

Melanie Tonia Evans knows the personal hell of narcissistic abuse up close and personal. More importantly, she has discovered a pathway out of this purgatory – and that is the Quanta Freedom Healing method which is outlined in this book. Having taken her online course, I can attest to the power of her approach. It is not enough to understand narcissism intellectually – though that is a first step. Eventually each of us must address the wounds deep within us – that make us a target for narcissists. We must heal emotionally and spiritually – at the deepest levels. We must turn inwards. We must give up on the narcissist and finally embrace the only life we can save – our own. In these pages you will find out exactly how to do this. You too can become a Thriver who is no longer afraid, sick, or downtrodden. Thank you Melanie for doing this work on yourself and for all of us.

Christiane Northrup, MD
5 May 2018

Author of *Dodging Energy Vampires:
An Empath's Guide to Evading Relationships That
Drain You and Restoring Your Health and Power*

PREFACE

My default setting has always been to let my life be guided and inspired by love, kindness, compassion and empathy. Seeing the light in everyone and everything and being sensitive to the needs of others is the path to heaven I recommend to my readers. I couldn't write my spiritual books if I stopped believing that spiritual approach to be true. But a few years ago my belief in heaven and the power of love to explain and conquer all was shaken to its core.

In 2014 someone jumped into my life with a powerful endorsement from a trusted source. I had no reason to doubt them but over the next two years I glimpsed hell on earth. The story is a long one and a book in itself so I won't share it here. Suffice to say I experienced the pain, confusion, emptiness and heartbreak that Melanie so movingly describes in this incredible book. I'd never encountered someone before who flattered with such intensity, believed in their own magnificence so completely and who brought such a promise of magic into my life ... but who also deceived with such relish, played with the truth so I didn't know what was real anymore, took greedily without any thought of giving back and whose promises meant absolutely nothing.

Despite the harrowing intensity of the confusion and pain and the obvious red flags, instead of valuing myself enough to walk away I went into denial. I found myself inexplicably trying to do all I could to help, support or impress them so the golden period of adoration, so harshly replaced with silent treatments, could return. I believed that by showering them with love, self-sacrifice and kindness they would change or see my worth again, but the more I gave of myself the worse things got. It was pitiful. I lost myself and I can honestly say that if I hadn't stumbled across one of Melanie's videos I may not be writing this Preface today. I certainly wouldn't be living the joyful, loving and fulfilling life I live now.

Being a spiritual author people often write to me asking for advice about why bad things happen or they want my spiritual guidance for dealing with the loss of a loved one or a crisis of belief in themselves. I care deeply about my readers and love nothing more than to teach, share my knowledge and see others grow in spirit, but during that dark period in my life I suddenly found myself for the first time simply unable to offer that guidance with any conviction. The reason was I needed help and spiritual understanding myself.

The situation was so agonizing and my heart cut into so many pieces I didn't know where to turn. I've always been self-reliant and asking anyone, even family and friends, for help when I need it doesn't come naturally to me. Fortunately, in the past when I've encountered tough times my spiritual beliefs and the energy of the love and joy I had in my heart has pulled me through and given me the strength and hope I need, but this time was dramatically different. My heart was dry. My spirit depleted. I urgently needed help so I did what I always do – I prayed for it. Heaven (with a little help from Google search) answered through the YouTube videos of Melanie Tonia Evans. Instantly I was mesmerised by her message. It resonated powerfully with me. I signed up to her NARP Program and my healing adventure began.

Four years on, thanks to Melanie, I'm at the end of the narcissistic tunnel and have reached the point when I'm actually grateful for the experience because it showed me that I was seriously lacking in the self-love department. Melanie helped me understand something I instinctively knew but clearly needed reminding of and that was that the understanding, validation, adoration and excitement I was seeking outside myself were all things I needed to discover from the inside out. I also have reached a stage when I truly don't want revenge because I know that for a narcissist – to quote Milton, 'which way I fly, myself am hell' – the law of karma will deal with them. Thanks to Melanie's spiritual wisdom I can let go and simply send them love and hope they find their peace.

Of course, I'm saying all this with the benefit of hindsight because at the time understanding, hope and any kind of loving resolution seemed impossible. That's why I'm utterly delighted to write this Preface because I know the healing, understanding, comfort, support, love and joyful hope it will bring to every person who reads it. Whether or not you have suffered from narcissistic abuse this book should be required reading for everyone as, sadly, narcissistic personality disorder is on the increase and, as Melanie explains, sensitive, empathetic people are the narcissist's drug of choice. If you haven't encountered a narcissist yet, chances are you will. The information here will help you spot the warning signs earlier and avoid a world of pain, heartache and confusion.

I don't believe in hell but being in a relationship with or getting tangled up with a narcissistic person feels very close to it. Fortunately, there is an earth angel in the form of Melanie Tonia Evans to show us that not only can life after narcissistic abuse be more rewarding than life before it, but that heaven on earth really does exist. The first place to look for this understanding and healing is within. That's an extremely difficult thing to do though, all by yourself, but you aren't alone with your suffering and confusion anymore. Melanie and her team are here to heal, guide and support you every step of the way.

You've done something incredibly empowering, loving and healing for yourself by reading this book. It could be the most valuable purchase you ever make. I'm so excited for you as you've now taken the first step towards escaping the black hole of narcissistic abuse. Along with Melanie's online Thriver community this life-changing book truly is your light in the darkness. It is a course in self-healing miracles, a return to love. It is your answer from heaven.

Theresa Cheung
10 May 2018
Sunday Times bestselling author of *Answers from Heaven* and *21 Rituals to Change Your Life*
www.theresacheung.com

INTRODUCTION

This book is for all of us. Most of us have either suffered some form of narcissistic abuse or know somebody very close to us who has. Yet until you have been narcissistically abused yourself, you cannot begin to appreciate what a silent epidemic this is, nor how the effects of narcissistic abuse can leave you reeling in a deeper state of despair than anything you have previous experienced, shocked that you just don't seem to be getting better.

Right from the onset I want you to know that if you have suffered from a traumatic relationship with anyone such as a parent, spouse, lover, friend, boss, co-worker, business partner – anyone at all, even your own child – this book is completely relevant to your situation, regardless of whether you are trapped in an abusive dynamic right now or still struggling to heal from what happened decades ago. You also don't need to know whether or not someone is a true narcissist to benefit from the powerful healing techniques offered in this book. The only criteria necessary for you to be here is that you have had enough of painful and disappointing relationships.

This book – although primarily about recovering from narcissistic abuse – is really about much more than this. It is about helping you explore and understand the dynamics of narcissism, and most importantly it teaches you how to make a full recovery from its insidious effects. *You Can Thrive After Narcissistic Abuse* is essentially about each of us forming part of a healed global whole; and it is about reclaiming ourselves – despite abuse and abusers. To do this requires diving deep into our selves beyond the workings of our rational thought processes, in order to reverse symptoms that we once thought untreatable. It's then that we begin to heal the unthinkable and let go of trauma that once seemed insurmountable, in order to create more rewarding lives than we have ever known – including before abuse.

If you are already familiar with, and have an interest in, areas such as quantum physics, spirituality and expanding consciousness, then this book is tailor made for you! It is one in which science and spirit converge. It explores cutting-edge, revolutionary ways to get well, regardless of how your life has been to date. If you haven't yet considered these sorts of subjects and are inclined to think 'I'll believe it when I see it!', I would ask you to keep an open mind and heart, because I promise you there will be enough information in this book to grant you serious food for thought as to how and why we can heal trauma in ways we have never done before.

Like all my work, this book is non-denominational and unconditional: it caters to people from all religions and from no religion at all. It acknowledges that no matter where we are from or what our beliefs are – political, religious, spiritual, economic or sexual – we are all in this together. If you have any particular religious beliefs, you may experience one or two challenges with my healing methods; that said, there are many Christians in the Thriver Community who use my healing system successfully and happily, and who believe it is consistent with much of their faith. Likewise, if you are an atheist you may experience some resistance too, but there are many others like you who have also healed the seemingly unhealable as a result of simply accepting and applying my system!

My healing system doesn't just include tapping in to a Higher Power; it actually doesn't work without doing so. Yet I'm absolutely not attempting to force you down any particular spiritual path, because the concept of a Higher Power can be defined as anything of your choosing; it literally could just be 'Life' itself. To keep things simple and standardised in this book, I refer to this Higher Power by names such as Life Force, Source and Creation, which I believe are all fundamentally the same thing.

I am aware there are many members of our community who sadly due to religious abuse (or other reasons) have an aversion to the term 'God' – and I respect that. Yet, for those of us who are comfortable with this, God is absolutely the context of Life Force, Source and Creation in the sense in which I will be using those words. If you have no belief in God, you may simply wish to acknowledge an 'Energy' instead.

The healing and transformation occur regardless of what we call it.

In this book I also mention past lives. The truth is that I thoroughly believe in them, and that whatever issues we have chosen to heal will keep on reappearing for us during our lifetimes until we tackle them. During my earlier work as a past-life regression therapist, I frequently received startling evidence from people who recalled historic events of which they had no previous conscious knowledge at all. This included names and dates and events that could be checked out in historical records, including birth certificates. I had this experience many times myself during my own regressions. I believe that the origins of many of our traumas and abuse patterns usually have their roots in particularly brutal times of history and are then carried over from lifetime to lifetime. This is why we need to expand our awareness and endeavour to see the bigger picture if we are to tackle the trauma of abuse at its core, which, if not cleaned up, can never truly heal.

The same applies to the epigenetic trauma that is passed on from generation to generation through molecular memory and the expression of our genes, until someone releases and heals it from within their own DNA, thereby breaking the cycle for themselves and for future generations. There is now a growing belief that trauma can be passed on epigenetically from our ancestors – that is, through our very genes.

At this stage, science has yet to prove the existence of past lives (even though there have been highly credible books written about them, including the classic work *Many Lives, Many Masters* by Brian Weiss); and please understand that it is not at all necessary for you to believe in past lives for my healing system to work: the programme will clean up the trauma from your past, no matter what that is, regardless of your beliefs. However, as we will see, the field of epigenetics is now gathering incredible momentum in terms of the scientific evidence that supports it, which I will be referencing in this book.

This book is about healing from the narcissistic abuse that results from any type of relationship with someone who has Narcissistic Personality Disorder (NPD). All sorts of other labels are sometimes applied to these individuals, such as 'psychopath' or 'sociopath'. Similarly, 'narcissist' has become such a buzz word that many people throw it around and attribute it to those who are perhaps unthoughtful and even selfish, yet who are certainty not narcissists.

The truth is that we can all be a little (or quite!) narcissistic at times – especially when we feel insecure, hurt and emotionally triggered. It's then that we may lash out, react without thinking and possibly say or do things that we aren't very proud of later. However, there is a huge difference between 'occasional narcissism' and 'malignant narcissism', which is when a person not only acts thoughtlessly and in hurtful ways, but their very essence is that of a malicious, pathological liar. Malignant narcissists don't possess empathy and use other people as tools with which to get what they want, often at the expense of those same individuals. And they don't behave in this way only occasionally, or experience deep remorse and regret afterwards (in the way that people with a conscience would); rather, narcissists *always* operate like this, with *no* remorse or regret. They can act as though they do possess these empathic human qualities if and when it suits their agenda, but in truth they don't.

Sadly, so many of us have allowed these sorts of harmful individuals into our lives, only to find ourselves shredded to pieces by them. Given that you are reading these pages, this is likely to include you too. That's why I have written this book: to help you reclaim those lost pieces of yourself and to heal for real in ways that you never dreamed possible, until now.

In Part One of this book, we will be exploring the nature of narcissist abuse, what it is and the effect it has on us and our relationships. Part Two will set out the ten Steps that will help you to connect with your own inner trauma and to heal from it, one stage at a time. Part Three looks at the lessons that can be learned from narcissistic abuse and the way forward – both for ourselves and for future generations. Throughout, you will read the amazing true stories of people who have healed themselves from narcissistic abuse and turned their lives around in unprecedented and miraculous ways; however, in the interests of privacy, some names and identifying details have been changed.

Before we continue any further, I'd like to reassure you that I understand just how convoluted and complicated narcissistic abuse is, just as I know how important it is for you to have the best support and assistance possible. Recovery necessitates getting to the truth of the matter, regardless of whether this trauma has been with you for days, decades or your entire life.

That's why I want to make sure you are aware of the free course I've put together for you. As a result of teaching people for over ten years online how to recover and create abuse-free lives, I've learned that for someone to heal the devastating trauma of narcissistic abuse, they need a defined system – a step-by-step process to follow. I've also learned how important a support system is, so that when you get stuck, you can ask for guidance and receive advice from someone who knows exactly what you are going through. This is why I've put together a free online course and community to accompany this book. It's called the 'You Can Thrive Program'. You can register for free here: www.youcanthriveprogram.com.

Please note that I'll be directing you to the resources within the 'You Can Thrive Program' as I accompany you throughout this book. All you need to do to access them is go to the website mentioned above and register your details.

Okay, so if you've had enough of the pain, insanity and sense of helplessness that go with narcissistic abuse, it's time to get started. Let's do this thing! I can't wait to help you heal and Thrive...

All my love,

Melanie

Melanie

1

HOW IT ALL BEGAN

Writing this book is very dear to my heart. In fact, this book represents my life – how my life nearly ended and how it has now become. At first I didn't realise that my story was so many other people's story. Initially I just thought I was trying to survive an isolated cataclysmic event in my life that was beyond the horrors of what I had ever known possible. It was only later that I discovered how many people had shared experiences similar to mine, and how many of us were silently in this together, feeling trapped, powerless, filled with shame, pain and fear and not having a clue about what we were *really* dealing with.

Like so many others globally, I have suffered narcissistic abuse, which means being abused by an individual who suffers from Narcissistic Personality Disorder (NPD). Such a person is pathologically self-absorbed, over-entitled and caught up in feelings and behaviours that most of us have never experienced, triggered by things that normal adults just don't get upset about. Relationships with these people are devastating and confusing; they strip their victims of their self-worth, personal rights and resources.

Sadly, narcissistic abuse exists in epidemic proportions. But until you have stepped out of what we think of as the usual struggles in life and heartbreak (which are challenging enough) into the literal bowels of hell with a narcissist, you can't possibly understand the levels of unspeakable confusion and trauma that this sort of abuse generates. And please know I am not saying this as a victim who wants to sensationalise her own life; I am simply saying what I and so many other people have discovered, which is how it feels to be pillaged, soul-raped, demonised and discarded by the very people that we have given our hearts and trust to. It's an experience that fractures one's soul and spirit.

I am very grateful to have been given the opportunity to write this book because help is desperately needed for those who have been narcissistically abused. What has been so sad and traumatic is that, until now, not only have there been no effective healing and other methods available to reform narcissists (mainly because they simply do not think there's anything wrong with themselves), there have been very few real healing resources for their victims. All too often, those who have been violated by narcissists are left suffering from significant trauma and diminished trust in themselves and others, alongside ongoing nervous-system disorders such as post-traumatic stress disorder (PTSD) and agoraphobia, with their only hope being to attempt to manage these terrible conditions for life. Additionally, I see the insidious cycles of narcissistic abuse in families everywhere, where the trauma is passed on from generation to generation, setting up harmful patterns whereby the children of those who have been abused may become victims or even perpetrators themselves.

As a mother whose son suffered terribly from this form of abuse, and who almost lost his life in his struggle to heal, I know how vital it is for our healing systems to update adequately and change in ways that allow real healing to take place – with recovering adults leading the way. Healing from narcissistic abuse, helping others heal and passing on a healthy and whole way of being to our children has become a passion of mine. Even more than this, the mission to 'heal for real' has become my *dharma* – my life/love mission – which now lies at the core of the work I do.

This is how it all started: at thirty-five years of age I met someone who I believed was the perfect man for me. He was caring, attentive and attractive. And he was so supportive and spiritual. I fell in love – quickly, easily and completely, experiencing a 'soul-mate' connection that blew me away. So much so, I remember telling him one day, 'I'm so in love, I can't even see straight.' This was uncharacteristic for me; and what also surprised everyone I knew, was that within six weeks of meeting him I was engaged, and four months later I was having my dream wedding.

Everything seemed perfect, yet at times the hairs on the back of my neck would stand up. It would be caused by a comment or a look from him that just didn't feel right. Before long he was monopolising my time, wanting me all to himself. Even though this felt a little controlling, I took it as an expression of how much he loved me.

Then I discovered that his cancer condition – a melanoma for which he told me he'd had chemotherapy in the past and which was in remission – had become fully blown again. I was devastated for us both, but I loved this man so much I was fully committed to standing by his side and doing all I could to help him beat the disease. What I soon discovered was his jealous behaviour had become fully blown as well. Behaviour that previously felt uncomfortable escalated into unreasonable demands for me not to speak to or look at any other men, not being allowed to do my consulting work with male clients and his questioning my every move, or bursting into a rage if I was late home because I was so much as held up in a grocery line.

I put his behaviour down to what he was experiencing with his cancer, yet no matter how much I tried to love and support him, and to reassure him that I wasn't going anywhere, his jealousy intensified and became complete paranoia. I soon found I was recoiling from any man, and that I would look at the floor if I was with him anywhere in public, terrified that some other guy might look my way.

Months later, when I discovered that the entire so-called cancer was nothing more than a hoax ingeniously created by him to glean sympathy and attention, he was remorseful for only one day. Then, without cancer to hide behind, the control and abuse became worse. I didn't know it at that time, but he was punishing me for exposing him.

Other things started to come to light. Much of his past was a forgery; his self-proclaimed financial success bore no resemblance to the truth. I began to realise that his default position about anything was to lie. One lie would cover up the previous lie – and I started to lose my grip on what was real and what wasn't.

What made things even worse was that I had no idea initially just how hooked on and enmeshed to him I had become. By the time it was obvious that there was something terribly wrong, and that I was being significantly abused, smeared and isolated by him, I felt powerless to leave. All of our assets were combined and he was racking up debt. There were numerous impending court cases because of his deceitful business misconduct and crooked activities, and I was constantly trying to perform damage control to keep the roof above our heads.

Being in overdrive, trying to sort out the disasters and mess, kept me distracted from what was really happening to me: my soul and my ability to define my truth, rights or needs were being torn to shreds.

So much about him that was not in alignment with my vision of him as Prince Charming came to light, and my adoration turned into criticism and contempt. That's when the violence started, verbally, physically and sexually – yet still I didn't leave. There was so much at stake, including everything I had worked my whole life to achieve before meeting him. I thought that was why I wasn't letting go, but as I discovered later, it was as if I was psychically possessed by him. Every aspect of my thoughts and feelings had been taken over by him. I felt like I didn't know how to breathe without him. There was also the threat of what he could do. He told me he had destroyed people's lives before, piece by piece, and if I tried to leave him he was more than capable of doing that to me too.

There were times over the next four years when my terror of staying became greater than my fear of leaving – and I would try to escape. But then he would stalk me and terrorise me, dismantling any structures I tried to create and attacking the people in my life, forcing me to return to him in a bid to stop him ripping my life completely to pieces. Or he would turn up, totally remorseful, and declare that he would do anything to save our marriage. Again and again I'd capitulate and go back. In amongst it all, I stubbornly held dear to the notion that I could fix and change this man.

Clearly, that was never going to go well. The cycle of violence only intensified. We would get back together and he would profess he'd do anything to change; and I would again forgive the unforgiveable acts he had committed, such as stealing my work computers and forging cheques on my bank accounts (the list goes on and on). Then the tension would build, the situation would explode and somehow I'd get away again, often fearing that if I didn't leave I would die.

Finally, I moved out into a rental property, but I was still hooked; I couldn't stop thinking or obsessing about him. He was living in the home I had paid for, renovating it and claiming it as his own. In spite of my horror at his behaviour, we still 'dated' occasionally, which led to unspeakably traumatic evenings. Some of these were so bad I actually have no conscious memory of them.

After another one of his 'I will do anything to save this marriage' bouts, I persuaded him to see a personality disorder specialist with me, who diagnosed him as suffering from Narcissistic Personality Disorder (NPD). Soon afterwards, he stopped going to the sessions and the specialist continued working with me, trying to help me leave him. The girl whose appointments were just before mine was pregnant by a narcissist, and told me his last three girlfriends had all committed suicide. I started to get a sense of how serious my situation was, especially when I was told by the specialist in no uncertain terms: 'These are your four options if you stay with him. Either he will kill you, you'll kill yourself, you'll have a psychotic breakdown or contract a horrible, possibly even terminal disease as a result of the stress.'

I asked her what happens when you have a psychotic breakdown. She told me about one of her clients who was taken away by a Crisis Assessment and Treatment Team (CATT) because she had thrown all her clothes out of the upper storey window of her apartment while shouting gibberish. This lady was still in institutionalised care some eighteen months later. 'It's a long way back from a breakdown,' my specialist said.

It was only a few weeks later that she told me how close she thought I was to having a breakdown myself. I weighed only 37 kilos (81 pounds), my hair was falling out in clumps and my PTSD was off the scale. I hadn't been able to eat or sleep properly for months, and I shook almost continuously. I was still meeting up with my husband like a drug addict, lying and making excuses about it because everyone was disgusted with me for still seeing him.

Not long after this, I was doing the catering for a workshop when a group of people arrived and started talking to me. I experienced the internal panic that had by now become my norm when engaging with people, especially men. The panic intensified and I realised that I was having a silent internal meltdown. There was nowhere to run, my exit was blocked by people. In the next moment, it was as if I was watching myself talking to people while looking down remotely from the ceiling. I knew something was horribly wrong, so I excused myself, walked to my car, and, in this relatively safe space, re-entered my body with a thud. But then the hallucinations continued in the form of horrific scenes of me smashing into a tree in my car – first of all in flickers, then as solid images that would not go away. Whether my eyes were closed or shut, it made no difference, and the feelings of dread and powerlessness that accompanied the experience were unspeakable. I knew this was it: my mind had finally snapped as I literally felt sanity dissolve away.

Somehow I drove home and called a girlfriend. I was rushed to an emergency medical centre, given a sedative and the images subsided. Tests revealed that I was suffering from an adrenal breakdown, where my body's adrenal glands could no longer cope with the amount of stress they were suffering. The accompanying psychotic breakdown was obvious. My options were explained: I was told I would probably need to take anti-psychotics for the rest of my life, as well as undergo close monitoring and possible institutionalisation depending on how I responded to the drugs. It could take up to three years' complete rest with ongoing psychiatry before I recovered and I would never again function as I had before the breakdown.

I felt like this was the end for me. I was no good with drugs; even paracetamol affected me badly. Additionally, I was forty years old and I had lost everything. I'd been wiped out financially; I'd lost credibility, family and friends; and now I was without the physical and mental health I needed to rebuild my life.

That night, while under suicide watch at home, I was lying on my bed contemplating how to kill myself, when a voice in my head said, 'No, there is another way.' I thought it was just part and parcel of my madness, and I argued with the voice, but it was persistent. In desperation, I got off the bed, walked into the bathroom and looked at the crazy, haunted, emaciated woman who stared back at me in the mirror. Then I crumpled on to the bathroom mat, tormented by the anguish of trying to live when I didn't believe there was any way to continue doing so.

In total despair, I raised my hands and, through a torrent of tears, screamed, 'Help me. I can't do this on my own!'

I felt everything collapse within me. I had let go of all that I had – my life, my being and even my soul. I had totally surrendered. Maybe it would have been impossible to let go at this level if there had been anything left of me to hang on to. But I felt like there wasn't; I even believed at this time that my son would be better off without me. I didn't surrender to be saved, I did it because there was nothing else to do.

Then it happened. The sensation was undeniable: it felt like my head had parted and a whole heap of stuff was being sucked out of it. Up until that moment I'd felt like a powerless victim. Now I didn't and within seconds I received a download that was so packed with clarity and illumination that there was no missing it. I had never known anything to be so real and true (at that point) in my entire life.

Instantly, I knew exactly why my ex had come into my life and what it had all been about. Then I had the incredible experience of being catapulted into the future. The vision was so real, it was not just like watching a movie; it was if I was there – feeling in every cell of my body what it was like to be happy, confident and free of any pain whatsoever. Then I snapped back into my body in present-time reality. That was enough to know this 'new me' was what lay in store for me.

Previously, I and everyone else I knew had made what had happened to me all about 'him' and 'narcissism'. Never before had I understood that it had anything to do with me personally. Yet now, as I was shown all the correlations and the deep soul-healing reasons as to why he'd had a role in the stage play of my life, I realised it was to help me heal the traumas I'd experienced before even meeting him. There was no shame and pain attached to this self-analysis. Rather, there was an incredible feeling of, 'Oh my God, I never realised – this is the key!'

Seconds later, I emerged from this 'divine download' and I was already changed. I had hope. I had received that vision and I had *felt* in every cell of my being how the new me, the new Melanie, would feel when she knew how to heal this trauma. I knew the new me of the future would be far superior to the one of the past, including the person I had been before I was narcissistically abused.

The next day a miracle happened: my doctor was blown away by my shift and agreed to release me from taking antipsychotics and psychiatry. From that day on, I never again contacted nor saw the ex-husband. I blocked all ways he could communicate with me. I still had a ton of trauma and nervous-system disorders to heal, but never again was I tempted to call him, because I now knew my healing had nothing to do with him. I had taken my power back – and it was gloriously all about healing myself.

As if someone had flicked a switch, the narcissist stopped trying to control, terrorise and hook me. All attacks ceased. And so I began an incredible eighteen-month divine assignment that I called 'how to heal abuse trauma for real'. I had been shown in my vision that the healing needed to take place deep within the subconscious mind, which resides not in the head but throughout the body. And to do that, the embedded trauma must be reached, released and replaced with another force that reverses the effects of that trauma. If I had not experienced the download as such a deeply felt truth, I would have thought this was crazy. But I never doubted it and followed my gut instinct; I researched and trained vigorously in several mind–body healing modalities such as Kinesiology, Theta Healing and Emotional Freedom Technique. The immediate relief I experienced when I started applying these tools was literally heaven sent. I could feel myself changing from the inside out. The shifts were felt and 'held' in my being, unlike the talk therapy I had tried for years, which had meant continually revisiting information in an attempt to get the healing to stick.

Even though I sometimes doubted that I could keep moving forward, my accumulated progress was startling, my adrenals and my mind had repaired in ways that were deemed medically impossible, and the rebuild of my external life was truly beginning to reflect the rebuild of my internal life. In less than twelve months, I had come such a long way.

By now I had become a fully fledged practitioner of mind–body healing modalities, and I was thrilled to see that the people I was treating for trauma were having wonderful breakthrough results as well. In many ways, despite losing so much and having to start my life from scratch, I was happier than I had ever been.

However, one of my conditions persisted: I had acute agoraphobia. So, even though I felt normal and even blissful in 'safe' spaces, I found going out into open areas – especially alone – terrifying. I would feel as if the very walls of my life were caving in and were about to swallow me up. I would barely get though the experience of being out in the open by repeating affirmations; then I would collapse inside my front door, sweating, shaking and crying, as soon as I got home. It was usually easier to ask someone else to go shopping for me.

I tried everything I could to heal this, contacting every advanced mind–body modality specialist I could find. I also made many attempts to cure my agoraphobia myself, because by now I had become proficient at performing healings on myself and professionally for others. But nothing stuck. Nevertheless, by this stage my research had reached a point whereby I knew it was possible to get better. If I could find the original wound that was causing my fear that 'I am not safe in life', and target it with the healing tools I had acquired, I knew I would go free. Like myself, lots of my clients had been improving in many areas of their lives through the healing work we were doing, yet occasionally a persistent condition would stay rooted in their subconscious.

One day, a friend invited me to meet her in Koh Samui, a beautiful tropical island in the southern gulf of Thailand. With agoraphobia, how on earth could I fly overseas on my own? But something told me I had to go, so go I did. After collapsing into my friend's arms at Koh Samui airport in a completely frazzled, traumatised heap, it took a few days for me to get back to normal while staying within the confines of the hotel perimeter. Then I wanted more – I wanted to go out and play in Koh Samui – but I knew that wasn't possible with agoraphobia.

A day or so later, while my friend was out shopping, I sat in the hotel room by myself and grabbed a pen and paper. I set the intention that I would find the answer to my problem. I opened my head and heart, and started to take dictation from something other than myself, which flowed through me. As I was writing down the healing protocols that came to me in that moment, I knew *this is the answer.* That afternoon, for two hours, I did the first ever Quanta Freedom Healing on myself and immediately afterwards walked out the front gates of the resort and into the busy streets of Koh Samui. No dread, no meltdowns; instead an overwhelming feeling of expansion, joy and loving connectedness with everything and everyone. Finally, I felt safe to engage with life and after several more sessions on myself the agoraphobia never returned.

I knew I had to share this unique healing method with others, so when I got back to Melbourne, I told my clients, 'We're not doing that anymore, we are doing this!' As for myself, the results of Quanta Freedom Healing were like jumping out of a family car into a Ferrari: people's healing accelerated beyond recognition, and persistent chronic conditions melted away – sometimes instantly.

Word of mouth exploded and before I knew it I had clients seven days a week, booked up for months ahead. Many of those clients were healing traumas caused by abuse; others, having recovered from abuse, returned to me to heal virtually any other health, financial or relationship issue that they wished to resolve. I soon discovered just how incredible and endless the applications for this new healing system were.

However, my real passion was healing people who, like myself, had been traumatised in abusive situations. This work was saving lives and enabling people to disengage from those who were hurting them, to heal their trauma and pull away and lose all interest in their abusers – even to stand up to them calmly and firmly in legal and custody battles, no longer terrorised or controlled by them. People were getting their lives back and narcissists were crumbling. These clients of mine were learning how to grow in confidence and know their own worth. Many quickly started to attract healthy relationships, and others even learned how to reverse a life of trauma when abuse was all they'd ever known. Children, even in co-parenting situations, were becoming empowered and healing, because now there was at least one healthy parent to lead the way.

When it became impossible for me to cater in a one-on-one capacity for all those who needed this healing, I created the Narcissistic Abuse Recovery Program, which contains the specific step-by-step Quanta Freedom Healings that enable sufferers to heal and recover from narcissistic abuse in unprecedented ways. And before I knew it, this revolutionary new healing system spread globally and is recommended today by a wide range of practitioners worldwide, including many in the medical profession.

It brings me unspeakable joy to know that the Thriver Mission has since touched the lives of over 10 million people in over 80 countries worldwide. There are now over 20,000 graduates of the Narcissistic Abuse Recovery Program who are presently Thriving in abuse-free lives.

I want you to know the following truth: there is a reason why you have found your way to this book. For you, just as it was for me, the information in *You Can Thrive After Narcissistic Abuse* will be more than just a tool to help you to cope; it will set you on a life-changing path, after which you will never be the same again, given the transformation that this journey entails.

The world I live in now is one of Thriving rather than just surviving, and I can tell you, from the bottom of my heart, it's been incredible to go from victim to survivor to Thriver. This book is an invitation to join me in my world, where you will no longer need to wait for those who have hurt or almost destroyed you to change their ways, or to be held accountable, or to have anyone else fix life for you. Instead, you will discover how to be in control of your own healing, your life and your future – regardless of whatever those people do or don't do.

To give you the greatest amount of support, and the transformational tools that make all this possible, please make sure you sign up for your 'You Can Thrive Program', which you can access for free here: www.youcanthriveprogram.com.

As you read this book and journey through the 'You Can Thrive Program', I am going to show you the step-by-step process to healing your relationship trauma and abuse patterns, just as I and thousands of other individuals in my community have done before you. And one thing I do know with absolute certainty: no matter how much you have lost, how old you are or how greatly you have suffered, you deserve to live the joyous, fulfilling life that you were born to enjoy.

It's my greatest heart-felt desire to show you how.

PART ONE

WHAT IS NARCISSISTIC ABUSE?

'Narcissus so himself forsook,
And died to kiss his shadow in the brook.'

William Shakespeare (1564–1616), 'Venus and Adonis'

When we consider our supposed civilised society and see the harm, deception and destruction that surround us, we know that something has gone dreadfully wrong with much of humanity. Despite spiritual and legal guidance regarding what is moral and right, we don't have to look far to realise that all too often scriptures and sanctions fall short and have little positive impact on our behaviour. I believe the true issue our world faces today is a dreadful unconsciousness in the form of a psychic disease, which causes people who are emotionally wounded to act out behaviours that are destructive to others. Moreover, this unconscious 'disease' – this compulsion to commandeer things and people outside one's self in order to 'be' a self – is narcissism and it exists in epidemic proportions. Excessive self-absorption has been recognised for centuries, and in the late 1800s the term 'narcissism' was derived from the Greek myth of the handsome hunter Narcissus, who fell in love with his own reflection. Today, I believe we live on a narcissistic planet.

*

Many people think that narcissism is the result of our over-entitled, selfie-taking culture, yet I believe it's the product of people not being able to form a solid and whole inner identity based on healthy self-love and self-acceptance. This might be due to the trauma of emotional neglect or abuse experienced while they were growing up, or the fact that they have only ever known conditional love. (Conditional love is based on the notion that you are only worth loving if your behaviour meets with the expectations of others.) Those who are suffering from the disease of narcissism often appear to be overconfident, yet underneath the brash façade – their mask – lies a seething pit of pain.

Many neuroscientists now believe that extreme trauma, such as that responsible for triggering narcissistic personality disorder, can be passed on from generation to generation epigenetically, and therefore influences the ways in which our genes are expressed. While not targeting narcissism, a study by New York's Mount Sinai Hospital in 2016 analysed the genes of thirty-two holocaust survivors and their children. A methylation tag (a common epigenetic signalling tool that causes cells to lock genes in the 'off' position) was found in a stress-related gene in parents and children alike, which caused them to have feelings of anxiety and hopelessness. Rachel Yehuda, who led the study, said, 'The gene changes in the children could only be attributed to Holocaust exposure in the parents.'[1] This is absolutely not to say that narcissism is linked to Holocaust survivors, but that, to my mind, this finding strongly supports the idea that suffering can be inherited within our very DNA.

In a related area, Michael Meaney, a professor and neurologist and neurosurgeon at McGill University, carried out experiments on rat pups that established a causation relationship between maternal care and behavioural epigenetic programming.[2] This research found that HLG (high licking and grooming) mothers create pups who are also HLG parents, whereas LLG (low licking and grooming) mothers create pups who have substantially higher levels of glucocorticoid receptor density, and are therefore much more frequently subject to flightiness and stress, as well as having different oestrogen receptor expression in the medial pre-optic area of the brain. Hence they experienced more difficulty in feeling 'good' or 'nurtured'. Meaney's early epigenetic research was instrumental in understanding behaviour in both animals and humans, and confirmed that stress and trauma can absolutely be passed on.

Despite the newfound science that supports the notion of generational trauma, the theory has ancient origins and is even touched upon in the Bible in Exodus 34:6-7: 'but who will by no means clear the guilty, visiting the iniquity of the fathers on the children and the children's children, to the third and the fourth generation', as well as expressed by those famous lines in Shakespeare's play *The Merchant of Venice:* 'The sins of the father are to be laid upon the children.'

These inherited wounds are then unconsciously projected onto others with devastating consequences. This can happen within romantic relationships, families and communities, even whole countries – and at the very highest echelons of society, with devastating consequences. According to psychoanalyst Michael

Stone, author of *The Anatomy of Evil,* Hitler was a world-stage psychopathic malignant narcissist, and he further suggests that Hitler's hatred for his father fuelled his hatred of Jews, who, after his father died when Adolf was only fourteen, served as scapegoats for his residual fury.

In the age in which we live, celebrities are granted more recognition than people finding cures for cancer. Psychologists even have a name for this phenomenon – Celebrity Worship Syndrome (CWS) – which causes people to lose their own identity while living vicariously through that belonging to a celebrity. In the United States and United Kingdom, psychologists have created a celebrity worship scale to rate the problems and in 2002 American psychologists Lynn McCutcheon, Rense Lange and James Houran introduced the Celebrity Attitude Scale. It stands to reason that narcissists are often celebrated, admired and encouraged in an age when physical beauty and material acquisitions appear to be revered above all else. Our culture of instant gratification and 'more, more, more' – as well as community values being overruled in favour of the individual – creates a fertile landscape that allows them to operate undetected.

So how do you know if you are in a narcissistic relationship? Join me as we discover in Part One what narcissism is, how to identify a narcissist and how we can find ourselves involved with them in all walks of life.

2

HOW DO I KNOW IF I AM IN A RELATIONSHIP WITH A NARCISSIST?

Virtually no one has any idea initially they are in a narcissistic relationship. You see, humanity has never been properly educated about it. Most of us tend to think that narcissists are merely self-absorbed people with over-inflated egos who are in love with themselves, but nothing could be further from the truth. It often isn't until we have suffered significant narcissistic abuse and have needed to find help and solutions to save ourselves, life and soul, that we realise there are people out there who are wired very differently to us. Many of us might never have imagined we'd come across individuals who don't feel remorse or guilt for their actions, and who will do whatever it takes to gratify the demands of their egos by securing money, attention, contacts, sex, attention and possessions – all without giving any thought for how their actions might affect others. We lack the means to understand how these people think, because we ourselves just don't think that way.

Sadly, when it comes to intimate relationships, another factor that allows narcissistic people to latch on to, abuse, undermine and exploit others to the level where their lives are virtually destroyed, has its roots in what we are told from a young age: that sharing our lives with a partner is everything. Indeed, religious marriage vows such as the Christian 'till death do us part' are ingrained beliefs for many. Women, historically, were educated to believe they 'need a man' and men were brought up to believe in being the 'head of the house'. Even though narcissism is not gender specific, old-world ingrained values such as offering selfless service without having healthy personal boundaries in place – sometimes to the extent of martyrdom – have caused people to hand over their power and allow others to abuse it.

For many people abuse started in the home at birth. If you grew up with narcissists in your family of origin, the abuse is familiar to you. Having your rights and voice squashed is all you might have known. If you had a narcissistic or emotionally damaged parent or family member, it was never modelled for you how to feel whole and solid inside yourselves first before having a relationship with another person. And because of this, many of us are at terrible risk in later life of hanging on to the myth that another person will 'complete' us in some way, despite the threat of abuse. In intimate relationships, we may gratefully accept whatever crumbs of affection we receive and we may try to salvage the image of the 'dream person' we hope the narcissist in reality will become, continually rejecting the truth – that our lives, sanity and soul are being destroyed by them. In business or friendships with narcissists, we become convinced they will bring something to our lives that maybe we can't provide on our own – such as prospects, abilities, success or fun – despite our guts churning, warning us instinctively against them, and there being all sorts of drama and issues popping up around them.

How Childhood Can Set Us Up For Narcissistic Relationships

Not all people who have suffered narcissistic abuse as adults were born into narcissistic families. I grew up in a family in which there was a symbiotic, co-dependent relationship between my mother and father, and between their parents before them, where both parties were essential for each other's real-life functioning and survival. My mother and father loved each other, and in many ways their relationship could have been seen as very functional. They had gender-defined roles: I remember my mother wearing her apron, baking in the kitchen, while my father was outside digging, planting and making paths around the garden. Despite her own chores, Mum was often focused on what Dad was doing, fetching him something if he called out for it; and no matter how hard my mother was working inside the house, when my father was hungry she would stop everything she was doing and make his lunch. Even if we children needed Mum at those times, she would say, 'I have to get your father something to eat.' Interrupting this vital task was unthinkable, as was making any noise or wanting to watch something else on TV when Dad was watching the news.

It was all pretty clear cut: my father was the most important person in the household and my mother's role was to tend to him. I can't remember my mother ever having her own interests, such as friends and hobbies. Much of what she did socially was with my father. Likewise, Dad would handle all the money and bills, and the whole family moved from state to state around Australia, following Dad's career.

This was very normal to me as a young girl growing up in the late sixties and seventies. Other families we knew did the same thing; I didn't have any female role models in my life who notably had their own identity or power. My mother simply didn't challenge my father about much at all. Even when she was feeling abandoned and ignored by him (he did a lot of overseas travel for work), it was inconceivable for her to leave him. Since she'd been a teenager my mother had never been without a man, and I grew up feeling I'd be worthless if I didn't have a boyfriend one day too. I remember splitting up with a boy when I was nineteen years old, and feeling like a total failure because I was single again. Little did I know that this sense of feeling fractured and incomplete if I wasn't in a relationship formed part of my susceptibility to narcissists – who ironically also feel chronically empty on the inside. (I'll be talking more about that soon.)

As children we learn by example, and even though neither of my parents was narcissistic, the old-school dynamic of their partnership, which in many ways worked well for them and those before them, was not helpful for me going into my own relationships. As a young woman, I lived in a rapidly changing world of emerging equality and shared power between the sexes. And I had the ability and the drive to be successful and a source of my own security and survival; yet my inner programming was to dim down my light and not behave like an equal. I was conditioned to rely on a man to take care of me, and to do whatever he said to ensure this happened. Just like my mother, I clung to men for my identity and sense of self-worth. If a man wasn't validating me or affirming my existence, I wasn't doing a good enough job – because my entire life was about securing the protection and approval of Mr Right.

As a consequence of my upbringing, I felt my father put a lot of pressure on me to succeed, and felt that his love was conditional on my performance. I was always trying to get him to love me and approve of me by improving my performance, yet because of the example set to me by my mother, I had no idea how to combine success with personal relationships, which I believed needed to be all about the man. As a result, I kept being drawn to men who seemed powerful and who were at first attracted to me by my capabilities, yet who would then dislike, compete with and even attempt to sabotage my accomplishments. Time and time again, I would find myself fighting to be recognised by these sorts of men through my achievements (the influence of my father), whilst struggling to feel loved within a relationship that I was too terrified to let go of (the example of my mother).

Like myself, I discovered that many other people who experienced a significant painful relationship pattern, including narcissistic abuse, could trace the origins of their trauma and their ingrained beliefs back to their upbringing. You too may relate to some of what I have just shared with you. Another example that comes to mind is a client of mine whom I will call 'Anne'. Anne's father was a high-achiever who was critical and demanding. Busy bringing up five children, and suffering from the anxiety of not doing a good enough job for her husband, Anne's mother simply did not have time to spend with her daughter and show her love. Exhausted and stressed, her mother's impatient catch-cry with her kids was, 'Please just deal with it!'

Anne tragically suffered three narcissistic relationships back to back, two of which involved bosses and one an intimate partner. These were all with men who represented her father – demanding, emotionally unavailable and hypercritical – while she accepted that her role was to serve them and not be respected or loved by them. Through her behaviour, Anne echoed her mother's words; she 'just dealt' with this too, feeling insignificant, unimportant and unheard as she always had, until the bosses' abuse or her partner's affairs became so rampant that she had no option other than to leave.

Tragically, just like my old self and like Anne, you too may be susceptible to being attracted to and becoming trapped in narcissistic relationships. If you grew up in a family with narcissistic abuse, or with values that diminished your personal identity and power, this will be all you have ever known, and the chances of repeating that pattern are almost inevitable. When we have inner unhealed parts, we are responding to our relationships from the 'child inside': our inner child. Not as a mature adult who has healthy boundaries and rights.

Unfortunately, whether they were narcissistic or not, many of our parents simply didn't know any better, and thought that providing life's physical necessities, rather than emotional 'inner' commodities, constituted healthy parenting.

To begin with, we may not realise we are in a relationship with a narcissist, either because we grew up with this person and know no different, or, in the case of any form of new relationship – whether it be professional, intimate or any other kind – because the abuse is gradual and insidious. A narcissist certainly won't present themselves to you without their mask in the early days – because you just wouldn't sign up for the ride if they did.

Five Major Signs of Narcissism

Having worked with thousands of people around the world, I have found that, irrespective of age, race, gender, race, religion, sexual preference or who the narcissist is (such as a spouse, lover, family member, friend, colleague or boss), narcissism is narcissism and there are some clear-cut definitions relating to how someone with narcissistic personality disorder behaves. If you are having any doubts about whether or not you are involved with someone with NPD, take a look at the following five points:

1. Emotional insecurity
Despite the commonly held belief that 'narcissists are full of themselves', the experience of living with a narcissist shows us a completely different reality once their mask has started to crack. Narcissists are hugely insecure and react on a hair-trigger to things that average adults simply don't get upset about. Their over-sensitivity is extreme. When narcissists erupt into a narcissistic rage, their anger is a reaction to a perceived threat to the narcissist's fragile self-esteem or self-worth. This type of threat is known as 'narcissistic injury'. Perhaps you spoke appreciatively about a colleague – and all of a sudden the narcissist is ripping your head off for being disloyal, or even accuses you of having an affair? If the narcissist

doesn't receive enough attention in a group setting, he or she may stir up trouble or exit the scene, only to chastise you later and degrade you and anyone else perceived to have stolen the limelight.

This insecurity may be so extreme that it provokes incredible jealousy and envy that can't be assuaged. A client of mine, Michelle, was ordered to strip down to her underwear every evening when she walked in the door from work, so that her narcissistic partner could check whether she was having an affair. He had access to all her passwords on her electronic devices, and placed a tracking device on her phone. No matter what measures she allowed him to take in order to prove she wasn't cheating on him, the insane jealousy continued. Another of my clients, John, told me how he was the 'face' of his company; at any presentations for business accolades and awards, his narcissistic business partner would get drunk and cause scenes to undermine the event, then rip strips off him in the car on the way home. Michelle and John, and countless others, shared the experience that I had. No matter how many times we tried to include the narcissist, share our lives with them and convince them that we were loyal to them, the abuse continued. It is devastating not to have the trust, love and support of a person who plays such a major part in your life.

It doesn't matter who the narcissist is in your own life – you will painfully experience their insecurities in the form of accusations directed at you. Taking it out on you is just something that narcissists do.

2. An extreme sense of entitlement

If you share your life with a narcissist, you will quickly discover they have an unreasonable sense of entitlement – it truly is all about them – and very poor peripheral vision when it comes to anyone else's needs. A narcissist's self-absorption, which is an integral part of their inner wiring, means they believe they deserve preferential treatment over and above all others. They will push people's boundaries without hesitation and go for whatever they can get away with, while their real agenda remains cloaked in charm, flattery and feigned care. No matter how good it looks to others, any deal brokered by a narcissist is underpinned by a desire to obtain the best of the spoils, regardless of who else might suffer in the process. Without conscience or as much as a backward glance, a narcissist will throw all and sundry under a bus when the time comes for them to collect, including their spouse, family and even their children.

The narcissist's sense of entitlement ranges all the way from normal everyday events such as 'I'm not listening to your conversation, let alone engaging with you in it – I will spin everything back to me' and 'I will watch whatever I want on TV and turn the volume up regardless of your trying to have a conversation on the phone', to major life decisions such as property settlements and the splitting of assets: 'I deserve all of what I want because...' (cue the narcissist's version of events).

If you grew up in a narcissistic family, this kind of behaviour constitutes your 'normal' version of life. When it comes to boundaries, you will be used to the idea that whatever is yours is the narcissist's; and as for your rights – what rights exactly? However, if connecting with a narcissist later in life, in all likelihood you didn't see this coming, because initially the narcissist made you believe they had your back; that they cared for you and loved you genuinely, and that they saw, heard and valued you. After trusting and allowing someone in to your life at the deepest level, it can be devastating to realise this person is actually gobbling up your space, energy, attention and resources, and emptying you out, without any remorse while doing so.

3. Circular arguments that don't make sense

One of the surest ways to identify an NPD sufferer is the way they argue. Over the years, I have identified numerous ways in which narcissists use diversionary tactics when in conflict situations. Their defence mechanisms range from being subtly manipulative to displays of downright nasty, out-of-bounds behaviour. These tactics are so common among narcissists and the expressions they use are so consistent word for word that it is almost eerily uncanny; frequently used phrases include refrains such as 'you didn't let me finish what I was saying' and 'just because I didn't say what you wanted to hear' and 'you are the only person I have any problems with'. (Believe me, there are so many others!)

Long before you have identified what is going on during these sorts of conversations, you may well feel terribly anxious and traumatised, and wonder if you are losing your mind. You will probably be bamboozled as to why you appear to be arguing over and over about basic points with someone who apparently refuses to get it. It's like disagreeing with an angry five-year-old who won't remain on topic, or be held accountable, or learn from previous behaviour. Finally, perhaps after hours, days or even weeks, you think you've won the debate and the narcissist really does understand your point of view, only then to discover evidence that, shockingly, nothing was resolved in the first place – and now you are back at square one.

The arsenal that narcissists draw on in arguments includes:

- excuses for their behaviour;

- minimising an incident altogether;

- accusing someone else of wrongdoing;

- offering a false apology and expecting you to accept it;

- flatly denying that whatever you have brought to the table even exists;

- confusing you with antics or trivia to take you off the subject;

- projecting the blame on to you;

- using allies, real or fabricated, to back up their argument;

- stonewalling you and leaving the scene;

- using 'tit for tat' behaviours relating to something you did in the past;

- stating how disloyal your accusations of them are;

- discrediting your observations, owing to your 'unstable' past.

There are many more tactics, including making actual threats or downright abandonment if you continue the conversation. All of the above are a part of the construction of the quintessential narcissistic three-ring circus, which makes you feel like your head is going to explode.

4. Pathological lying

In his or her grandiose self-delusion, a narcissist is covering up a fragile inner identity – and thereby creating and acting out a different script of 'who' he or she would like to be.

The lies begin very early on in relationships with narcissists, because lying is an ingrained part of their identity. A narcissist is likely to lie and brag about accomplishments in his or her past, as well as complain about how poorly they have been treated by those with whom they have had fractured adult relationships – which is usually a gross projection and distortion of what the narcissist has done to others. Moreover, narcissists believe their own lies, which is why they can be such convincing deceivers, often attracting a host of minions who believe in them. Grown adults with integrity can't imagine why another grown adult would say such terrible things about anybody else – in explicit detail – unless it were true. Especially when that person appears credible and can look you in the eye while doing so.

Many narcissists lead double lives. They are attracted to breaking rules and subverting authority. Likewise, the sanctity and exclusivity of marriage threaten to reduce them to 'normality' (which feels like emotional annihilation to a narcissist). Therefore they are often associated with criminal and extra-marital activities, behaviours that are concealed and lied about so that they can retain the things in their lives that provide them with enough stability to remain functioning. In over a decade of helping people to recover from narcissistic abuse, I can't count the number of times I've been told about narcissists eventually being caught out having affairs, or being involved in dodgy business practices and even illegal activities. Due to the falseness, lies and deception associated with narcissistic behaviour – forever seeking more acclaim, notoriety and the envy of others – no matter how successful a narcissist's life looks, scratch beneath the surface and you will often find a countless number of disasters waiting to strike.

And narcissists *do* get struck down: they get caught out, people leave them, they go bankrupt and they are prosecuted. Yet many will divorce themselves as effectively from this sort of unwanted exposure – and everyone involved in it – as an actor moving from one movie deal to the next. These things and people simply don't serve a purpose for the narcissist anymore and he or she may just up and leave.

When you have fallen prey to a narcissist, it is beyond shocking if the façade cracks and their lies start unravelling – and you find yourself confronted with sordid truths that sock you so hard you don't think you will survive. My friend Allen found out that his narcissistic bookkeeper, a supposedly lovely, trusted family friend who also babysat his children, had been embezzling money from three of his businesses for the last five years. And then there was a client of mine, Jody, who moved interstate to marry and live with her narcissistic partner, who was a builder. After marrying him, she found out that while his men were busy building he was booking motel rooms and having affairs. Within a two-week period, two separate women surfaced and contacted Jody after she announced who her husband was on Facebook. Previously he had pledged how strong a value monogamy was to him.

I know that if you have been narcissistically abused, you too will have discovered shocking truths that you never thought could happen to you. Your life becomes a surreal bad dream and the person standing in front of you bears no resemblance to the person you thought you were having a relationship with.

5. Blaming you for their problems

One of the most insane and devastating parts of narcissist abuse is the projection tactics that narcissists use. Narcissists, quite simply, accuse you of all the things that they do themselves. I can't remember the number of times I screamed at my ex, 'Have you looked at yourself in the mirror?' when I was accused of being selfish, uncaring, moody, using people to do my bidding, wanting him for his money (what money!) and of course adultery, which I later discovered he'd been guilty of all along.

With narcissists, you are damned if you do and damned if you don't. Nothing you do will ever be good enough. As far as they are concerned, your actions will all too often represent a personal affront or even a direct attack, intended to hurt them or undermine them – and they claim this is the reason why your relationship is experiencing problems.

In these situations, it's easy to feel like you will never win, and that you are losing your mind. If, for example, you have discovered what narcissism is and accused a narcissist of being one, he or she will in all probability twist that accusation back on you until you seriously start to question whether you are the narcissist instead. Too many people misguidedly end up staying in a relationship while suffering this sort of abuse in an attempt to prove to the narcissist that they are not to blame, or because they are genuinely trying to unravel who really is the abuser and who is the victim – while feeling great shame and confusion in the process.

Rest assured, a narcissist will have no qualms about throwing you metaphorically to the wolves if they think the need arises. They will talk about you in disparaging ways to others – labelling you as the abuser and smearing you to the key people in your life. Narcissists are used to operating within the thresholds of drama and pain, and even in extreme situations which would stress out normal people, they appear high functioning and therefore credible. In stark contrast, you are likely to seem like a lunatic while you struggle to hold it all together. Devastatingly, the important people in your life will often start to believe the narcissist. You might even lose your job because of discussions that a narcissist has behind your back with your boss and colleagues.

All of this isolates the victims of narcissists yet further, pushing them into a deep abyss of helplessness and powerlessness, while, like a stealth bomber, the narcissist continues to pillage and rape their soul and life.

I totally understand how even after reading the information in this chapter, your head may be spinning with questions such as: 'But is s/he really a narcissist?' To make sure you are crystal clear about what you are dealing with, I've created 'The 50 Traits of a Narcissist Checklist' which you can access for free in your 'You Can Thrive Program'. Register here for instant access: www.youcanthriveprogram.com.

How Does Narcissism Develop?

Far from narcissists suffering from too much self-love, they traditionally come from families where love was severely lacking or which suffered from parental engulfment – in which a child's relationship with a parent becomes suffocating. Through mental, emotional, physical, spiritual or sexual abuse, the child's boundaries become merged with the adult's and overruled by them. This can cause the potential young narcissist to suffer such intense inner disintegration that they then bury their true self, deeming it unable to have its needs met, and create a false self in its place. Yet there are also cases where narcissists have emerged from families headed up by loving, decent parents and in which the other children have never developed narcissism. In these cases, I believe epigenetic trauma is the explanation: the parent's epigenetic and/or childhood trauma was passed on.

The narcissist's false self is a fictitious character who can act as a buffer against the trauma felt: 'If it's not me, it won't hurt.' The same 'splitting off' from the true self can be caused by severe neglect and rejection, as well as by the 'golden child' syndrome, whereby the child is granted special attention and favours, which leads to a sense of over-entitlement – creating children as the clones of narcissistic parents who regard their offspring as extensions of their own egos. Whatever the cause, the truth is that the narcissist's core identity becomes damaged and disowned, because, once their inner child has been buried alive, they are left with what resembles a black hole inside. Yet this is more than just a gnawing, dreadful feeling of emptiness: that void becomes an echo chamber for a terrifying inner critic.

Imagine if the inner critic that exists in your own thoughts were to tell you on a low volume that 'you are defective' or 'you are worth nothing' every minute of every day. You might be able to keep busy and distract yourself enough from this inner voice to operate. Now imagine the volume turned up so loud that you have no choice but to do whatever it takes to survive. One narcissist recently wrote to tell me:

> I live with my deep self-loathing that I can never escape. I want to die, but death terrifies me. Yet to live, I know I have to continually pretend I am someone I am not – because everyone would recoil if they knew the truth. And no matter what I pretend, I know I can't really connect to people or even experience the feelings that they can. I know I am already dead on the inside. I have no idea how to escape this hell that means I have to hurt people to try to momentarily feel better.

These words offer some insight into the narcissist's world. There are times during narcissistic injury when something so bad happens to the narcissist that the defences of their egos collapse and humility is present. But as soon as enough outside attention is gained, those defences shoot back up and it's back to narcissistic business as usual. This happens quickly – usually within hours and rarely more than days. Many narcissists, having made a revealing confession such as the one above, would complete deny they wrote the statement as soon as their ego reasserted itself.

A classic example is what happened to my client James. After he left her, his narcissistic wife hit rock bottom and wrote to him at length, admitting she had serious issues and needed help. He loved his wife and was relieved that she appeared humble, honest and apologetic, and he said he would do everything he could to support her. Within two days of moving back in with her, her narcissistic rages and threats started again and she spewed at him how it was him who needed therapy, not her.

How Does a Narcissist Survive?

There is only one thing that can drown out a narcissist's terrifying inner critic and allow the narcissist to somehow feel 'alive' – and that is narcissistic supply. Narcissistic supply consists of attention, significance, acclaim, notoriety, money, possessions, sex and the ego-boost of knowing that other people are hooked on the narcissist, affected by them and obsessing over them. Narcissistic supply is the number one thing that motivates a narcissist, as it temporarily grants the narcissist's false self enough strength to block out their inner demons. But it doesn't last. Once the 'thrill' or 'conquest' is over, those relentless inner demons return and the narcissist needs to tap into fresh sources of narcissistic supply.

Narcissistic supply is the narcissist's drug, and as such it's a form of pain relief. It's a distraction from that self-annihilating inner critic, which is always threatening to eat the narcissist alive; the narcissist is as addicted to narcissistic supply as a crack addict is to crack, both using their drug of choice to block out the horror of their inner traumas. When the buffer of the narcissist's false self is compromised and can no longer block out suppressed emotions, a narcissistic injury can detonate at any moment. To let their defences down and be engulfed by their damaged true self feels worse to a narcissist than death; the reality is, many narcissists would rather physically die than dismantle their false self. The real truth is, I believe, that the parasitical, psychic virus that is 'narcissism' has overtaken the narcissist by this stage – and he or she has no choice other than to serve it now.

Just like the myth of vampires, those undead who need to feed off human blood if they are to survive, and the accounts of black holes in space that have no real composition yet which ingest celestial bodies, including entire planets, to maintain their existence, narcissists empty out everything and everyone in their wake, yet never genuinely feel 'alive' or 'whole' as a result of doing so. The narcissist's quest to escape their inner demons is never ending.

Although the narcissist's struggle is inescapable, luckily for us – the people abused by them – there is an end in sight. Now that you can understand what you are dealing with, you know that this goes way beyond trying to deal with a person who is being unreasonable. The solution to dealing with a narcissist starts with understanding the real nature of the individual that we are coping with as the first step; yet, ultimately, it involves nurturing a deep and necessary understanding about ourselves – which we are about to explore.

3

WHY WE ATTRACT NARCISSISTS

The strong consensus within many online groups whose members have suffered abuse is that narcissists are evil predators who will seek out and latch on to anyone they can find. Yet I find that this view, and the popularity it has gained, severely disempowers people. In fact, my frustration with it is one of the driving factors behind my writing this book. I believe this sort of attitude means that, rather than attempting to heal the inner unconscious reasons that make us vulnerable to narcissists in the first place, the focus remains instead on trying to learn more about these sorts of individuals in order to avoid them. Yet sadly information about narcissists doesn't offer people protection, because the reasons we get involved with them are not logical: rather, they are to do with the unhealed parts of our inner selves. Moreover, if it were true that absolutely anyone could be taken in by a narcissist, there would be no need for self-reflection, nor any opportunity for us to evolve and move on to a different love and relationship trajectory – processes which we are going to be delving into deeply throughout this book.

There are some people who are simply not susceptible to narcissists, just as my present self isn't – yet once upon a time I was as appealing to a narcissist as an injured gazelle is to a predator. My realising and understanding *why* I was susceptible, and healing my susceptibilities, were what set me free. There are those who might confuse taking personal responsibility for healing ourselves with a form of victim-blaming; however, the Thriver Way – the philosophy of taking back our power to activate our true healing potential – is not about shaming and blaming ourselves; it is about finding truth, relief, resolution and freedom from the unconscious belief systems and traumas that have previously been causing us so much pain.

What were my susceptibilities? To start off, I had scanty, if not almost non-existent, boundaries. I struggled to say no to people because of my fear of them criticising, rejecting, abandoning or punishing me. (I like to call this fear by the acronym CRAP!) I was a people pleaser, trying to be what other people wanted me to be, so that they would love me and approve of me. I had very little idea of my own needs or rights, much less the ability to speak up for them. Unconsciously, I was always trying to play it safe, not rock the boat, and to be nice to people so they would look after me. I also believed other people had much more authority and made better decisions than me – so best let them make them.

And I wasn't connected to my intuition. I didn't trust it and I was not investigating, confronting, asking the right questions, setting boundaries or walking away if something seemed off. Rather, I'd bury my gut feelings, make excuses for how I was feeling (even when red flags, such as receiving two conflicting stories, presented themselves), and think, 'Everything will be okay, and I can deal with it even if it isn't.' Time and time again, my life ended up in pieces because of my self-abandonment.

I was the perfect dish on a silver platter for narcissists: hardworking, trying to seek approval, capable of providing a good lifestyle, lacking any sense of personal rights, self-love or self-worth, and more than willing to go along with anything that anyone wanted from me so that they might love me. I was also the prefect candidate to stay hooked to abuse, even when it reached unthinkable levels, because I was terrified of life without a man. In my narcissistic relationship, I felt like my very survival depended on convincing my partner that I was worthy of his love, and that I was not the things he accused me of being. I fervently believed that somehow my devotion to 'us' could pull him out of the darkness and into true loving harmony with me. As I have explained, there were many deep, vulnerable, raw truths of my inner programming that I was later to discover, heal and evolve from. Yet people thought I was outwardly strong and capable – and the truth was that I thought I was too, because I was successful at everything else I put my mind to.

Once we emerge from a relationship with a narcissist, we start to realise that our susceptibility to narcissists does not mean we are a weak person. Incredibly, often the exact opposite is true: most people who find themselves connected with a narcissist are very intelligent with high integrity. We are generally people who can make our life work, and we get up and go even when the chips are down. It is our resilience rather than our weaknesses which keeps us involved with narcissists: we believe we can fix this, and we certainly don't want to give up on the significant investment of love, time, energy and money we put into the relationship.

Even though many of us who are abused by narcissists are the type of individuals who are trusted by others, and who are capable and reliable, it may not be until we experience the utter powerlessness of being hooked on and addicted to a person who is tearing us to shreds, that we realise something is not right with us. Then we find ourselves obsessing over and over: *I'm an intelligent capable person, so why on earth can't I get it through my head to get out, stay out and leave this person for good?* We are dismayed and astounded to discover that still we don't go, despite experiencing things no one should ever stay attached to.

I promise you there is a reason why we are susceptible to narcissists: as we saw in Chapter 2, in our own childhoods we did not receive the love and support that allowed us to grow up with whole and healthy inner identities. It became our 'normal' to be highly functioning and capable – strategising, fixing and applying ourselves to challenges whenever they arose. Yet we didn't realise this high-functioning behaviour represented an unconscious attempt to self-medicate and treat the inner anxiety and depression we suffered as a consequence of never believing we were 'good enough' just as we were.

Maybe, like myself, you were parented in ways that involved conditional love, and you became convinced that affection and approval had to be earned. Perhaps you only received attention when you granted your parents what they wanted, or when you achieved top academic marks or sporting results. Maybe you had high-functioning parents who were anxiously operating in their own survival 'doing' mode, so you never had a role model for how to just 'be'. Nor were you taught how to recognise your own needs or tend to your emotional wellbeing, so your ability to self-soothe (meaning to meet, support and process your emotions to their healthy completion) and to love and accept yourself unconditionally were severely compromised.

Maybe, like a narcissist, you were parented in abusive ways, yet rather than bury your true self and adopt a pathological false self to survive, you took on the role of the fixer and giver – trying to keep your unhealthy family sane so that they would have enough resources to love and take care of you. Perhaps, because your survival depended on your being hyper-vigilant around other people and supplying whatever they needed, you never developed an awareness of your own needs, boundaries and rights – or how to take care of these.

All of these experiences are commonplace. Many people experience unconscious parenting as a consequence of much of our formal education being about cognitive intelligence rather than emotional intelligence. We were taught in our early formative years – and beyond them – how to read, write, calculate and think, yet not how to feel, self-partner (meaning to 'be' with our inner emotions with love and without judgement) and establish an inner relationship with ourselves. This was left to our parents to model for us, yet often they had never learned it themselves. In this way, unconscious parenting can be passed on from generation to generation – and we carry the scars with us into our adult lives.

If you've ever been abused by a narcissist, you know they will attack your most painful wound, your deepest insecurity, your most troubling scar, at the worst possible time. The reason for this is that narcissists are attuned to finding your weakest points. Paradoxically, in a new relationship sense, whether it be intimate, business or friendship, they will at first use your insecurities to manipulate you into becoming involved with them. If you feel insignificant and unworthy, this person will 'see' and 'validate' you like no other. If, for example, you feel that you don't have the nerve to succeed in your own business, this person will present themselves as having the essential courage you lack. Yet they will then turn the tables by attacking your inner wounds mercilessly, ripping them open all over again whenever the narcissist's false self does not feel it has been appeased enough by you. Rather than you leaving as a result of the abuse, the narcissist now has you hooked, because you then try to turn them back into your original saviour figure, and of course they don't comply. This in turn grants them copious significance (i.e. narcissistic supply) in relation to you: *Look at how much I can affect another.*

It is only by finding and healing these old, original traumas that the narcissist has been using against you that you can break out of the insane emotional prison he or she has trapped you in. The irony is, this necessity brings with it an incredible opportunity: it can enable your evolution into the version of yourself that you have always wanted to be. It can allow you to free yourself at last from those wounded parts of your inner being that have prevented you from becoming your highest and best self. As the thirteenth-century Sufi poet Rumi wrote:

> What hurts you, blesses you.
> Darkness is your candle.
> Your boundaries are your quest.[1]

Those people who were lucky enough to have parents with the time and insight necessary to validate and help build their child's inner identity are not susceptible to narcissists. The reason is simple: they already are a source of love, approval, security and survival for themselves. They don't accept scraps of affection riddled with abuse from people, or mistake these for real love. When you are no longer dependent on someone else for your love or happiness, why would you settle for anything less than a partner who loves you unconditionally and who wants to see you thrive in every aspect of your life?

The Nine Traits that Make Us Susceptible To Narcissistic Abuse

I would like to share with you the nine main susceptibilities that I believe lead us unconsciously into narcissist abuse. Once we understand these emotional susceptibilities, we can work at repairing them, and finally change our relationship patterns beyond what we previously believed was possible. My deep due diligence of my own inner being, as well as my work with thousands of people for over more than a decade, has led me to believe there are certain common traits shared by virtually everyone who has been narcissistically abused.

1. You have already suffered abuse, you fear abuse or you have a strong aversion to abusers.

When we still carry the pain of past abuse, we unconsciously seek out people who represent what is familiar to us. The abuse we previously suffered becomes the version of attachment that creates the most emotionally charged feelings for us, and therefore establishes a pattern – a trajectory of 'love' – that becomes part of our inner programming.

2. You find it difficult to speak up, stand up for yourself or create healthy boundaries.

If you suffer from an inability to assert yourself because of your fears of criticism, rejection, abandonment or punishment (CRAP), this means you will hand your power away. Rather than confront, investigate and honour yourself when needed, you would rather go along with others despite how wrong this feels for you. This classic self-abandonment allows narcissists through your boundaries, and means you will struggle to kick them out of both your life and your psyche once they start abusing you.

3. Your integrity level is high and you are dismayed if anyone questions it.

When we believe our worth is dictated by what other people think of us, rather than what we think of ourselves, we are in for a very hard time. Life will feel precarious, especially if you are attached to a narcissist who accuses you of things you would never fathom thinking or doing, while you frantically try to force them to think differently about you so that you can feel okay again. This lack of self-worth means we are vulnerable to being abused over and over again.

4. You work hard to sustain a sense of security, and you clean up the mess made by other people that could threaten your security.

When you take financial responsibility for people who refuse to take responsibility for themselves, it is like watering their garden while your own is dying. You are being drained of your energy, sanity and resources. Narcissists attach to people who have resources and with whom they can enmesh their lives, and who will take responsibility for cleaning up after them. The narcissist syphons out your resources while you are busy sorting out their mess.

5. You feel, deep down, that you can only be loved for your efforts and accomplishments.

If you keep trying to prove your worth by taking on the burdens of others, being generous to a fault, giving till it hurts and doing all the things we do when we don't believe we are loveable or worthy simply in and of ourselves – narcissists will be magnetised to you. You are the perfect source of narcissistic supply, as the narcissist gets to live out their preferred scenario: *It's all about me at your expense.*

6. You unconsciously feel others will only love you and care for you when you tend to their needs first.

If you grew up in a household where you tried to placate or keep others sane so that they would have enough resources to love and care for you, you are likely to be attracted to unsafe people. Rather than identifying your own needs, asking for what you want and laying down boundaries that define how others treat you, you will have a high tolerance for unacceptable behaviour and a propensity to cater to it in order to stay safe. Narcissists are the perfect fit for this tendency.

7. You are very hard on yourself, and are never happy with what you have achieved. You continually feel anxious about what you haven't accomplished yet.

It is a totally false premise that people will treat us how we treat them. The truth is that people treat us in ways that reflect how we treat and truly feel about ourselves. If you are your own terrible inner critic, then you will gravitate towards relationships with people who deem you as 'never good enough'. Additionally, most of us won't stay in a relationship in which the level of love is below the level we hold for ourselves. (Narcissists generate and stay in painful, dramatic relationships, because chaos is the state of their inner being.) One of the reasons we stay with a narcissist is because the narcissist mirrors the ways we truly feel about and talk to ourselves. We have seen how, with narcissists, we are damned if we do and damned if we don't, yet how many of us treat ourselves with unappeasable conditional love?

8. You have a tendency to want to fix and sort out other people's problems rather than examine and sort out your own uncomfortable emotions.

If we have never learned how to self-partner, self-soothe and heal our own emotional triggers, we will tend to look to the outside world for relief from our uncomfortable feelings. Yet if we try to control others in a bid to assuage our own out-of-control emotions, we in turn will become more vulnerable to being controlled. By focusing our attention outside ourselves, we effectively drain ourselves of power, hand it over to others and enable somebody like a narcissist to receive A-grade narcissistic supply from us and power up against us.

9. You see yourself as an empath, and put other people's needs before your own in the belief that this is virtuous.

If we are an empath (i.e. we feel the energy of others intensely and we try to assist others as a way to feel better about ourselves), we may pride ourselves on how we show concern for other people's needs and wishes, and cater to them. However, if we are not capable of defining our own needs and wants, nor of asking for these to be met healthily, we will not receive back the care and love we crave. This can cause us to become resentful and to hold other people responsible for our unhappiness. We might righteously lecture others on how we think they should behave, instead of accepting the way they do. This attitude can inadvertently keep us hooked on narcissists as we try to change them into 'good' people, whilst offering them copious amounts of narcissistic supply.

*

It can be such a revelation to understand how many of us possess a lot, if not all, of these nine traits. All of these susceptibilities were the old me to a 't', and the truth is that if I hadn't freed myself from them I would not be alive today. In a nutshell, I used to try to define myself from the outside – the ways in which other people perceived me – instead of being self-loving and self-defined.

I sincerely hope this list of nine susceptibilities has helped you identify where your emotional susceptibilities are too. Please know that these fractures don't make us bad people; they just mean that we can become very disconnected from ourselves in ways that end up self-harming, which then of course allows others to hurt us too.

Just as narcissism is an epidemic, the victims exist in epidemic proportions too. This is because many of us have been brought up to believe that the nine susceptibilities we've looked at are virtues. Sadly, all too many of us have been taught to focus outside ourselves and thereby hand our power away, rather than looking inwards and learning how to become healthy, whole individuals with the power to generate healthy, whole relationships.

The Healing Opportunity of Narcissistic Abuse

I realise you might be in shock right now; you might be even thinking, *Why me? Why did I have to go through this nightmare?* I want you to know I truly understand what you are going through and how terrible it feels, but I promise you that you can heal from this.

A couple of years ago I worked with a client named Josie, who had been told by a psychologist that what had happened to her was 'just terrible bad luck'. When she joined the Thriver Community, a global group of individuals who embrace my Thriver Way to Heal (which I will soon explain in more detail), she was overjoyed to learn there was a reason why she had experienced a narcissistic relationship. She exclaimed: 'Why on earth would you go through all that for nothing? That never made sense to me.'

We go through this for a reason, and this is: when we suffer narcissistic abuse as adults, we have as yet not become a solid source of love, approval, survival and security for ourselves, and we hold other people responsible for meeting our needs. As children, this might have been the only option we had to survive, as we were dependent on the grownups in our lives (i.e. completely reliant on an adult to provide us with love, approval, security and survival), yet as adults ourselves, it is vital to become our own source of these things. When we feel empty inside and try to fill that emptiness from outside sources, we will gravitate towards and connect with other empty components, such as false sources who are trying to achieve a sense of inner wholeness themselves, i.e. narcissists. Yet when we start learning how to generate inner wholeness, working with our Higher Self and our emotional inner guidance to connect to the healthy components of life – such as genuine people and situations who add to our wellbeing, rather than subtract from it – this is when our life starts to take off in incredible, fulfilling and inspirational ways.

Narcissistic abuse is the absolutely traumatic make-or-break experience that occurs when we try to generate our inner missing pieces through others. We thought the narcissist was the healer of our wounds – but they weren't, they were the messenger instead. After narcissistic abuse, life can no longer go on as normal. We have hit rock bottom and now is the time to dissolve or evolve...

The Thriver Way to Heal

I want to introduce you now to my Thriver Way to Heal, which is important to grasp in order for my healing processes to work for you. At first, elements of this method may seem counterintuitive, because it is human nature to want to point the blame at someone who appears to be hurting us. Yet I'd like you to park that thought for a moment and open up to another possibility – one which, when you grasp it, will start to create feelings of relief rather than powerlessness in your body.

This is a Thriver mantra: whatever happened was for a reason and if you can find out and heal that reason, then not only will this situation never happen to you again, but you will evolve and heal, and your life will improve and expand way beyond how you were living previously – even before the abuse took place. All the dreadful trauma symptoms that you are suffering will leave you. You will feel more empowered, safe, solid and confident than you ever have done in your entire life.

I promise you this is not some wild statement; it is completely true. This is the Thriver Way, and it has saved the emotional and physical lives of thousands of people worldwide, often when nothing else has worked. In my own case, my intense focus on the narcissist and what was wrong with him, rather than on my own healing and evolution, nearly took me to my grave. When we stay focused on who narcissists are and what they have done to us – even though this is very important to understand in the beginning – we are not loving and healing ourselves back to wholeness. And if we are not healing ourselves, we will have to wait for circumstances outside ourselves to change in order to find relief: circumstances such as abusers atoning, making amends or being held accountable. I promise you that in the thousands of cases I have come across, including my own, this seldom ever happens; and even when it very rarely does, victims who have not healed themselves and released their own trauma will only experience momentary relief before their symptoms return. Why? Because the trauma in their being has yet to be addressed and healed.

Who Are Thrivers?

Thrivers have courage, because they are revolutionists. As Thrivers, we don't accept the standard beliefs and prognoses that often come with being a victim of abuse. We don't wish to remain victims whose very existence is undermined by anxiety and terrible nervous-symptom disorders, suffering from a reduced ability to engage with life, experience love and fulfil our dreams.

We don't wish merely to survive, despite what has happened to us; we choose to do all that we can to Thrive *because* of what happened to us.

As Thrivers, we acknowledge a Quantum Law, the law of energy, the 'consciousness' that underpins all of creation, which is the very foundation of the Thriver Way to Heal; and that is: *so within, so without.* Put simply, this means that if we experience something on the outside that hurts, there must be a corresponding unresolved trauma inside us; otherwise, emotionally and energetically, we would never have unconsciously attracted and accepted this outer event into our life.

As Thrivers, what we discover is this: once we give up our intense focus on the narcissist, and stop trying to control life on the outside in an attempt to find peace and security on the inside; and if instead we turn inwards, and focus on self-partnering, loving and healing ourselves back to wholeness, we rapidly start to feel better. It feels 'right' in our body.

At first, we might not realise what this really means: that by turning inwards, *finally we are on our way home.*

I hope you are beginning to get a strong sense of what it means to be a Thriver. In the next chapter, we're going to take a look at how abuse can take many different forms, which is important because toxic and narcissistic individuals can appear in all walks of life. The good news is that there are commonalities between all narcissists, so after reading Chapter 4 you will be able to identify narcissists in any area of your own life.

4

ABUSE IN MANY FORMS

Back in 2007, when I was intently focused on healing from narcissistic abuse – from the inside out – I had some powerful revelations about the key reasons why narcissistic abuse happens to us and how to reverse our symptoms, and I felt compelled to reach out and share my experiences over the internet.

At that time a wonderful woman called Janara came into my life, by pure synchronicity, to help me build a website and publish articles to assist people who had been through similar experiences as myself. When I met her, I was amazed to discover that she too had suffered narcissistic abuse. Likewise, as soon as I started publishing articles documenting the common experiences my clients faced, I was astounded by how many people related to them and began to contact me. They wrote things like: 'This is exactly what I am going through. Were we with the same person?'

In 2008, after returning from Christmas in Koh Sumui, Thailand, I was working with my new healing system, now officially called Quanta Freedom Healing, and I was overjoyed to be able to help people shift incredible amounts of trauma and claim their freedom in powerful and fast ways. This was important, because as I learned from my own experience, and from those of others, people who are abused by narcissists can suffer from serious emotional, mental and physical health issues, which can be so excruciating that it can sometimes feel like it's impossible to live with them.

One of my clients at this time was Janine, who, despite being successful, owning her own property, having a large friendship circle and being a manager at a large firm, was desperately hooked on her narcissistic off-and-on boyfriend. He regularly discarded her, threw other women in her face and verbally, physically and sexually abused her in graphic, degrading ways. What was astounding, was that Janine had incredible self-worth in other areas of her life, but none whatsoever when it came to her relationship with him. Janine was on anti-depressants and seeing a psychologist, yet she still couldn't stop seeing him and was regularly feeling suicidal.

Janine was as dangerously hooked as anyone I had ever met. So addicted to him was she that she could see no way out of her torture other than to end her life. I worked with her in the same way that I do with every client: we didn't go into the logical story of the events that took place or 'what happened'. Instead we accessed what hurt in her emotional body, applied Quanta Freedom Healing to it, and found and released the traumas that were embedded in her subconscious.

During this process, Janine discovered that she was only attracted to men like her father – a military man who was stern and unavailable to love her. She was subconsciously trying to get 'Daddy' to love her this time round. Once those wounds were cleared from within her subconscious programming, Janine felt no attraction towards, nor obsession about, her ex-boyfriend at all. She stayed away from him, blocked his contact and kept working on her healing without the trauma of her old addiction to him. She was soon well on her way to being free forever from her previous horrifying relationship patterns.

Janine's wasn't an isolated case; many abuse victims who were finding their way to me were dealing with all sorts of narcissists, such as parents, siblings, their pastor or healer or even friends. Some were in terrible situations that involved domestic violence; others were severely traumatised as the result of emotional, mental, financial or spiritual abuse. The commonality amongst all of them was the distress caused by their being caught up in toxic power struggles, and from feeling addicted and bonded to the people who were hurting them – and not knowing why they were feeling like this.

My clientele was dramatically increasing via word of mouth from my own clients and from psychologists, doctors and other therapists who were now referring their abuse clients to me. Because Quanta Freedom Healing is an energetic healing practice that is performed without touch, I had been doing healings successfully by phone with clients for a while, some of whom lived great distances away, and even though I was able to help more people this way, I realised I was only dealing with the tip of the iceberg. Narcissistic abuse existed on a much bigger scale than I could ever have imagined, yet I still didn't comprehend the full magnitude of it.

That year, I received an email that jolted me to my core. It was from a lady in the USA, who had just lost her sister to a narcissist. Her sister had been depressed and trapped for years, and had taken her own life, leaving three small children behind. This lady was devastated and said she had been trying to get her sister to read my articles, but now it was too late.

Something inside me bubbled up with intense ferocity, and late into that night I researched suicide, and substance abuse and terminal illnesses and the causes, and I was fully convinced that the death rate from narcissistic abuse must be astronomical. I knew my healing work was saving lives and that many people like Janine were healing from chronic depression and helplessness, but now I started to think about our future generations too. What would happen to that poor lady's children now that their mum was gone? Were they to be single-parented by a narcissist? Would they take on their mother's path of helplessness and powerlessness in their relationships? Might they become abusers themselves? What about their children and their future generations?

Wider Healing Is Needed

My waiting list for one-on-one sessions was now six months. So, after hours, I started to create the Narcissistic Abuse Recovery Program (NARP). This consisted of sequential recorded Quanta Freedom Healing Modules, which laid out the step-by-step processes that I used in my one-on-one sessions, so people could listen to them at any time in the comfort of their own homes.

Creating this course was an incredibly channelled experience, similar to what had happened in Koh Sumui when I originally was 'shown' how to put the Quanta Freedom Healing process together: once more, I was guided all the way. I knew exactly how to put it together and what order the healings had to be in. The visualisations and the words needed to create energetic imprints, so that the healings would work on people, were literally 'given' to me. And work they did, beyond my wildest expectations.

News of the programme broke out globally, and I was approached for interviews and radio segments. More and more people were finding their way to my website and joining NARP. In a very short time after the release of NARP, I was receiving thousands of hits daily on my website and hundreds of emails were streaming into my inbox.

Due to the incredible amount of contact I had with those abused by narcissists and my awakening out of my previous wounded trance, I saw the truth. Narcissism is, sadly, prolific. This was confirmed for me by an interview I once did with my dear friend and colleague health expert Dr Christiane Northrup about 'energy vampires', in which she said she believed that 1 in 5 people suffer from Narcissistic Personality Disorder and that 1 in 25 is a sociopath. However, the published statistics concerning narcissists are frequently completely inaccurate because narcissism is mostly underdiagnosed and often undetected. By virtue of its very nature, the disease of narcissism entails a state of unconsciousness when it comes to personal accountability; narcissists take zero responsibility for their behaviour. Instead, the narcissist is likely to blame everyone else for their troubles and is therefore highly unlikely to seek professional help.

You Are Never Alone

Regardless of who the abuse has come from, it is serious, and I hope that by now you are gaining an understanding that helps you feel like you are not going crazy – and that you certainly are not alone.

I want you to know, with all my heart, that it is precisely through the catalyst of situations such as these, involving narcissistic abuse, that we can find and release our deep-seated inner trauma – and then begin to live free of it. This means that we do not have to remain stuck with the ongoing suffering – those terrible symptoms of abuse that take up so much of our energy, joy and life force. Healing ourselves takes dedication and it takes courage; however, it offers us a way out – a light at the end of the ghastly tunnel that we simply couldn't see previously. I and so many other people like me are the living, breathing examples of how people's lives can be healed and changed as a result of meeting and healing their inner trauma; and it is my greatest wish that, like us, you too escape from the bowels of hell into the true life that is your destiny.

If they only involve talking and exchanging information, many traditional forms of healing can leave us feeling stuck, trying to manage the symptoms of our trauma for years, decades or even a lifetime. However, the Thriver Way to heal allows us to heal deeply at our core, tackling all that is generating our symptoms, so that we can finally live free of them.

5

WHAT HAPPENS TO YOU WHEN YOU ARE ABUSED

Narcissistic abuse breakdowns and breakups are not experienced as regular relationship pain and disappointment. Time tends to heal those wounds, yet with narcissistic abuse, time is irrelevant. Unless you have personally experienced it, you can't even begin to fathom feeling like your 'being' is not your own any more, while trying to survive the all-consuming anxiety and deep depression that are now your everyday life. People commonly report that, even though they have previously been through horrific events, nothing affected them as badly as narcissistic abuse.

Some say that the narcissistic abuse experienced in childhood is the worst to get over because it's all you have ever known; whereas others state that giving up the dream of a soul mate, and the life you believed you would share with that special someone, is the worst trauma to overcome; and others declare that your child being a narcissist is the worst experience imaginable – because how do you turn your back on them?

Despite these various claims, I have seen all types of narcissistic abuse bring people to their knees, wondering how they will ever survive what has happened. And the terrible trauma continues regardless of whether they have been able to remove the narcissist from their life or not. The absence of a narcissist doesn't necessarily bring relief and closure; it is like the trauma is a living, breathing entity within them that has a presence of its own. I have worked with many people who have continued to suffer from the effects of narcissistic abuse long after it has occurred to them.

Thirty-five years ago, Grace had been married to a narcissist for a period of three years. When I met Grace, I was shocked to behold a woman who looked eighty yet who was only in her mid-fifties; she was frail and weak and shook continuously. She explained to me her constant need for medication since her marriage, as she suffered from anxiety, depression and panic attacks. She hadn't been able to work or engage in life in the ways in which she used to before the abuse. Grace was told by medical professionals that her mental illness was depression but that it was not necessarily related to her previous marriage, even though she was adamant it was. Until she found my information online, Grace had no idea she had been narcissistically abused, yet after relating the list of narcissistic characteristics to her ex-husband's behaviour, she was positive she had been. Suddenly, it all made sense and she was able to begin the healing process.

And then there was Mark, who had been single for fifteen years, but who desperately wanted to meet someone to share his life with. When dating, he often came across what he described as 'red flags' and he would not proceed. Even when he met nice ladies who he believed were decent, he just couldn't let them into his life. He knew he was finding every excuse not to connect with people who were available to love him. The cause lay in the trauma of 'the love of his life' leaving him for another man and alienating him from their children, which had caused deep emotional fractures that he just couldn't seem to overcome.

It's not just intimate narcissistic abuse that sabotages people's ability to lead healthy lives. As discussed in Chapter 2, childhood trauma – especially when caused by a narcissistic parent – creates incredible obstacles for people to be whole and healthy and capable of generating love, success and joy for themselves. If you have suffered narcissistic abuse from a boss, colleague, neighbour or even friend (actually anyone at all), the damage can still be horrifying, leaving you bamboozled and deeply concerned about the state you are in.

One doesn't have to look very far when Googling community boards for victims of narcissistic abuse to discover there are so many people stuck in an ongoing trauma that they believe they may never escape.

Sadly, there is a great deal of information available on the internet and from health professionals regarding the 'breakdown' experience, but very little research, understanding and application of the 'breakthrough' opportunity – which (thank goodness) is what the Thriver Recovery system is all about.

What also doesn't help matters is that many people, understandably, just don't know what to think or how to support someone who is going through narcissistic abuse. Logically, especially when a person has been separated for a time from the cause of the abuse, acquaintances think they should just recover from the experience. As Robin said, 'My family and friends are sick of me. They have all pretty much yelled at me to stop moping around and feeling sorry for myself – and to just get on with it. I wish I could, it's been two and half years now, but I just can't.'

I understand this perfectly; before experiencing narcissistic abuse myself I used to think people like this were simply blaming others for their problems and using excuses not to take responsibility for themselves. However, after being floored myself to the point of not knowing how I would remain upright, alive and breathing, now I totally understand: the trauma level of this experience is something else; it really is indescribable.

There are various reasons why people can't 'just get on with it'. Deep, powerful, soul reasons that belie everything we may ever have thought about how we can simply use positive thinking to overcome the pain and tribulations in our life. In his book *The Body Keeps the Score,* PTSD expert Bessel van der Kolk says: 'Neuroscience research shows that the only way we change the way we feel is by becoming aware of our inner experience and learning to befriend what is going on inside of us.'[1] In an online interview, Dr Bruce Lipton, the internationally acclaimed neurologist and bestselling author of *The Biology of Belief,* notes: 'Some people think that the conscious mind and the subconscious are directly connected with each other, so if I change the conscious mind I will change the subconscious program. That is totally incorrect and actually causes a lot of problems.'[2]

New Healing Methods Are Required

If we have suffered significant narcissistic abuse and the trauma levels are very high in our bodies, it might be difficult for us to achieve a shift through conventional talk therapy. That is because this approach's healing suggestions may not be able to get past our highly activated brain and filter down into our bodies. As a result, we may be left trying to manage the horrible trauma trapped inside us, rather than being able to release it and live completely free of it. In *The Body Keeps the Score,* Bessel van der Kolk states, 'The more intense the visceral, sensory input from the emotional brain, the less capacity the rational brain has to put a damper on it.'[3]

I was told after my adrenal and psychotic breakdown (which is where so many narcissistic abuse victims end up) that I would never again function normally and my only hope was to take anti-psychotics in order to achieve any standard of living. Similarly, I have encountered countless people globally who are in the traditional system of psychology and medication, yet who are still barely surviving their constant struggle with anxiety, depression, adrenal fatigue and post-traumatic stress disorder – and who are certainly not Thriving.

Please note I am not anti-therapy and I know many wonderful therapists who understand and work with the body–brain connection. I also love the fact that more and more healthcare professionals are catching on to this truth (which is consistent with narcissist abuse recovery): that it is only those people who undergo an internal shift, deep within themselves, who become different. They are the ones who, as a result of releasing trauma from within their inner identity at a cellular level, experience their mind following suit. Freed up from toxic trauma, they have the room in their cells now for new ideas, fresh ways of being, inspirations, solutions and true healing to enter. Without this inner work and shift, it is like trying to change what is happening in a car's engine while the hood is closed! The work simply doesn't get into the engine for the repair to take place, and we can only guess what is really going on. For many trauma victims, concepts, information, strategies, study and even intensive cognitive coaching just don't provide the conditions necessary for deep internal change to take place, because the logical mind does not operate on the same wavelength, frequency or communication channel as the subconscious mind.

Regrettably, it seems that more 'thinking' and 'talking' are often not the answer for abuse victims. In fact, they can sometimes inadvertently make matters worse by cementing our inner identity as being that of 'an abuse victim'. As Rachel so eloquently put it: 'There is only so much that talk therapy can do when the trauma we've experienced that's attracted toxic relationships began at a pre-verbal time in our lives.' And as Dee Dee wrote in: 'I've been in talk therapy for quite a while, but I walk out frustrated and in tears. While my therapist means well, and understands the hallmarks of emotional abuse, she doesn't have the tools to offer me to make the deep inner shifts that need to happen in order to heal and let go.'

I concur; it was totally the same for me. Nothing I heard, spoke about or learned allowed me to do the one thing we all need to do to get well: to let go of the trauma and be able to live without its horrifying effects inside me.

Why People Couldn't Heal

During 2008, as I was working on myself at a deep level with Quanta Freedom Healing and sharing its incredible benefits with others, I became immersed in a mission to understand and create a better way for people to heal. I frenetically researched all I could about the brain and body connection as I was perplexed as to why so many intelligent people, who were trying to do everything they could to heal, weren't able to free themselves from abuse symptoms until they accessed the subconscious healing modalities offered by Quanta Freedom Healing. I was also fascinated by the primal, all-consuming addiction to narcissists that we all suffered from, and why it seemed to be totally untreatable with logic.

Standard science and psychology weren't granting me the answers, whereas quantum physics and neuroscience and global thought-leaders like Dr Joe Dispenza, Dr Bruce Lipton and Dr Candace Pert did. I was amazed that no one else appeared to be accessing this information or talking about it for trauma recovery – despite the fact that it resonated powerfully with this area and made incredible sense to me. (Later, I also discovered the ground-breaking work of Dr Bessel van der Kolk, mentioned earlier.) From these neuroscientists' studies, I learned about emotional addictions and why people stay attached to abuse and become hooked on narcissists – and then can't let go. And why, even if they do physically leave, they often stay stuck in the terrible cycles of obsessing and still feeling addicted, powerless, unresolved and traumatised.

I came to understand the difference between the subconscious and the conscious mind and how they both operate. As Dr Bruce Lipton says, 'The major problem is that people are aware of their conscious beliefs and behaviors, but not of subconscious beliefs and behaviors ... the fact is that the subconscious mind is a million times more powerful than the conscious mind and that we operate 95 to 99 percent of our lives from subconscious programs.'[4]

The picture was starting to come into focus as to why mere thinking couldn't overcome the powerful feelings that were triggered by the subconscious – and then there was more. In an interview for the film *What The Bleep Do We Know!?,* Dr Joe Dispenza noted: 'We know physiologically that nerve cells that fire together wire together. If you practise something over and over again, those nerve cells have a long-term relationship. If you get angry on a daily basis, if you get frustrated on a daily basis, if you suffer on a daily basis, if you give reason for the victimisation in your life, you are rewiring and reintegrating that neural-net on a daily basis. That neuro-net now has a long term relationship with all those other nerve cells called an identity.'[5]

From this, I started to realise that our emotional trauma was being 're-lived' by our thoughts: a revelation that was signed, sealed and delivered for me when I researched the work of the late Dr Candace Pert, a neuroscientist and a pharmacologist, who explained the body–brain connection in this way: 'Your mind is in every cell of your body.'[6]

The Healing Key

When we have significant trauma, as Dr Joe Dispenza puts it in his audio workshop, *Breaking the Habit of Being Yourself – How to Lose Your Mind and Create a New One,* 'The brain follows the body – always',[7] meaning we can only think within the range of the trauma. I had come to understand – as I also experienced – that unless a shift happens at the core level of our being, within our subconscious programmes, the 'stinking thinking' (i.e. thoughts that match the painful nature of the inner trauma) of feeling powerless, shell-shocked, deceived, cheated and victimised didn't ease. In fact, as the years go by, some people like Grace get worse and not better as a result of the neuro-nets in their brains becoming more practised at asserting a particular self-identity that is embedded in painful emotions and thought patterns.

I was discovering that the reason Quanta Freedom Healing was working so effectively in my own and other people's lives was because, by engaging with theta brainwaves (which I will explain), its process is in direct contact with the subconscious programmes that are responsible for driving the trauma we are feeling.

This is what the Theta Healing Institute, created by founder Vianna Stibel, have to say about theta brainwaves: 'Theta brain waves can be considered the subconscious; they govern the part of our mind that lies between the conscious and the unconscious and retain memories and feelings. They also direct your beliefs and your behavior. It is believed that this mental state allows you to act below the level of the conscious mind.'[8]

With regard to trauma recovery, it is important that we do access the subconscious, because, as Dr Bruce Lipton says, 'I want to be clear that merely reading your book – or any self-help book – and being able to comprehend the concepts does not provide what's necessary for someone's subconscious to be rewired, for a reader to achieve their own healing. Understanding the concept is very different from integrating it into everyday life. It's only in constantly interrupting the tapes, or through an extraordinary experience like a deep, emotional transformative moment or a powerful hypnosis that you can achieve self-healing.' He goes on to say, 'Or a series of reprogramming modalities collectively referred to as energy psychology.'[9] The latter – 'energy psychology' – is exactly what Quanta Freedom Healing is.

As I kept applying Quanta Freedom Healing to myself and more and more trauma was leaving my inner being, I discovered an innate, organic wisdom emerging within me. I started connecting to natural states that I didn't know I was capable of feeling. Freed from my internal trauma, these wonderful feelings arose spontaneously. The same thing was happening for many other people as well. And I realised what 'unconsciousness' really means: it means that when we are locked into painful subconscious programmes that have become our core identity, we don't even know that we are trapped in them. It was exactly those subconscious programmes of learned helplessness and powerlessness that we acquired as children which were causing us to hand over our power to abusers and to stay traumatised. It isn't until we start shifting out of these ways of being that we can unravel the old self and begin to be released into our true self.

This was when I started to understand at a profound level what the addiction to the narcissist and to narcissistic abuse had truly been about: it was trauma bonding.

How We Become Trauma Bonded to Narcissists

The addiction to narcissists is anything but logical; it is in fact a deep cellular physiological process. The manic pulls can be so extreme, it feels like you will literally die if you don't reconnect in some way with the narcissist – even if just through your thoughts.

In her book *Molecules of Emotion,* Dr Candace Pert describes how our brain creates neuropeptides (amino acid chains) which are distributed throughout our body. There is a different peptide for each emotion, and the cells of our body literally get hooked on the ones that they receive regular rushes of. If we regularly experience powerlessness, victimisation and all the other terrible feelings that go with narcissistic abuse – feelings that are consequently chemically coursing through our body in large amounts – our brain pushes us to go to the source of that neuropeptide and to interact with it, hook up with it or think about it in order to generate more of the chemical that our body is addicted to. Pert states that when rats are fed neuropeptides, they can become so addicted to them that they will forgo food, water and all self-care in order to obtain the peptide; and that neuropeptides are more addictive that any synthetic drug.

Pert's work was so ground-breaking that many, including her husband and collaborator Dr Michael Riff, believed she had 'established the critical link between mind and body'. One of the greatest takeaways I ever got from Candace's work is her statement that: 'Your body is your subconscious mind that you can't heal by talk alone.'[10] From the moment I heard those words something within me knew this was the truth. I absolutely knew that real healing had to be done through the body, and that our trauma programmes are not caused at a logical level; they come into being at the emotional level.

For real recovery to take place, the peptide cycle has to be interrupted and healed, and that can't take place at the level of logic. The roots lie with the original trauma that existed before this more recent hurt; that is the cause of the old self seeking more of the same. And it's this sequence that needs to be broken.

It helps to understand that addiction, the urge to reconnect with something that is damaging us (in this case the narcissist), is not the real issue – it is a symptom. It is the existing trauma that has never been resolved within the body which is causing that addiction. Let me explain it this way: imagine you've given in and eaten a large slice of chocolate cake that you had been denying yourself all day. Now you feel self-disgust. You know you've blown your calorie count and you say to yourself, 'Why did I do that? I have no self-control!' Then an hour later you crave another piece, and you wrestle with your craving and make the excuse 'I'll go to gym twice tomorrow' – and you eat the cake and feel even more shame.

Logically, you might think the first 'telling off' would have kept you away from another slice. But it didn't. Why not? The reason is that, as you probably tend to beat yourself up a lot (boy, did I used to do that!), your peptide rush of self-disgust was so intense that the cells in your body responded to it by gearing themselves up to get another fix of their drug of choice. So you were forced into eating that second slice as you tried to self-medicate (which is the addictive urge) the pain of self-disgust. Your brain enabled all of this to take place by conjuring up the excuses necessary to take exactly the action that would feed those urges.

Your mind is an ineffectual tool when the almighty urges of your entire body are pitted against it. As Dispenza says, 'The brain follows the body': your chemical addiction will trick your mind into coming up with all the excuses it needs to gratify it 'just one more time'. I know how many times I was forced by my addiction to go back to the narcissist again, or to stalk him on social media, or call someone who knew him, or think about him 'just one more time'; even though logically I knew that connecting to his energy again would pitch me into traumatic obsessions whereby I could lose entire days of functioning. Of course, I came up with every excuse to justify my behaviour, but it was really my brain wanting to manufacture more of the terrible emotional cocktails that my body was hooked on.

Now think about the narcissist in your own life and any urges you have or intense emotions that your connection with him or her creates, and you will start to have an understanding of what is really going on. Think about the emotions that cause the most powerful emotional rushes for you. It may be the narcissist invalidating you, verbally abusing you, abandoning you, betraying you, not trusting you, accusing you or hurting you in some unspeakable way that devastates you. Whatever it is, these are the emotions that your entire cellular being is addicted to the most. Now let's take it a little deeper: these powerful surges of pain represent the unhealed, unfinished stuff from your past. Therein lie the traumatic wounds that are the root cause of the painful chemical rushes which your body was already used to before the narcissist came into your life; these include the fractures that we have acquired from our ancestors and which have been developmental in our childhoods. If the narcissist is your parent or a family member, these are the chemical cocktails that were already a part of your nervous system, even pre-conception, meaning they were inherited as part of your ancestor's painful traumatic beliefs being carried family to family.

Okay, so back to present day ... logically of course you would *not* play a part in manufacturing more of those same traumatic experiences. You would never logically pursue and stay attached to more feelings of powerlessness, victimisation, abandonment, being unloved, dismissed, invalidated, overlooked, replaced, irrelevant, worthless, betrayed and deceived – yet unconsciously what is really going on here? What is really driving your part in not breaking away for good, and then staying away?

I know when I first discovered this information, like you may be feeling, I was astounded as to why this isn't common knowledge. Then I realised a lot of establishments would be non-existent if it was. Surely, if people knew how to unhook themselves from their peptide addictions to terrible emotions that were destroying their lives, there would be a much reduced need for Big Pharma. My own case alone resulted in one less prescription for anti-psychotics.

My personal belief is that the greatest authority we can have comes from examining our own lives. If you apply this information regarding peptide addiction to the areas of your life in which you have struggled to make healthy choices, it will resonate deeply with you as to why you have been unable to make them. It will also explain to you why, until now, you may have battled terribly to heal your abuse symptoms and patterns.

For many people in this community, understanding exactly how peptide addiction works and how to break free from it has turned out to be the missing key in their Thriver Recovery. For this reason, I will be covering peptide addiction in greater detail in your 'You Can Thrive Program'. Register for free access: w ww.youcanthriveprogram.com.

The Thriver Way to Heal

The Thriver Way to Heal might appear to be totally counterintuitive when compared to the ways in which many of us are used to trying to heal from trauma: no longer do we share the story and talk about what happened to us. We move away from the realm of logic and stop searching outside ourselves for the reasons something happened 'to' us; instead we go inside, into our emotional centre, and start doing the core work at that level. Effectively, what we are doing is creating a shift within our inner being – our subconscious – to then produce a shift in how we feel and think about this topic in our life.

When we start to understand the Quantum Law of *so within, so without,* we realise that we are powerless to try to change things and people outside ourselves in order to feel better. Attempting to change other things and people is a false premise which means that rather than feeling better we only hand away more power and feel even more powerless as a result. Instead, when we take full, radical responsibility and embrace the notion that 'no matter how this was caused, only I have the power to change myself and then I will feel better', we are finally pointing in the right direction.

Today, with Quantum Tools such as Quanta Freedom Healing, we can access and release trauma, break our peptide addictions and heal our emotional being in order to generate better evolved and healthier thoughts. As Bessel van der Kolk states in *The Body Keeps The Score,* under the subheading 'Accessing the Emotional Brain': 'The rational, analysing part of the brain, centred on the dorsolateral prefrontal cortex, has no direct connections with the emotional brain, where most imprints of trauma reside, but the medial prefrontal cortex, the center of self-awareness does.'[11]

At first, the idea might seem fanciful that we can completely heal our trauma by going within and doing specific work on our inner being. I get that; before I started working with body energetic healing, I firmly believed that we could only use our mind to heal and that nothing in our emotional body was the issue. I thought the body came after the mind, but now I know it is the other way around.

At the time, I also believed that visualisations were not real enough to make a difference; that they were far too ethereal to make certain things happen within our DNA and unconscious programmes. Now I know that when you have the code to contact and communicate with your subconscious, and to instruct it, then you can shift yourself from 'who you were being' into 'who you would like to be' in pretty spectacular and powerful ways.

Many people who access my healing system are already familiar with subconscious healing modalities such as Reiki, Kinesiology, Theta Healing or EFT (Emotional Freedom Technique), or they have witnessed the real-life results of people who all of sudden changed dramatically – seemingly overnight – as a result of using Quanta Freedom Healing. These sorts of results are the reason why so many psychologists, counsellors, health professionals and global relationship experts have contacted me, endorsed QFH and now recommend patients to this work. Then there are those people who come to it who have had enough of the trauma of abuse, who have tried 'everything' to heal but to no avail – and who would be willing to bang two fishes above their head if they thought it might help! These people often sign into my free webinar, have a Quanta Freedom Healing experience with me and irrefutably know something has happened to them.

This is what Jayne said about her webinar experience: 'I am in disbelief how my shellshock at his betrayal – which I have been seeing a therapist for over year about – melted away in a heartbeat. That night I slept, the next day I ate and went for a walk. These were things I was still struggling with. It's been a week and now I can't even access the thoughts I used to have about what he did.'

I personally never grow tired of the feeling I receive whenever I do Quanta Freedom Healing shifts on myself. Naturally, at the start of my narcissistic abuse recovery journey, I was cleaning out tons of trauma and pain, but now I use Quanta Freedom Healing techniques to tackle any confusion, negative triggers, health issues, fatigue – literally anything at all when I know I'm not at my optimal best. I know that by clearing trauma I automatically reset to wellbeing and I grow in consciousness, health, wisdom, love, insight and even youth! I also know that when I clear the blocks within me that separate me from my highest goals, aspirations and contributions to my life, these start flowing in again.

The Quanta Freedom Healing 'shifting' process starts like this: the accessing and gathering of trauma via specific visualisation processes. This part feels heavy and toxic as we draw trauma out of the subconscious memory and from those connected parts of the body that are holding that trauma. We then release the trauma from three specific areas:

1. The emotional pain body, that part of our subconscious of which we are most aware and where we can name what we feel the most easily when triggered.

2. The past-life level of trauma, which includes any previous trauma we have accumulated on our journey. (If you don't believe in past lives as such, then for you this level can relate to any trauma in your past.)

3. The epigenetic DNA level, which is the stored trauma connected to our ancestors and to childhood wounds caused by both nurture (our conditioning) and nature (what was inherited).

When the release from these three levels of the subconscious takes place, we feel a relief and a lightening of a previous emotional burden. For most people, these feelings are very real. Then we bring in the 'Light' – our super-conscious/God/Source Energy/the Universe (or whatever form you believe a Higher Power takes), which has the power to heal what our logical mind simply can't. And this is when we experience an instant shift from unconsciousness (fear, pain, powerlessness and trauma) to consciousness (love, peace, wholeness, wisdom and powerfulness) concerning the topic where the trauma previously lay.

It feels like resolution; it feels complete. For me, it feels like bliss and an opening up within and emotional freedom. The previous trauma feels gone. We have done no less than midwife a breakdown of the old order to achieve a breakthrough of the new order. We have moved from a false self (of trauma and false beliefs) to a true self (an alignment with Life/ Source/ Creation). This is what Marija, a member of the NARP Community, says about it: 'The healing is so deep and profound and the shifts are noticeable immediately.'

Yes, this healing method is incredibly spiritual. It is Quantum; it is where science, consciousness and spirit meet. It grants us the power to be our own healers in ways that we might never have dreamed possible until now. It truly is an incredible solution for any disease, and is especially effective for recovery from trauma. Why? Because our mind is far too shattered and worn down to try to overcome the force of the regurgitating traumas and peptide addiction that has completely hijacked our being. We therefore need a way to heal that keeps our logical mind out of the equation, because as soon as the mind is involved it gives rise to 'stinking thinking' and the obsessional loops we become trapped in, that are only making matters worse.

This is a personal testimony that Vanessa shared on the internet about her shift as a result of accessing Quanta Freedom Healing: 'I tried all my life to change my thinking *by* thinking – but it didn't work. I was hospitalised for a suicide attempt and three weeks after my release I have already experienced major positive shifts in my inner being. Now I truly believe that energetic healing is the only way to change our thinking. I owe my life to this discovery.'

Annise, another member of the NARP Community, described her first ever Quanta Freedom Healing: 'I had just connected to an intense feeling of being a worthless dirty rag that could be discarded at any moment. I felt so worthless I literally felt like there was no place for me on earth. Then the shift happened, and I realised I could take my power back and that I am worthy of love and so much more. That dirty rag feeling that totally consumed me, was now a million miles away. That shift happened in only a half an hour!! Delving into the pain and acknowledging wounds on a subconscious level and learning how we have actually created our lives to heal ourselves, and that we are not victims is the most powerful thing anyone can experience.'

Get Ready To Take Your First Step

Now that we have approached the path that leads to healing for real, it's important to prepare for the first steps along it. The next chapter is therefore about a stage of the recovery process which is so important that your chances of healing might be sabotaged if you overlook it. Join me as we begin the journey and discover why.

6

THE VITAL FIRST STEP TO THRIVING

One of the most important things that we will ever have to do to make the space to heal for real is ironically the most incredibly difficult to do: to detach from our abuser *and really mean it* – meaning, taking our focus off what the narcissist is or isn't doing and turning our attention fully inwards to heal ourselves.

This part of the recovery is not just important, it is critical. Time and time again, I have seen people who are not serious about No Contact or strictly Modified Contact (which are two commonly used terms in abuse-recovery circles that I will explain in this chapter) continuously sabotage their chances of healing for real. It is vital that you understand how wanting to recover and then reattaching to the narcissist is as disastrous as it is for an alcoholic or a drug user to capitulate and take up drinking or drugs again.

When healing from narcissistic abuse, the most important thing is to break the addiction to the abuser and to grant ourselves enough love and self-value so that we say no more to allowing ourselves to be continually hurt. If we go No Contact, this involves cutting off all forms of communication with the narcissist in our life. In essence, No Contact means that we stop hurting ourselves.

The following self-healing motto is essential at this stage:

> I declare to myself and to all of my Life that no matter what the narcissist does or doesn't do, I am now removing myself to heal and look after myself.

Many of us know the Serenity Prayer, and its message is highly relevant to understanding how to heal from narcissistic abuse:

> God grant me the serenity to accept the things I cannot change,
> Courage to change the things I can,
> and the Wisdom to know the difference.

The truth is that we can't change narcissists and the more we try to control them the more we are changed and controlled by them. At this stage, you may feel miles away from serenity – more like you are trying to escape a warzone within and without! The healing, peace and sanity come only after we start to control the one entity we can – ourselves – by releasing the terrible triggered traumas that are erupting to the surface from within.

How Difficult No Contact Is

From a logical perspective, it may be easy to realise that No Contact is the only way to heal; however, most people are completely taken by surprise by how hard it is to get away and then stay away from their abuser. This is what Margaret said about what happened to her when she purposefully stopped all contact: 'I was shocked by how traumatised and terrified I felt. Not so much about what he might do to me, but rather how I felt like I was going mad. I thought I was losing my mind and like I was going to die. Every minute of every day I was white-knuckling it. Being in the hell house and having my self-worth battered by him felt preferable to what I was going through now. I wanted to return to him constantly.'

Margaret was experiencing what every narcissistic abuse victim goes through when they go cold turkey: the horrific peptide addiction, which is not getting its fix (i.e. via the narcissist) anymore, hits at full force. As does complex posttraumatic stress disorder. When caught up in the battle of day-to-day survival with a narcissist, you don't have time to feel the trauma fully from yesterday, let alone last week or month. Yet when you are out of the situation and no longer in the warzone, it all has a chance to hit home – and it does, like a freight train. This is when your mind – propelled by the peptide addiction in your body –

will try to convince you, with any reason it can offer, to reconnect.

Kevin, one of my clients, said this to me after two weeks of No Contact: 'I know now how much I love her. This has to be a soul contract. I can't eat, I can't sleep, I can't function. I am supposed to stay with her and work this out because there is no way I could be feeling feelings like this unless she was my true soul mate.' I knew it wasn't true, and after Kevin went back for yet another round of unspeakable abuse, and returned to me completely suicidal and barely alive, he conceded that if he didn't turn inwards and heal he was not going to survive. Once out on the other side of his recovery, he saw the truth clearly – it was never love at all; it was all about his need to heal the traumas within himself that were on repeat in his relationship with her.

In standard recovery programmes, people break No Contact continually because of the terrible traumas that surface when they try to leave narcissists. A relapse is commonly and easily caused when the addiction urges become too strong – when those feelings of needing resolution, accountability, apology and amends (all equalling lack of closure) strike. Or, we can cave in when the narcissist 'hoovers', 'hoovering' being a term commonly used in abuse-recovery communities to refer to the narcissist's attempts to suck you back into a relationship with them for more narcissistic supply.

Narcissists know how to draw people back in very easily; it's simple: hit their identified weak spot. Mark had always been a rescuer of women because his mother had died at an early age from mental illness. Whenever Mark tried to pull away, his narcissistic abuser, Lucy, would get a message through to him that she was in trouble and needed him. Because Mark had never healed his original trauma, he got emotionally hooked back in every time.

Xavier's narcissistic boss took advantage of Xavier's superior work ethic by telling him he was uncaring about his team members unless he took on their unfinished work as well. This always got the better of Xavier, echoing his father's words that he was selfish when he wasn't giving up his life to look after his younger siblings.

Janelle, on the other hand, had left Rob many times because of his narcissistic abuse. They had lots of joint friends, and Rob only had to ask another woman out on a date and let a friend of Janelle's know, and Janelle found herself manically begging him for another chance. Janelle's father had left her and her mother for another woman, and because Janelle had never got to the bottom of her terrible panic whenever she thought Rob was moving on with someone else, she continually fell for this ploy.

For you, the triggers may be the narcissist breaking down and crying – and your heart aches for them. Or maybe you can't get past the guilt of leaving them the way they are and not being able to protect and look after them. Or maybe they leave abusive, insane and unfair messages – and you can't help but retaliate.

This is the bottom line: even if you become strong enough to stay away from them, your evolution may not come that easy. Whatever it is that the narcissist is in your life to help you heal, this needs to play out. Marianne said to me, 'This man is like a terminator. I can't get rid of him and his harassment. How long is this going to go on for?' I replied, 'When you heal what you need to and his behaviour becomes as disinteresting as a slug on a pavement to you – that's when it'll all stop.' She got it: she stopped focusing on his attempts to abuse her by proxy with the authorities and cleared her own terror of persecution within herself, and everything fell flat for him. And, true to form, he left her alone. Narcissists simply can't go without their payout: narcissistic supply.

So this is the deal: not only do we have to contend with the peptide addiction when it hits at full force, as well as the narcissist possibly 'hoovering' to try to get us back into the ring to hand over more attention to them; there is also all of society's conditioning, which tells us to focus on the problem and to try to change it.

And with narcissistic abuse, there are tons of problems when we leave or are discarded by a narcissist. We don't just split up from narcissists with a respectful hug while wishing each other the very best. What is more usual is that you have been devastated beyond measure – the narcissist has raped and pillaged you emotionally and mentally for sure. Also possibly physically, sexually and spiritually, and more than likely financially.

While we may have been taught by society to seek retribution and to insist on accountability and justice, we are not dealing with a soulful being; we are dealing with a heartless and cruel false self who has no concept of playing fair. To add insult to injury regarding what the narcissist has already taken from you, deceived you about or destroyed in your life, he or she may then not allow you to claim what is rightfully yours, and might do unspeakable acts to those remaining things and people that mean something to you, or assert ownership of them – all to hurt you.

Of course the injustice and violations of the situation are eating you alive and you want to make it right, yet the narcissist knows that this grants him or her attention – good or bad, it makes no difference. It's like those peptide chemicals: it's the intensity that counts, and, to the narcissist, the ends justify the means if the result is to get you hooked in again. If you retaliate, you hand over narcissistic supply; if you break down and plead for the narcissist to do the right thing, you hand over narcissistic supply. If you try to cut a deal, the narcissist knows that they have you cornered now for narcissistic supply for as long as they want.

There is only one solution: pull away, establish No Contact, cut your losses – and heal. Yes, absolutely, if you have legal recourse and have healed yourself beyond triggers, and are able to walk a straight and powerful line, you can and will do well in court. I have seen many a narcissist be defeated by Thrivers in court who have done this. Their situation stands in stark contrast to those people who stay connected with narcissists, who walk on broken glass, who try to appease them or play them; or who delude themselves into believing the narcissist will come to their senses and 'do the right thing'; or who just remain plain terrorised and heartbroken by them. This is like being in the spider's web and getting yourself well and truly tangled up before being devoured as the narcissist's meal.

Can I say it to you enough times? These are the vital points: paying any attention to the narcissist is like handing them the metaphoric bullets with which to shoot you; you will only become more hurt, sicker, more drained and even more powerless. There is no relief, closure, sensibility, sanity or wellness to be gained from connecting to the narcissist, just as there is none to be gained from a heroin needle. We can't have it both ways: keep taking our drug while expecting to recover from its effects.

One of the most powerful things I started to do for myself, when I was fully invested in my healing, was to imagine that my abuser was deadly poison and, in my mind, I visualised placing a red cross over the top of him. He was lethal and if I had continued with him there is no doubt I would be dead. Narcissistic abuse is that serious for nearly everybody.

Hanging on to Hope

I would really like to talk to those of you who are still clinging on to hope. I understand this totally: once upon a time, I used to believe that if there was one chance in a million that I could fix the relationship, then I would stay and try to find it.

It is so hard to get past the idea and the version of this person that we have projected on to them. This person was supposed to be our soul mate, our life partner for the rest of our lives. Or they were supposed to be a genuinely loving and supportive mother or father, or sibling. Perhaps this person was meant to be the business partner we hoped they would be, or the healer genuinely wanting to help us, or the friend we'd always wanted. But they are not. And it is time for us to let go of the dream and the sentimentality, and to face reality. So many of us like to think that our good nature and love could conquer anything, but it doesn't.

Healthy relationships need components like honesty and trust and shared values. And the truth is this:

the narcissist is never after love, harmony or teamwork and a peaceful, happy existence with you. Regardless of who this person is to you, the narcissist can't be loving and genuine, no matter how much we believe they should be.

He or she is only ever after narcissistic supply and for a time you were hooked in as the dispenser of that drug. It's not personal. Wanting and expecting a narcissist to be different is like expecting a crocodile to roll over while you scratch its tummy. A narcissist doesn't want to be loved back to health by you. A narcissist does not want to engage in successful and healthy teamwork with you. A narcissist doesn't want to get better. A narcissist only wants to extract your energy, and the more you stay connected, the longer you offer yourself up as prey.

This is something that you need to get very clear about, and when you are, you will know there is no possible way forward other than to detach and heal yourself.

No Contact (When Possible)

No Contact means No Contact. This means that you change phone numbers and email accounts, or you use any app necessary in order to block the narcissist from getting in contact with you. It means you stop that person from connecting with you in all ways possible. It means that if they do try to get a message through to you, you don't accept it; you delete before reading or listening to it and you don't answer the door if they come calling.

I don't recommend doing No Contact while leaving any ways in which that person could contact you in any shape or form, because this means you will be constantly checking whether they have or haven't. Remove all possibilities. It's a pain to change your contact details, yet I highly recommend it; or, at the very least, set up blocks and diversions so that you don't even know if the narcissist has tried to reach you. You want to remove not only all physical contact possibilities but any reminders of this person in your life.

Importantly, there is more to this. The following example shows how we need not only to create boundaries with that person, but with ourselves. Mandy had left Chris and she meant it; she knew he was toxic and she was sick of his constant affairs and porn addiction. She was done and blocked all contact possibilities. Yet then Mandy went and created a fake Facebook profile and befriended Chris! Several times a day she would stalk his Facebook page and the pages of the women connected to it. Many months later Mandy was still doing this and would even wake up in the night to check up on him. Mandy was feeding her addiction and using it to self-medicate, rather than facing her traumas, healing them and thereby evolving beyond relationships with men who cheated on her like her father had done to her mother.

Tara had blocked her mother's contact because she had had enough of her rages, guilt trips and demands for money. Yet Tara remained obsessed with speaking to other family members daily to find out what her mother was up to and what she might be saying about her. The small unhealed child inside Tara was still craving her narcissistic mother's attention and love.

The moral to the story is this: delete all social-media connections with the narcissist and block their account so that you don't look at it. Don't get in contact with people who know the narcissist in an attempt to find out through them what he or she is doing. What the narcissist is doing is none of your business; what you are doing – and how you are healing – is what needs to be your business.

When we are orientated towards Thriver Recovery, we take No Contact one step further: we apply it to our thoughts. Rather than give in to the usual 'stinking thinking' and obsession that occur because of our peptide addiction, whenever the terrible pulls try to force us to obsess, we apply this rule instead: 'less thinking, more shifting'. Rather than surrendering to obsessing about it, we use Quanta Freedom Healing to track that terrible urge back to its origin, and release it from there. We stop trying to work it out logically; rather, we work it up and out of our bodies instead. As a result of doing this, our mind then automatically shifts into relief from those pulls. Then it gets easier and easier to be away and stay away, and before we know it, all attraction, obsession and unresolved feelings dissolve away.

We are finally putting things right in the place where they really need to be addressed – within our inner being – and the accompanying sense of relief, solidness and empowerment lets us know how right this inner orientation is. And the wisdom comes, a deep, organic understanding about the journey with the narcissist: that he or she was really only a catalyst to help us do this.

As St Paul said in Ephesians 5:13: 'But everything exposed by the light become visible – for everything that is illuminated becomes a Light itself.'

Modified Contact (If You Can't Go No Contact)

Now, of course, there may be circumstances that mean you can't just leave and go full No Contact. You might run a business together, or you might still be living under the same roof and need to work out some arrangements first. You might be parallel-parenting with a narcissist (co-parenting isn't possible because narcissists aren't cooperative) and/or going through court battles with one. Also maybe, emotionally, you just aren't ready to do this yet; you don't feel clear or strong enough.

Please know it is possible to detach and to start powerfully healing yourself even if you are still in contact with a narcissist or even living under the same roof. This is when applying Modified Contact can be used. It means detaching emotionally as much as possible, and not feeding the narcissist any energy, conversation, emotion or attention other than what is absolutely necessary. 'Grey rock' is commonly talked about in recovery groups as an effective way to be as bland, dull and uninteresting as possible when dealing with a narcissist, so that they don't get fed any drama or energy from you. If you give them nothing, they have to find their narcissistic supply elsewhere. This is powerful, because when you withdraw your energy from the narcissist, then you have the energy available to love and heal yourself back to wholeness, as well as to work on any triggers that are coming up for you, as you disengage from the narcissist and set up your new life.

Many people have used Modified Contact successfully in joint businesses, shared living arrangements, parallel-parenting or when buying some time before leaving. When Joanne, for example, announced that she was moving into the spare bedroom, her partner Tony started stonewalling her, making snide remarks and changing the plans for their garden design – things he knew would hurt her. Before, these sorts of behaviours used to hook her in and make her react to him, but now she was determined to let go of her life with Tony, heal her inner wounds, get herself organised and leave in an empowered way. As far as she was concerned, let him play his games! When

Tony realised these tactics weren't getting her attention, he tried begging her to return to him and promised he would change. With the help of Quanta Freedom Healing, Joanne shifted out those traumas that might otherwise have compelled her to reconnect and feel sorry for him. She stayed strong. After Tony made a few more attempts to win her back, which ranged from showering her with gifts to being downright nasty and threatening her with violence, Joanne looked him fair and square in the eye and told him that if he laid one finger on her, she would prosecute him. She had done so much work on her inner being that she was no longer scared of him.

Tony backed off, left her alone and started flaunting other women in front of her. Joanne went to the NARP Modules and shifted out the now-emerging trauma – those triggered hurt feelings – as well. By the time she left Tony, she had set up funds, got a promotion at work and created a strong support network of friends and family around her. She planned her escape while he was out of town, didn't tell him she was going, and was able to remove everything from the house that was hers. She already had an attorney force proceedings to sell the house. Tony capitulated; he signed a fair agreement and, because he was energetically defeated, just wanted to be free of the injury to his ego caused by her not being intimidated by him. This is what happens when there is absolutely no narcissistic supply to gain and the game is up.

Modified Contact can be a lot more challenging than No Contact, in that you have to deal with the constant triggers around you. However, if you are determined to be incredibly disciplined and to say 'no more' to your addiction of obsessing, and not to hook into the narcissist, but to look inwards instead to heal yourself – then it can be done, as Joanne proves, very successfully.

Creating healthy boundaries is a very important part of successful Modified Contact, which might well entail intervention by the law, third-party mediation and contact points if necessary to settle matters concerning settlements, property and custody disputes.

You may wish to arrange neutral handover places for the children, and to use a portal such as 'Our Family Wizard' for communication when parallel-parenting. Do not allow the narcissist to visit your home and children whenever he or she wants. It will be very important that you go through the legal system to have definite orders in place about custody times. And don't be tempted to do family time together, because your children are a part of your susceptibilities and narcissists generally will not hesitate to try to use them against you. Your children are much safer with a narcissist when you are not there at the same time, because when you are absent they won't readily become pawns in the narcissist's games to make them see you come undone.

Leaving Safely

Most narcissists are bullies; they will feed off your fear and attack you with it. This means that when you have no fear, they are powerless to affect you. In my own case, and in those of many other people, I discovered that when we took out intervention orders against narcissists who threatened us or even harassed us, and used these in conjunction with working on our own inner wounds, the narcissists backed right off.

However, if you can't get beyond your fears and/or the person you are dealing with is dangerous, it could be time to get professional help. I totally acknowledge that there are some people out there who find themselves in very dangerous situations, and who are undergoing serious physical threat and abuse, perhaps even living with psychopaths. If this is your situation, please make sure you contact the police; they will help link you up with domestic violence resources that are available to help you leave safely and protect you once you have left. Public awareness, strategies and support are getting better all the time – there is help available for you. And also know that someone does not have to physically threaten or harm you for you to take out an intervention order against them. If you have told somebody not to contact you but they continue to do so, and you feel immense anguish and torment as a result, then this too is harassment; it is abuse, and you have a right to live without it.

Getting Ready To Heal For Real

Now that you have an understanding of how vital detachment from your abuser and creating your space to heal is, we can move on to Part Two, which explores the practical application of each stage of healing the Thriver Way.

PART TWO

THE STEPS TO HEALING

You may write me down in history
With your bitter, twisted lies,
You may tread me in the very dirt
But still, like dust, I'll rise.

Does my sassiness upset you?
Why are you beset with gloom?
'Cause I walk like I've got oil wells
Pumping in my living room.

Just like moons and like suns,
With the certainty of tides,
Just like hopes springing high,
Still I'll rise.

Did you want to see me broken?
Bowed head and lowered eyes?
Shoulders falling down like teardrops.
Weakened by my soulful cries.

Does my haughtiness offend you?
Don't you take it awful hard

'Cause I laugh like I've got gold mines
Diggin' in my own back yard.

You may shoot me with your words,
You may cut me with your eyes,
You may kill me with your hatefulness,
But still, like air, I'll rise.

Does my sexiness upset you?
Does it come as a surprise
That I dance like I've got diamonds
At the meeting of my thighs?

Out of the huts of history's shame
I rise
Up from a past that's rooted in pain
I rise
I'm a black ocean, leaping and wide,
Welling and swelling I bear in the tide.
Leaving behind nights of terror and fear
I rise
Into a daybreak that's wondrously clear
I rise
Bringing the gifts that my ancestors gave,
I am the dream and the hope of the slave.
I rise
I rise
I rise.

Maya Angelou (1928–2014), *I Still Rise*

In this section of the book, I will be walking you through the ten key Steps for freeing yourself from narcissistic abuse. These are the same ten Steps that saved my life and which have been implemented by over 20,000 people in the Narcissistic Abuse Recovery Program.

*

Each Step corresponds to clearing different levels of trauma that are relevant to you at each stage of your recovery journey. Before we begin, a word of caution: while the exercises in Part Two might seem very straightforward, they are extremely powerful and could bring up some highly uncomfortable and challenging emotions for you. I will be guiding you through these exercises, but as I can't be with you in person, please seek any other support you need. Be aware that this book is not intended as a replacement for professional medical advice.

You may or may not have worked with meditations and visualisations before, or perhaps you feel like your mind is just too busy to meditate successfully. (This is especially true when we are dealing with the day-to-day traumas of narcissistic abuse.) Nevertheless, in order to transform your inner being back to health, it is important to be aware of the difference between 'informational' healing and 'transformational' healing.

Informational healing means that we are taking in information at the cognitive level and, for example, we might be reading material which, although it makes sense to us, is not necessarily reaching or being absorbed by our subconscious programming. As Bessel van der Kolk writes in *The Body Keeps the Score,* 'No matter how much insight and understanding we develop, the rational brain is basically impotent to talk the emotional brain out of its reality.'[2] This means that information alone will not shift us from our old, traumatised self to our new healed self.

In stark contrast, transformational healing means purposefully doing the work within our inner being – in our subconscious – and therefore achieving a major internal shift. This creates an adjustment within our inner identity, which means we truly change. This core understanding is the foundation of the Thriver Way, in which we focus our attention on transformational healing in order to break free and Thrive. It is this approach that makes Part Two the most challenging yet liberating part of the book to work through and to take your time over.

The Link Between Visualisation and Our Subconscious

Visualisation is an essential tool for changing our lives, because this is how we can start communicating with ourselves in the language of the subconscious. To do this, we need to be in a theta-brainwave state, as this is the thought frequency of introspection (when we take our attention inwards, to what is going on inside ourselves). As Bessel van der Kolk states in *The Body Keeps The Score,* 'Only by getting in touch with your body, by connecting viscerally with your self, can you regain a sense of who you are, your priorities and values.'[3] When we practise visualisations and enter this state, our brain slows down into slower and more powerful brainwaves. These brainwaves in turn relate to the ways in which we form our inner identities by creating belief systems and establishing thought patterns and associated behaviours. It is no coincidence that these are the brainwaves in which children predominately operate up to eight years of age, when they are learning sponges, soaking up information from everything and everyone around them at an incredible rate in order to create an inner identity that can function in the complexities of the human world. These early formative years set up most of a child's instinctual, ingrained patterns for life; hence the famous quote often attributed to the Greek philosopher Aristotle: 'Give me the boy until he is seven and I will show you the man.'

It is in this state of deep introspection, of theta brainwaves, that we can access these inner programmes, change them and completely transform our inner identity and the future trajectory of our life. We can literally shift from being an abuse victim to an empowered person who no longer suffers abuse or abuse symptoms.

That is the Thriver Way!

We Can All Visualise!

Even if you have never done any visualisations before or you don't believe you can visualise, I promise you can! You don't need to actually 'see' anything concrete. Truly, visualisation is not about sitting there, impatiently waiting for a vision to arrive and then complaining, 'It's not coming!' It's about directing your thoughts by setting your intention and allowing your mind to make up things through engaging your imagination. Even if you can't 'see' anything, your body will start to respond with emotions. And here's the thing: it is not the *seeing* we are going for; it is the *feeling.* That is how we learn to speak the language of the subconscious: by accessing and adapting our feelings, and by keeping our attention rooted in how our body feels whilst directing the visualisation, or as my lovely friend, award-winning author Arielle Ford, calls them, 'feelingizations'.

The crazy thing is that once we start working with this, it becomes so powerfully natural that we are astounded at how we ever became disconnected from being emotionally self-partnering in the first place. Of course, because we have been trained out of introspection by individuals, who – like the generations before them (especially in the Western world) – were also trained out of self-partnering, visualisations can take some practice at first!

In the exercises in Part Two, you are going to feel into where dense, painful energy lies trapped in your body (your emotional traumas) and speak to your inner being about them, as well as learn how to start clearing these traumas out of your body. The exercises include elements such as visualising dense matter (i.e. the trauma) leave your body, and then allowing white Light (representing Life Force, Source or Creation, which has the power to heal what we can't) enter where that trauma once was. When performed correctly, these exercises will enable a shift to occur deep within your inner identity, yet it is worth remembering that there are no rights or wrongs in terms of what you 'see' during them; rather, how effectively the exercises work depends on choosing what resonates individually with you when working with setting intentions and preferred visualisations – and feeling into that shift. I promise you, you will find your way and your rhythm!

So, welcome to Part Two where your powerful healing begins – and I can't wait to get started with you!

7

RELEASE THE IMMEDIATE PAIN AND FEELINGS OF LOSS

I want to extend my love and support to you right now for making it through Part One. You should be really proud of yourself because this is no easy or light journey, and it takes great courage and commitment and self-dedication to make it this far!

Let's just recap. In Part One, we covered the essential foundational steps necessary to achieve a Thriver Recovery from narcissistic abuse. These were:

- Getting clear about the situation that you are dealing with.

- Understanding the difference between normal and narcissistic relationship breakups and breakdowns.

- Knowing that Thriving requires going No Contact or implementing the most absolute version of Modified Contact you possibly can.

Now you are ready for the really exciting part, where you can begin to experience the inner transformation necessary for recovery from abuse. Coming up in Part

Two are exercises designed to get to the root of the pain that has been keeping you unconsciously trapped in abusive situations with toxic people.

At the end of each chapter I will provide you with exercises that will help you find and release your trauma in order to gain inner freedom and relief. However, be aware that changing anything about ourselves and our life that isn't serving us can be challenging. It involves facing, investigating and letting go of uncomfortable and even painful parts of ourselves. Yet if you have had enough of the pain, and you are willing to be courageous, you will discover that self-partnering and shifting your wounds becomes easier the more you do it, and your healing will accelerate dramatically as a result.

Let's dive now into Part Two, starting with the four pillars of Thriving, which are:

1. Taking back our power by removing our focus from the narcissist and whatever he or she is doing, and concentrating instead on carrying out essential inner work on the only person we can: ourselves.

2. Making the shift from our mind into our bodies in order to access, release and shift the traumas and belief systems that are unconsciously trapping us in abuse.

3. Continuing to up-level our lives from the inside out, addressing each trauma as it arises in order

to start living in the emotions, thoughts, ways, opportunities and higher trajectories that we never had access to before.

4. Becoming our radiant, expanded, true self who shows up lovingly, powerfully and authentically; we are then able to unfold our life from our wisdom within and thereby attract into our lives those people and events that are real, true and wholesome – naturally, calmly and powerfully confronting and repelling anything and anyone that isn't.

So let's get started!

The Dangerous Trauma of Narcissistic Abuse

When you have been narcissistically abused, regardless of whether or not you have been able to maintain No Contact (or Modified Contact if necessary), you may be feeling the intense agony of what the narcissist did to you. Because you are reading this book, it is likely that the relationship is, or was, toxic and the cycles of abuse have become more frequent and intense. It is important to understand what these cycles look like: the build-up to the abusive event, the actual abuse, the fallout or separating, the coming back together, the period where all seems better, the build-up, the abuse ... and so on, and so forth.

What is characteristic of narcissistic relationships is that there is no durable relief from, or actual rebuilding of, the relationship; the same issues occur over again, and get worse. What is for sure is that your emotional and mental states will be suffering. If you've seen a medical professional they may have diagnosed you with various conditions such as complex post-traumatic stress disorder or adrenal fatigue. It's likely that you will be experiencing great difficulty functioning in day-today life when it comes to eating, sleeping, working, socialising and generally being able to take care of yourself.

What I discovered from my own recovery, and while helping many others reclaim their souls, sanity and lives, is that there are aspects of narcissistic abuse that activate grave emotional triggers and traumas which are so severe that you feel like you can barely remember how to boil a kettle, let alone function amidst the complexities of human existence. This is consistent with people towards the end of their narcissistic abuse experience, and, as I have previously discussed, it often worsens after leaving the narcissist – when the aftershock of the compounding abuse catches up with you.

With narcissistic abuse, there are things we experienced we can't possibly assimilate, decipher, reconcile and file away. They bang around inside us constantly in the form of trauma. Additionally, the terror of the unknown doesn't cease, because everything we thought about ourselves, our lives and all that we believed in has been smashed to pieces. Narcissistic abuse doesn't just threaten our sense of stability; it shatters our inner identity to pieces. We have no idea who we are anymore.

Andrea said after leaving her narcissist: 'I went home to my mum because he wouldn't leave the house. He moved the new woman in the next day. While we were joint parenting our infant daughter, he sent me photos of his new woman holding our baby. I ended up in ICU with panic attacks that were so bad I couldn't breathe and thought I was having a heart attack. It's been two months; I've lost my job, I've had a car accident and I can't function. He is now mounting a case against me and going for full custody. I fear that I'm going to lose my daughter.'

Andrea's case was extreme, as are those of many people dealing with malignant narcissists, because once the narcissist has discarded them, or believes this person is threatening to expose who they are underneath their false self, he or she becomes vicious and hits hard at your most vulnerable point. In Andrea's case, not only did she suffer the incredible trauma of discovering her husband's affair, she was on the receiving end of attacks that were designed to eliminate her as a threat. If Andrea became the broken and deranged one who was to blame for his plight, then the narcissist could save face. It's simple to a narcissist: things are black and white – destroy or be destroyed.

Here are some of the common traumas that bring people to their knees with narcissistic abuse.

- Being replaced as if you never existed, despite decades of marriage or proclamations and promises of total devotion.

- Being smeared to all and sundry, and accused of unspeakable acts that you couldn't even imagine doing, let alone actually execute – with the added twist that these are all things the narcissist did.

- Having no one believe your version of events and being alienated and persecuted by those who used to be your people, after the narcissist has turned everyone against you – causing you to be isolated even further.

- Discovering that the real individual with whom you were in a relationship bears very little resemblance to the person you believed you were with, and there is a history and emergence of activity that shocks you to your core.

- Finding that people whom you suspected and who are close to the narcissist, perhaps even your friends, are having close intimate relations with the narcissist.

- Discovering that the narcissist has been mining you and taking your money and resources for their own self-serving causes.

- Realising that the narcissist has been organising and plotting against you for some time.

There is zero accountability, responsibility, remorse or atonement displayed by the narcissist for what they did, and are doing, to you.

My mother once said to me, 'What has happened to you is like being in a bad movie. No one would even believe it!' She was right. So many of us who are narcissistically abused hope to wake up one morning and discover the whole thing was only a nightmare. Yet it is absolutely real, because we have often invested our whole lives in these people. Additionally, now there is the trauma of trying to retrieve out of the relationship what's ours – things the narcissist now declares he or she is entitled to.

All of this is serious – deadly serious. The levels of disorientation are horrific. It's dangerous health-wise and accident-wise. Many people in states of triggered panic make very poor decisions that put them at risk emotionally, mentally, physically and sexually, in an attempt to dull the all-consuming trauma. The greatest horror of it is, the narcissist just doesn't back off. It is chilling how when a narcissist feels your fear, they become as energised as a shark that smells blood and hones in for the kill.

How Your Trauma Is Being Used Against You

And there it is in the nutshell, the psychic, energetic and spiritual phenomenon of narcissistic abuse: with no true identity or energy of his or her own, he or she is a no-self who reflects back to you exactly your deepest fears and insecurities – namely your unhealed inner parts. The narcissist needs fear, pain and drama from others in order to avoid his or her own inner demons and survive. Whatever is stuck in your craw, hurting you the most, provides exactly the boost of energy that fuels the narcissist's attack on you.

Here's an example of what I'm talking about: Marcy's narcissistic son constantly accused her of not caring for him and of being an unloving mother. He used this as his reason to ignore her pleas about his behaviour; instead, he carried on doing his own thing, expecting her to clean up his gambling messes. She continually hooked into his accusations, arguing with him and trying to get him to stop using her as a scapegoat. Yet the more she tried to get him to be reasonable and take responsibility for his gambling, the more he would use her as his excuse to take zero personal responsibility and to keep behaving in a way that was hurting her and ultimately himself.

Marcy told me that she constantly obsessed over 'the unfairness of what he accuses me of as his excuse', saying, 'Of course I'm busy trying to keep everyone on track while he is destroying us. Of course I'm so hurt and angry. It drives me crazy.' Marcy did not yet know the real solution – the one that I am about to explain – which is to heal and diffuse the emotional trauma within ourselves. At this point, like so many of us, she was continuing to hand power over to the narcissist by trying to tackle external problems – which ironically is where none of us has any power – rather than focus on her inner world.

From the Bowels of Hell to Our Liberation

At the start of our healing journey we are going to be feeling high-level trauma. Maybe we aren't functioning, eating or sleeping. But 'stinking thinking' doesn't work – we know that. When we experience intense trauma, beta brainwaves are activated. These are different from the slower theta brainwaves, the ones necessary for communicating with our subconscious mind. Beta brainwaves are of the conscious mind: the higher the levels of trauma, the more our waking mind goes into overdrive trying to tackle it. When this happens, we are thrown into the survival centres of our brain, which are concerned with the manufacturing and release of cortisol and adrenalin, generating the 'fight-or-flight' response.

Amy F.T. Arnsten of the Department of Neurobiology at Yale University School of Medicine writes: 'The prefrontal cortex (PFC) – the most evolved brain region – subserves our highest-order cognitive abilities. However, it is also the brain region that is most sensitive to the detrimental effects of stress exposure. Even quite mild acute uncontrollable stress can cause a rapid and dramatic loss of prefrontal cognitive abilities, and more prolonged stress exposure causes architectural changes in prefrontal dendrites.'[1]

I have to confess that in my times of high stress during narcissistic abuse, rather than make a decision that would honour my wellbeing, I was much more likely to make really unintelligent decisions – such as hook in to him harder in an attempt to force him to be accountable. This of course just lined me up for more abuse. Sometimes, even though I *knew* what I was doing was bad for me, it was as if the rush of chemicals in my system made me do it anyway.

This sort of disruption of the cognitive faculties by stress is confirmed by Due Quach, founder of Calm Clarity, who writes: 'Unfortunately, the fight-or-flight cascade also reduces blood flow to the frontal lobes, thus impairing our mental processing capacity and our ability to regulate our impulses. When we can't think straight, we tend to react to stressors in ways that create even more stress in our lives by impulsively doing and saying things we later regret.'[2] Therefore access to calm, sophisticated and rational thinking and solution-finding is simply not available to us in times of stress, and our terrorised thinking compounds the surge of terrorising peptides throughout our system

– not helping us but allowing the narcissist to defeat us on every front.

The real solution is to take our attention inside and make our way into our bodies, opening them up and breathing deeply into them, as in meditation and visualisation, entering into a theta-brainwave state, then feeling and loading up the inner trauma, and shifting it up and out. We then bring in the Light, the Higher Power healing to fill where the trauma previously was. Then the neural pathways in our brains shift to reflect the body shift – meaning our previous brain synapses literally break off their connections and immediately form more evolved, empowered and wise ones. With respect to whichever topic we are shifting the beliefs of our inner identity about, we literally move from 'survival' to 'creation' mode.

The grand irony of all of this is that the journey into deep unconsciousness that narcissists force us into – the facing of our darkest and most painful inner places (those parts of ourselves that we try to bury and hide from) – necessitates making these unconscious parts conscious and releasing them. This inner alchemic act then grants us the gift of reaching the highest state of consciousness we could dream of: the shift from a life with significant emotional wounds and trying to survive them, to a life of joy, energy, purpose, inspiration and love (the state of Thriving) without them. This is the metaphoric journey from the underworld – rising from the bowels of hell to our own personal heaven on earth.

From the darkest of pain, we mine our brightest light – not just for ourselves but for our future generations and the collective consciousness of all humans – yet this can only happen one person at a time, as we purge the fear and pain from our individual inner universes.

How to Shift from Fear and Powerlessness to Healing and Power

You may be so blocked up with junk and toxicity from narcissistic abuse that the very idea of healing still feels overwhelming. You may simply be trying to survive and function despite the pain and trauma, which is excruciatingly difficult. What you must understand is this: these intense thoughts and feelings are blocking you from beginning the recovery process. Step 1 of your recovery is to release these emotions: not only will this grant you emotional and mental relief, it will begin to dissolve many of the powerful hooks that are keeping you connected to the narcissist. As we talked about in the previous chapter, detachment from the narcissist with the use of No Contact or Modified Contact is essential to get your healing work underway.

You may feel terrified of turning inwards and meeting your trauma. But, as the late Louise Hay wrote in *Life!: Reflections on Your Journey:* 'We are often frightened to look within because we think that we will find this terrible being. But in spite of what "they" might have told us, what we will find is a beautiful child that longs for our love.'[3] We have all been trained to self-avoid and to repress our inner emotions and traumas. We're encouraged to do things like look at social media, eat more food, drink, smoke, distract ourselves with sex, sleep, work – yet after narcissistic abuse we don't have those 'numbing out' privileges anymore. Now the trauma is so huge, nothing switches it off and there is no avoiding it if we want to get out of this nightmare. I promise you that when we turn inwards and learn to love and heal ourselves back to wholeness the Quantum way (which I am going to help you achieve), the relief, love and solidness we feel inside is indescribable.

Andrea, who I mentioned earlier, was terrified of losing her daughter to the ex-narcissist and his new partner, yet she suffered her greatest fear. Full custody of her daughter was awarded by the family court to him. After being hospitalised for suicidal inclinations, Andrea started working with NARP while she was an in-patient. As well as working with the Program, she was in contact with me as a client by phone. Initially, she was terrified about going inwards to be with her inner being. I helped her come to this realisation: 'I am stuck in so much trauma that I'm feeling it all the time anyway, so why would I be scared of purposely feeling it, being with it, loading it up, releasing it and then being free of it? At least then dealing with it can be on my terms, and it may stop hunting me down relentlessly.' She worked with Module One of the

Program several times a day for two weeks, in bed with her headphones on, with her notepad, and shifted tons and tons of trauma. Andrea worked with NARP as if her life depended on it.

Everything now centred on Andrea's total dedication to healing herself and she started to find relief very quickly, with which came energy, power, hope and new plans. Within three months of starting NARP, she was allowed supervised access with her daughter, and within six months she had 50 per cent access. Two years on, Andrea was divorced, remarried with a loving, supportive partner, had received a great property settlement and had won fulltime custody of her daughter. Her ex had moved overseas for work after several relationship breakdowns.

Would any of that have happened without Andrea shifting trauma and painful beliefs out of her system and directly reprogramming her subconscious? I don't believe so. What I do know is that it would have been much more likely for Andrea to have ended up being heavily medicated and barely functioning – as was going to be my fate too – and having only supervised (at best) contact with her child, had it not been for the Thriver Way to Heal. Really, the truth is that I doubt whether either of us would have been alive today without Quanta Freedom Healing. I know the same is true for many of the NARP Community.

When we use Module One, as per the specific guided visualisations in it, we can go to 'what hurts the most right now', connect with that feeling in our body, relax, open up our body and, by following the specific visualisation instructions, draw that dense energy literally out of our cells and into the 'holding bay' created inside us – and then release it. We let it go, powerfully, somatically (from our body, unrelated to the mind) and in Quantum ways, giving it back to our Higher Power (God, Creation, your Higher Self, the Universe or whatever you wish to call it) for recycling into love. As we do this, we see the dense energy leave us and dissolve, and this creates a shift deep within our subconscious programmes for letting go and opening up 'space' within us.

We feel it emotionally as a lightening of our burden, fear, pain or confusion, and we experience relief. Then we bring in to ourselves, through specific visualisation processes, Source Energy, which is the Light of Higher Consciousness. This represents our healed and whole self. Again, this is your understanding of whatever a Higher Power means to you; yet whatever form it takes, it is very simple to bring it in, because we only need to acknowledge this force as Light. There is nothing more to it when you have the right intention and processes to work with.

As we fill ourselves with this Higher Consciousness, it brings with it the power of resolution: a power that exists beyond the cognitive state and which we simply can't arrange, create or comprehend at a logical level. This is a force that is not available to us through the conscious senses; it is a power that just *is,* and we all are coded to have direct access to this energy when we know how to make the space in which to receive it – and then do just that.

The truth is that these sensations are impossible to connect with logically, and are much easier to understand when experienced physically. I know that some of you might be reading this, thinking, 'What on earth is this wacky woman from Australia going on about?' I promise you that once upon a time I would have thought I was stark-raving bonkers as well! However, I know that if, like me, you experience Quanta Freedom Healing and start living with the effects of it, you can't possibly dispute that it works – even if you have no idea how or why it works. The great thing is that this type of healing is completely unconditional: you don't need to believe that it works for it to work; all you have to do is to keep an open mind and heart and follow the instructions.

PRE-EXERCISE DETAILS AND INSTRUCTIONS

Please note that it is VITAL to read the following information before attempting the exercises. (Before proceeding please also ensure that you have a journal and a pen to hand.)

Very soon you will start transforming your inner trauma, which is where the true healing work begins!

In Part Two, you will find ten exercises – one at the end of each chapter – which correspond with the key Steps in the Narcissistic Abuse Recovery

Program (NARP). These journaling exercises offer strong and effective ways to access trauma and then release it. You will see that in addition to performing the exercises, you have the option of applying a specific Quanta Freedom Healing process to each Step, which you can learn about in the free 'You Can Thrive Program'. While the journaling exercises represent a powerful starting point, they don't work with energy imprints in the ways that Quanta Freedom Healing does. I therefore strongly encourage you to explore my Quanta Freedom Healing resources as well, along with all the other powerful healing supplements I have to offer you in the You Can Thrive Program. Access your free Program here: www.youcanthriveprogram.com. These practical elements provide you with the tools to shift your subconscious and are very important to me, as I was keen to make *You Can Thrive After Narcissistic Abuse* a powerful hands-on guide to healing, rather than just another information-heavy reference book.

The repetitive nature of the exercises

Over the years that I have worked with people recovering from abuse, I have found there are only certain journaling processes through which trauma can be accessed as safely as possible while still connecting with it strongly enough to grant us a shift. This is why you might find the journaling exercises somewhat repetitive at times. However, rest assured (and you will realise this when you really connect to them) that each exercise is carefully tailored to bring about a healing shift on the topic of the chapter in question.

Feeling your emotions safely

We are all initially scared of meeting our painful emotions. However, the 'dragon in the cave' (the emotional pain that is eating you alive) is actually your wounded inner being wanting you to turn inwards and come to him or her; and indeed once you *do* turn inwards – with love and devotion – to meet your inner trauma face to face, you will discover a hurt, terrified self who needs you and your love.

I totally understand how frightening it can be to go inwards for the first time to connect purposefully to our traumas. Some people feel instant relief as a result of doing so, while others believe that feeling the pain is somehow 'wrong' and this is only going to make matters worse. I promise you with all my heart that the pain is only terrible because it is chasing us down constantly – like a traumatised child who is being ignored, screaming, 'Please come to me!'

If you feel the pain intensely, just stay with it and approach it like you would a physical cut on your leg, for example. Emotional pain without the head story is somatic, we experience it physically as a dense, visceral sensation in our body. If this were a real physical injury rather than an emotional wound, it would feel awful enough – but in no way would your accompanying self-talk be along the lines of 'I'm hopeless, I'll never heal' or 'I'm unlovable, defective and I'll never be good enough.' If that happens, stay out of the story, open up your body as much as you can – and breathe. Ignore any terrible thoughts that come in to hijack you. Imagine sending them away to your Higher Power to be dissolved back into love. You will find this helps how you feel just by the process of doing it.

If, for any reason, you feel unable to connect with your inner being through the journaling exercises, I highly recommend accessing your 'You Can Thrive Program', where I offer an entire workshop dedicated to taking you step-by-step through the self-partnering process: www.youcanthriveprogram.com.

Getting out of your head and into your body

To start tuning into your inner being, I recommend closing your eyes, as blocking out the external world will aid the process of introspection. It's much better if you don't try to analyse what you are doing or feeling. Instead, simply follow the instructions in the exercise. While doing so, keep your intention as being one of fascination, love and devotion. Yes, you may be scared to meet your wounds, because, as I mentioned earlier, we have been conditioned by society not to self-partner. But I promise you this: the agony of your wounds is there only because you have been avoiding them.

The best way to understand my healing processes is to *experience* them. When we do the inner work, the less we try to puzzle it out rationally and the more we settle into the experience the better, because it is not the cognitive mind we wish to engage: it is the subconscious which requires contact, communication and a shift.

The meaning of self-partnering

Self-partnering is about being present with our inner experience, unconditionally and lovingly. How we self-partner is this: we stop looking outside ourselves for answers, and instead we take our attention inwards to find and heal the original traumas that are a match for the abusive people and patterns we have been living with in our lives. Self-partnering means that, as adults, we respond to the call of our inner being, who does not wish anyone or anything else to come inside and heal it. It has been waiting just for us all along.

Your inner being and your inner child

In the exercises in Part Two, you will come across the terms 'inner being' and 'inner child', which we've encountered earlier. Our inner being relates to our inner experience, where our subconscious is operating throughout our cellular being. Our inner being uses emotions to communicate with us. If you are instructed in an exercise to connect to your inner being, what I am really saying is: 'Go to what you are feeling inside yourself.' The sort of question you might ask yourself in order to connect with your inner being is one like this: 'How does that feel in my body?' Really this means: 'What am I emotionally and somatically feeling (i.e. including my physical sensations) when I take my attention inside me regarding how I'm feeling?'

Accessing our inner being takes a little bit of practice, because we have become so used to thinking about our feelings instead of feeling them! However, when you do start to connect to your inner being lovingly, you will find it extremely natural and even soothing to do so.

When I use the term 'inner child' in these exercises, this refers to those young, unhealed and underdeveloped parts of ourselves that lie within our inner being. Our inner child often holds trauma, and is not yet solid or mature. These wounds represent those parts of our childhood selves that we wish to reach and heal back to wholeness. It is important to understand that when we hand our power away and feel helpless and unable to change either how we feel or something else in our life, we are operating from the centre of our wounded inner child. If we are to heal for real, I believe there are always inner younger, epigenetic and past-life selves holding trauma that need to be transformed.

How to communicate with your inner being

In the Part Two exercises, when asking your inner being/inner child questions, or communicating with it in any way, please do this as lovingly as possible. If you are female, you could for example address your inner being/inner child as 'sweetheart' or 'darling' or whatever term feels endearing to you. Talk to this part of yourself exactly as you would someone you adore with all your heart. Likewise, if you are male, perhaps use a term like 'mate' or 'buddy' with all the love that you can muster.

I urge you to do this from your heart as if your life depends on it. Because it actually does: your entire future life is going to reflect the quality of the relationship you create with your inner being. None of us ever shamed, blamed or attacked ourselves back to wellbeing; it is only the force of your loving self-devotion and some powerful Quantum Shifts that are going to get you there.

In your healing journal, please write the heading 'My True Self Declarations'. Next, write underneath: 'I am now in the process of speaking to my inner being in loving terms at ALL times.' Now sign and date this intention.

The order and sequence of each exercise

In many of the exercises in Part Two, you will be asked to connect to the intensity of the emotional charges you feel in your body and to list these from highest to lowest. The highest-rated trauma is the one you start working with first. You then complete all stages of the exercise relating to that particular trauma before proceeding on to the next highest-rated charge, and so on. (This is explained further in the exercises themselves.) It is highly recommended that you clean up each painful emotional charge in turn, until it feels benign in your body, before going on to tackle the next trauma that you will be working on.

The only time you might stop working on a charge in your body until you can no longer feel it, is when another trauma becomes so highly charged that it has now taken centre stage in your emotional body. When this happens, put the one that you were working on aside for the moment (to come back to later) and move your attention on to shifting the charge that is now most intense within you.

The amount of traumas to clear in one sitting

This is totally a matter or preference, time and energy. Trust yourself as to how much work you want to do on yourself and know that you can come back to unhealed traumas another time. They are faithful – they are like housework – they will wait for you! There is no rush to have everything within you healed immediately.

The order of the healings and when to go on to the next one

My ten-Step process is a specific formula that delivers powerful healing results if the healings are initially done in order. Even if you feel like a particular healing Step is not relevant to you, I can assure you that when you access your inner being you are very likely to discover that it is *totally* relevant! I highly recommend working through all Steps in sequence, one at a time, until you arrive at a sense of completion and peace before preceding to the next Step.

Step 1 is a little different, however. This first Step is to do with the incredible and painful trauma that is crippling you at the start of your healing journey. Keep working with Step 1 until you feel like you can eat, sleep and function again, then it is time to move on to Step 2. However, please note that Step 1 can be used at any time as a multi-purpose healing to shift trauma that you can't specifically relate to any of the other Steps.

Repeating the exercises

Last but not least, it's worth mentioning that these exercises are usually not just a 'one off'. During your recovery, you will find that healing is generally a spiralling process rather than an ordered straight line. I always recommend that people revisit any relevant Steps whenever they are triggered by a corresponding trauma.

For example, Linda had progressed to working on Step 4, 'Release and Heal the Pain of Injustice and Betrayal', when she was triggered into beating herself up again over her choices and what she had lost. This meant she needed to revisit Step 3 again, 'Forgive Yourself and Life for What You Have Been Through'. When you return to an earlier healing topic, please don't feel like you have failed, or allow yourself to become weighed down in the feelings of 'Why has this come up again? I've already healed it!' The higher we evolve, the deeper the layers of trauma that will come up to be released – which is all perfect. Our body knows at every stage of our journey what is ready to be released, and that is what will come up to the surface next. There is a sequence for this and all we need to do is trust our emotions about it, meet it and do the work without judgement.

Okay ... it's time! Let's get started with the first Step!

EXERCISE: STEP 1 – LETTING GO OF WHAT HURTS THE MOST RIGHT NOW

1. Take your journal and go by yourself to a quiet and safe space where you will not be disturbed. Spend a few minutes breathing deeply in and out, then close your eyes in order to help you connect with your inner being. Focus on relaxing and opening up your body. Ideally you want to create a sense of space within yourself – and this means letting go of tension.

If any thoughts arise in your mind, don't wrestle with them or fight back: simply treat them as if they were somebody at the side of the room who you're not interested in right now. Just keep breathing and opening up your body.

2. Now take your attention inside yourself, and ask yourself lovingly, 'What emotionally hurts right now?' Allow your inner being to supply you with the answer. This will surface as feelings, thoughts, any words that come to mind and/or images. Just trust what arises. Is it about their new lover? Is it the terrible way the narcissist discarded you as if you didn't exist? Is it the shock of losing the life you thought was your dream? Is it the betrayal and smearing of you to other people? Is it the fear of losing your job? Is it the fear of losing your friendship? Is it the shock of how a family member could do this to you? Is it the fear of how you are going to carry on with your life? Is it the property and money you lost or are about to lose? If a lot of things come up for you, open your eyes and record them all in your journal under the heading 'Things That Emotionally Hurt Me Now'.

3. Go through your list of 'Things That Emotionally Hurt Me Now' and feel them, one at a time, inside your body. Rate the emotional intensity of each one out of 10, with 0/10 meaning 'it's just information, but I can't feel it in my body', whereas 10/10 means 'the pain is so intense, it totally consumes me'. In your journal, number your list in the order of highest to lowest.

4. Starting with the highest-ranking issue on your list, ask yourself where you feel dense energy emerge in your body when you connect with the thought of it. This could be a sensation of somatic, visceral heaviness, or of sorrow, anxiety or anger, or some other form of uncomfortable energy. It may be actual physical pain that 'lights up' in your body somewhere. (Please be aware that the communication with your inner being might be faint at first. Trust! The more you trust what arises – no matter how faint the sensation – the stronger this communication will become.) Where do you feel it? It might be in your heart, your solar plexus, anywhere at all. It might be so big, you feel it everywhere under your skin. Record where it is in your journal after you have located it.

5. Now, with your consciousness focused on this trauma, *feel* what it's like: is this trauma dark and heavy? Does it have a shape? Is it solid or porous? There is no need to understand what the trauma is 'about' in order to clear it from your being, your subconscious programmes and your life. Our subconscious is not interested in logical information; it responds to visceral feelings. *Trust yourself* even if you feel like you are making up what the trauma 'looks and feels like'. (Intuition and imagination are deeply connected – and sometimes it can feel like 'why would I be making THAT up?!') In your journal, describe how your trauma appears and feels.

6. Now we are going to visualise letting go of the trauma from your body. Imagine letting the dense energy that you have described leave you, out through the top of your head. This is where it is important to see/feel the appearance of the trauma, rather than focus on any particular information about it. If you focus on information, you will come back out of your body and into your head, where the healing won't take place. Stay with the language your subconscious understands, which is the visual nature of the trauma itself (trusting that your subconscious knows all about the inner painful programmes it represents). See it leave your body and, when it does, watch it dissolve back into native nothingness. *Feel this happening as strongly as possible.* Don't try to work any of this out logically; just do this in any way that feels right for you – even if you are simply setting an intention for it to be so, or feel like you are making it up. (I myself don't actually 'see' anything when I visualise; I simply set an intention and feel that intention unfold.) The key thing is to be willing to *let it go!*

7. Now imagine and feel the space that has opened up where the trauma once was, and bring down Light (which relates to your understanding of a

Higher Power) via a pipeline that connects from the top of your head to a big ball of Light above your head. All you need to do is to imagine the white Light as being exactly that. You don't need to think about what it contains (in fact, if you do, that is going off track). 'See' yourself fill up – in every cell of your body – with this white Light. Allow feelings of relief, warmth and healing to wash through you and know that, if your body registers such feelings, this is really happening.

8. In your journal, record how the experience went and how that old trauma feels now in your body. If you can still feel into it and an emotional charge still registers, there is more trauma to clear out. Keep repeating the process until you have cleared all of it.

9. Now repeat the process with the next highest-rated trauma on your list.

Please remember that this exercise serves as an introduction to accessing and releasing your trauma with Quantum Tools. To help you get started I've created a free healing training session which you can access in the 'You Can Thrive Program'. Register for free here: www.youcanthriveprogram.com.

Meeting Your Inner Being

If you have never done self-partnering like this before, this might be the first time you have connected with your inner being, and of course this could have been quite emotional for you. It may be such a relief to feel like you have finally come home to yourself and that there is hope you can heal.

Regardless of what your experience was like during this exercise, you have taken an incredibly important and courageous first step, and I realise that it is scary. Also know that you have my and this community's love and support all the way, because we want with all our hearts for you to experience what we have: the relief, healing and freedom that occur when we powerfully release the dense energy that has been trapped in our being.

Self-Partnering Results

By completing this first exercise, you will start to find relief from your pain. As a result of knowing you have finally 'showed up', your inner being will begin to relax and to stop panicking. Instead, it will be saying, 'Thank God, you're finally here!' By self-partnering, turning inwards by 180 degrees and meeting yourself with love, you will start to 'come home' – which is the path toward health, sanity, clarity and regaining your power.

Now it's time to look at the second level of trauma that we will be clearing in order to free ourselves from narcissistic abuse. This next Step allows us to give up those false sources that we thought could grant us our sense of self-worth and our identity, and we start to become the force that generates our own life healthily instead.

8

RELEASE THE ILLUSION OF THIS PERSON AS MY SOURCE OF SELF

As mentioned, it's usual to carry on working with Step 1 for some time, and this is especially true when we are experiencing big rushes of trauma. It depends how often you decide to work with this Step, but even if daily, you might be on it for a few weeks. The way to start regaining control of your emotions, and consequently your life, is to be really diligent about self-partnering, meeting and healing your emerging traumas as often as possible when they arise. By doing so, you will find that the trauma eases considerably, and as space starts to open up in your feelings and thoughts, you can start to gain some clarity about your situation and operate in healthier ways.

Okay, so once you have connected with your inner being and have been able to obtain significant release and relief from the first level of traumas that were derailing your recovery, now you can consider the next stage of your journey: releasing and healing the illusion of your narcissistic abuser as your source of self. I would suggest committing yourself to this next Step once you feel like you can eat, sleep and go about your daily life fairly normally – meaning that even though you are still getting triggered by narcissistic behaviours, you have cleared enough trauma in Step 1 to be back to everyday functioning.

One of the deadliest hooks in narcissistic abuse is when the narcissist becomes a symbol to us of one (or all) of the following four essential human commodities: love, approval, survival and security. These four commodities weave the very fabric of our inner identities, and if we are not yet secure within our subconscious programmes about these aspects of our inner beings, we unconsciously seek a 'parent' to provide them for us – and tragically this is when a narcissist might well become our parent figure.

If the narcissist in our life is our actual parent or another family member, then of course we might naturally feel a deep need for this person to validate us, support us and genuinely care for our wellbeing. And there may be times when we believe they really do care; however, this is usually short-lived, given the cycles of narcissistic behaviour that will inevitably impact on our relationships with these individuals.

Understanding What We Are Not Providing for Ourselves

With respect to every narcissist in every circumstance who we feel wronged and traumatised by, we don't realise that we have assigned them to act as our source of self. This includes narcissistic business partners, family members, friends ... in fact, any narcissist at all. I adore what my good friend and colleague Katherine Woodward-Thomas says: 'We are only upset with others not providing us with something, to the extent that we are not providing that for ourselves.' When I first heard Katherine say this, I thought back to how angry I had been with my abuser for telling me he loved me beyond measure – and then doing the things that confirmed, point blank, that he certainly didn't. I remember screaming at him, 'You said you loved me!' Later, I discovered the love that I was really missing and screaming out for, was me loving me, and once I shored that up by meeting my inner wounds and healing them, it mattered not one iota whether he loved me or not – because that was to do with his stuff, not whether or not I was loveable.

When we are still unhealed and unconsciously dependent, we may feel that we are nothing without a partner; or defective because we don't have a parent who is lovingly supportive and reliable; or we may feel incapable without a business partner who will go out and get contracts for us – the list goes on and on. It all comes back to understanding the Quantum Law: *so within, so without.* If we want something in our life then we need to 'be' it for it to 'come'. If we don't feel confident, whole and worthy because we still have unhealed, unfinished childhood business, we will hook up with people and cling to them while repeating the patterns that relate to whatever has been missing from our lives.

Jess had always had a feeling like her life was on hold without a partner. She didn't like travelling alone or even with a girlfriend. She hated socialising and being seen without a partner. The truth was she felt like she didn't have any value without being the other half of a relationship. She literally felt like a defective outcast as a single person.

When she met Anthony, he seemed to be everything that she wanted. He travelled, he dined in fine places, he mixed in circles of interesting people and often socialised through his work. What also came with Anthony was arrogance, impatience and raging episodes when he didn't get his own way, but because he provided all the stuff that Jess missed so terribly when she was single, she overlooked this.

After eight months of significant abuse, he hit her and Jess knew she had to leave; yet she was in incredible trauma at the loss of the life she now had – the life that she was not providing for herself. Before she could make up her mind to leave, Anthony discarded her and moved on with another woman. And suddenly Jess was back at square one, without 'a life' but with substantial abuse and traumas, now fully activated, to resolve.

Jemima's father controlled her life. He used his wealth and influence to get her the best contacts, social engagements and publicity for her business. Yet the emotional price was heavy for his assistance: total compliance with his opinions and demands, just like her mother had been beaten down to accept. Jemima didn't want the life he had chosen for her; she dreamed of travel and of meeting a young man and falling in love. She knew defying her father would mean becoming an outcast. She was terrified about the thought of trying to survive on her own.

Similarly, Patrick's narcissistic boss had become so abusive that working conditions were mentally unstainable for Patrick, yet he froze at the very thought of trying to start his own business or having to apply for other positions elsewhere. His town was firing not hiring and didn't nearly all small businesses fail?

The incredibly addictive thing about narcissists is this: they appear to be exactly what is missing. Such was the case when Rebecca came into Robert's life. Initially, Rebecca was very soothing towards Robert's tendency to be so hard on himself; he was always on his own case about how he didn't do a good enough job, and how he needed to do better. When

Rebecca first arrived on the scene, she seemed to be extremely complimentary, supportive and loving towards him. Not long afterwards, her loving gestures turned into condemnation and criticism. By this stage she had already moved in with Robert and was enjoying living with him in an expensive inner Melbourne suburb. Rebecca fell pregnant, stopped work and wanted Robert to keep funding her expensive tastes, which he did.

Nothing Robert could ever do was good enough. Robert knew he was now married to and shared a child with someone who bore no resemblance to the woman he fell in love with. Rather, he was face to face with a person who treated him exactly how he had always treated himself: harshly and with no clemency whatsoever.

Growing Up Our Inner Selves

It doesn't matter which way we slice it or dice it; when we engage in Thriver Recovery we seek the truth that will set us free, and it is this: when we are adults who hold another adult, or set of circumstances, responsible for acting as our source of self, we are handing away our power dangerously. It means we are not creating a solid, healthy relationship within ourselves or directly with life itself.

It also means we are not yet taking responsibility for growing up in those areas where we are broken and unhealed. Jess's clinginess around having a partner to fulfil her life was an exact replica of how she saw her mother behave: miserable without a man and focusing everything on her need to have one. Her mother had never established a solid sense of self and didn't have the resources to assist Jess in developing hers. Similarly, Robert's father was hard and critical, and Robert had internalised his critical parent's voice and applied it to himself. Jemima and Patrick both lacked the confidence, as adults, to take charge of their lives, their wellbeing and their security. When our insecure and damaged parts remain unhealed, we don't behave like healthy adults who seek out other healthy adults and situations; we are, in fact, unconsciously behaving like damaged children seeking a parent.

As children, we start off as critically dependent; we need caregivers in order to survive physically and to model for us the ways in which to develop our own inner identities – meaning what we come to believe about ourselves, life and others. If we develop healthily beyond these dependent, formative years, we start to reach independence, where not only do we have the skills to survive and provide for ourselves, but we have the ability to feel whole emotionally without requiring other people to complete our feelings for us. When we have established an inner solidity, we make relationship choices that reflect this; we no longer put up with abuse and bad behaviour as the payoff for whichever commodity we feel needy for and that we are not healed enough to provide for ourselves.

Narcissists Identify What You Need

Meredith didn't work, and couldn't do so because her anxiety was so bad. Greg, her partner, met all her survival needs and in exchange insisted that they had an open relationship so that he could take part in group sex orgies with other men and women.

This is the thing with narcissists – they zone in on what people need and are not providing for themselves, and hook in that person by providing it for them, yet sometimes even this doesn't last for long. In the case of Meredith, Greg needed to keep providing the essentials to keep her alive, but in the case of Robert, whom we met earlier, as soon as he was hooked and Rebecca had secured her position, the acting could end and her true narcissistic personality appeared.

A highly intelligent, self-professed narcissist called Dan wrote to me to gloat about how he would secure new sources of narcissistic supply. He explained: 'All I have to do with women is be attentive, caring and act like I am interested. Women tell me how men have hurt them in the past and then I make some intelligent comment about how I am not like that, demonstrate it in a gesture to them that links in with what I have said, and I have that woman eating out of my hand. If I meet a woman and I can't find out what still hurts her, or can't overly impress her, then I move on. I know I can't reel her in like the others and I can't be bothered winning her over in other ways.'

So many people, before Thriver Recovery, believe that once they have been taken in by narcissists, it's too late and they can't heal what has happened to them. This isn't true, because when you experience a Thriver Recovery, not only will you be immune to becoming ensnared by a narcissist again, all of the pain from the previous abuse will dissolve away too.

The great thing about being human is that we have the capacity to learn from our experiences. But we can only learn if we recognise the lesson that is being shown to us, and if we want to stop that lesson being repeatedly presented in our life. That is exactly what this is about: your narcissistic relationship is providing you with a powerful lesson. With this in mind, one of my most favourite quotes of all time comes from the Buddhist nun and teacher Pema Chödrön:

> Nothing ever goes away until it has taught us what we need to know.

Attraction and attachment consist of a strong chemical mix of emotions and unconscious currents, the neuropeptides that produce the emotions love, lust and bonding. These determine the pull and the feelings we have towards other human beings. Narcissistic relationships provide two big chemical cocktails unconsciously in our inner drivers, our instincts. They offer the promise of all of the love, approval and security that we missed out on from our parent(s) and other relationships, and that we are still trying to receive from them; and they also carry the exact components of the past hurt and pain that we experienced, and have not yet healed, from other previous relationships, including with our parents.

The Healing Work Has to Be Done Within Ourselves

We are comfortable with our unconscious wounds because they feel familiar. We are also unconsciously drawn to individuals who will deliver these wounds, because we are unconsciously trying to fix the people and the relationships that did not stay with us, love us and support us last time round.

We are unconsciously trying to right the wrongs. The problem is we are unknowingly still using the wrong formula. We unconsciously believe 'if I can just fix this person I can finally have the love/approval/security/survival I want'. The correct formula to create the inner commodities we want is to do the work on healing ourselves first – not trying to fix someone else.

The belief that the narcissist is our source of self is universal. Virtually every person who has been narcissistically abused in an intimate relationship reports that they have never felt a relationship to be so right, they believed this person was 'the one', and they couldn't imagine ever being able to meet someone else they were this attracted to. The connection and enmeshments with any other narcissist, including those in our family of origin, can likewise be incredibly intense.

Step 2, which follows, will help you to start identifying and shifting your dangerous dependencies on narcissists no matter who they are, whether family members, friends, colleagues or even your boss.

EXERCISE: STEP 2 – BECOMING A SOURCE TO MYSELF

1. Take yourself to your quiet space with your journal and allow some time to centre yourself with deep, slow breaths. Close your eyes, imagine relaxing your body and ignore any thoughts that pop into your head. Just keep coming back to your breath and imagine opening your body up as you do so.

2. Tune into your fears about what it is that you will lose if you let go of the narcissist. Really feel this in your body. As an example, these fears could relate to losing love that you will never find again. Maybe they are about a loss of security or your ability to survive by yourself in the world, or a fear of facing the unknown on your own. You might fear the loss of your social life, travel or the lifestyle you had with this person. Whatever answers come up for you, open your eyes and record them in your journal.

3. Really feel into your body as you ask yourself, 'Is there another time in my life when I have felt the same losses, fears or insecurities?' (It is important to be vulnerable and honest with ourselves. Remember, we have to be real to heal!) Hold your attention in your body, keeping your body open and relaxed while you breathe deeply in and out, and allow the answers to surface. The information that your inner being/inner child supplies you with may be something like: 'Ever since I can remember I have feared not being loved, or losing someone's love.' Or, 'I am scared to take responsibility for my own decisions, I prefer other people to do that for me.' Or, 'I don't believe I can make my life work.' Or, 'I don't believe I can survive without a man.' Or, 'I always feel uncomfortable doing anything social or travelling or particular activities without a partner, it makes me feel like the odd one out.' Write down the details of what comes up for you.

4. Look at the list of what you fear losing if you let go of the narcissist, and ask yourself this: 'Which of these things am I not providing for myself?' Again, be really honest with your answers. What is it specifically that you are not providing for yourself? Then ask yourself: 'Why don't I believe I can provide this for myself now?' Really feel deeply into the answer and write down as much as you can.

5. Go to the page in your journal headed 'My True Self Declarations' (see box entitled "PRE-EXERCISE DETAILS AND INSTRUCTIONS") and write down a declaration that relates to each thing you think you can't provide for yourself. A True Self Declaration could take the following shape: 'I am in the process of becoming whole to feel true devoted love for myself' or 'I am now in the process of becoming whole to find real security for myself.' You might wish to write these declarations out eleven times each, as eleven is a powerful number for manifestation!

6. Record how you feel in your journal after doing this exercise. Do you feel more solid and hopeful about moving forward in life as yourself? If you know there is more healing to be done, then keep working through Step 2 at your own pace until you feel that each trauma has been shifted.

Becoming Your Own Source

As you work through Step 2 and begin to release and heal the illusion that the narcissist is your source of self, something powerful happens. You will find you are no longer attracted to or obsessing about the narcissist. By coming home to yourself, you become the energy and the creation of a source of self – and this healing process allows you to finally start really loving, accepting and nurturing yourself.

The pain, the fear and the feelings of loss, and the emptiness of believing that your love and life were dependent on the narcissist all dissolve away, and you realise that what you sought outside yourself was within you the whole time; you have simply been disconnected from it. You start to find the power and inspiration to come back to yourself, and begin to feel adult and capable in your own body.

Becoming your own source of love, approval, security and survival is such a key component of the Thriver Journey, yet I know how hard it can feel in the early stages. We feel so broken and empty that mere survival seems like a mammoth task, let alone being able to be whole and complete on our own. This is exactly why I've put together a step-by-step training plan, as well as many other resources, to ensure that you make it out the other side. If you haven't yet accessed your 'You Can Thrive Program', you can do so here now: www.youcanthriveprogram.com

Once you have worked through Step 2 (which I strongly suggest doing before moving on to Step 3), you shift from seeking others to grant your sense of self, to becoming the very source of love and Life Force that you seek. This creates a great deal of relief, peace and freedom as it dissolves away your addiction, clinginess and desperation towards the narcissist and other people. It also brings with it the knowing that by becoming true to yourself, you will one day attract people in all walks of life who have the real resources to support and love you.

And now we move on to another key stage of the recovery journey – Step 3 – which grants us an additional level of empowerment, meaning that our recovery is well underway.

9

FORGIVE YOURSELF AND LIFE FOR WHAT YOU HAVE BEEN THROUGH

Now that you have come this far, you will have started work in earnest on releasing yourself from the unhealed traumas that lie within you, which have their roots in your childhood and which were causing you to feel like the narcissist was your source of love, approval, security and survival As a result of this work, you will have a much greater understanding of how to undo the emotional ties you feel towards this person. If you have joined me in the free workshop, and begun NARP, and started to shift out the specific traumas related to these wounds, you will notice that many of your needy feelings will have dissolved. Detachment is the goal you are heading towards, and it should seem much more tangible by now.

You may have also noticed that you have started to perceive painful events in your past differently (even those that didn't involve the narcissist). And rather than continuing to feel like a victim, you may have realised there was a greater gift to be taken from these experiences – the gift of coming home to finally loving and accepting yourself regardless of what other people do or don't do in your life.

You may have also started to feel a sense of comfort and solidity inside yourself, which is something that you haven't known for a long time, or which you have perhaps never previously experienced. This is because your feelings, energy and emotions are no longer being generated purely in reaction to what is or isn't happening in the world outside you; they are starting to be generated *inside you.*

Mourning the Significant Losses

It is time to consider the next Step of your healing journey. This next stage, Step 3, is a powerful shift for breaking out of the victimisation mode that can otherwise hold us hostage indefinitely after narcissistic abuse.

Losses are synonymous with narcissistic abuse and one of the hardest things with which to reconcile ourselves. Even after we have shored up our original traumas through Step 2, addressing whatever it was that the narcissist wasn't providing us with in our life, we still have horrific losses to grieve. In many ways these losses can feel as impactful as experiencing a death.

As Norman Cousins, an American political journalist, author, professor and peace advocate, said: 'Death is not the greatest loss in life. What is the greatest loss is what dies inside us while we live.'[1] When we have experienced narcissistic abuse we may feel like a part (or many parts) of ourself has died, because so many of the things we thought represented 'us' are gone: many people who suffer narcissistic relationships are robbed of not only their support networks, family and close friends, but often their capacity to work, as well as their money, possessions, previous investments and property. These individuals may feel like they have taken a step backwards and fallen years behind in regard to where they thought they would be; their losses may be so extreme that many feel they will never recover what they have lost. You personally may have lost everything you've worked for; or you may have had your family and friends turned against you; or you may be experiencing severe debilitation of your health or even have lost custody of your children. Maybe you have suffered all of these things and more; lots of people have.

Significant losses are incredibly traumatic to come to terms with. Certainly, one of the hardest things for me was trying to accept that everything I had worked so hard for all my life – all the things that I thought defined who I was and my worth – was now gone. And it wasn't just about possessions, as you may have experienced too. The losses on a personal level were enormous as well: friendships and connections that it had taken me decades to establish – all smashed to pieces by narcissistic smearing and drama.

What is also devastating is the hindsight and the knowledge that there were so many times when our inner voice was screaming 'warning, warning!' to us about the narcissist. We know we should have taken more notice of what was going on, trusted our inner voice more, left the relationship earlier and got off the ship before it sunk completely. But we didn't; we stayed, we rationalised away what we were feeling, and we were too worn out and beaten down to do anything about it anyway. We were barely surviving, let alone dealing with what was going on.

Nancy wrote this to me: 'I really believed Dean was the love of my life, and after marrying him I thought I was doing the right thing by standing by him. After discovering he had unpaid parking tickets amounting to thousands of dollars, I sorted them out for him because he didn't have the money to. When his car's engine blew up, I used part of my dad's inheritance to buy him a new car, because he needed it to work for me and the kids. When he was sued because of uncompliant work, I used more of my inheritance to pay for the legal costs. Before long, one way or another my entire inheritance was gone – and now there is nothing to show for it. Now that we have separated, he is saying that I am entitled to nothing and he wants the house and the kids. I am beyond devastated at how I supported this man, year after year, at my own expense, and he has turned on me like this.'

Nancy's story is not unusual; in fact, when it comes to narcissistic abuse, it is extremely common: victims mopping up the narcissist's messes for them and paying for their screw-ups is standard behaviour (I did it too), only to receive absolutely no gratitude or clemency at the time, and then to be attacked ferociously when everything falls apart.

Of course it is hard to forgive ourselves for getting into that position – throwing more and more good resources after bad, trying to offset disasters and fix our relationships, only to receive total destitution and devastation in return for our efforts.

The Difficulty in and Necessity of Forgiving Ourselves

The truth is, if we have suffered narcissistic abuse, we often feel completely devastated about the choices we made and how we didn't look after ourselves. When it comes to our healing, this is significant – really significant – because one of the hardest things we can ever do is to forgive ourselves. And forgiving ourselves is not just about what we did to ourselves; it's also about what we have done to the people we love.

My guilt around what I had put my son through was horrific before I worked with the healing processes in Step 3. There was no way that, as his mother, I could have possibly let myself feel exonerated from what I had put him through as a by-product of the relationship with my abuser, if it hadn't been for Quanta Freedom Healing. My son saw things he never should have seen. He and I found ourselves escaping out of windows, and at times stranded with no place to go. We were thrown out of our own home, and moved from place to place like refugees, not knowing what the next day might bring. And he witnessed his mother teetering on the edge of life and death, totally unavailable to look after him.

Thank goodness I did fully commit to the processes to forgive myself, because I later discovered that being a parent clogged up with toxic emotions would seriously compromise my ability to be a healthy, loving mother. We cannot shame and blame ourselves into shape – and if we are not healthy our children will suffer.

This is what Carmel said about releasing her guilt in Step 3: 'Before I forgave myself I was overcompensating for their narcissistic father, who I was co-parenting with. I was interrogating my children and trying to force them into therapy. They resisted, they pulled away from me and were starting to side with their father. The truth is I was toxic, anxious and full of shame. When I healed and released my guilt, my anxiety fell away and I was no longer trying to fix them to ease my guilt. I realised that by healing myself, they healed with me organically. They are doing so well now.'

Our guilt and shame can extend into many areas besides our children. When we are narcissistically abused and addicted to the abuser, we are horribly unavailable, easily triggered and defensive. We sneak around, lying and deceiving in order to keep seeing the narcissist when others have stopped supporting our toxic relationship. Naturally, people observe there is something seriously wrong with us and they are concerned, but rather than trying to alleviate their feelings or connect with them, we continue delivering our lies, unreliability, unpredictable moods and unavailability.

Greg said this about his shame and guilt: 'I am in shock about how ill I was. My relationship with my brother, who I was in business was, was terrible. I was anxious, angry and quite frankly manic. I was forever chasing after him when he called me and abused me, and I couldn't stop myself doing it. I would do everything I could to stop him interacting with clients. I neglected my wife and my kids, missing their important school and sporting events. It nearly caused a divorce. I let myself and so many people down who I cared about, in abysmal ways.'

Self-forgiveness is even harder than working through our forgiveness of others, and I believe it needs to come first. In fact, it's absolutely vital – which is why it is a focus at this stage of our healing journey. If we can't forgive ourselves, we can't forgive the processes of life that led us here. As Louise Hay advises: 'I forgive myself and I set myself free.'[2]

She is right: we can't move on from the horror and ongoing traumas within us unless we forgive ourselves.

Forgiving Life/Source/Creation

It's at this stage of the journey that we can also release ourselves from those terrible feelings of being struck down by Life, Source, Creation or whichever term you prefer to use for a Higher Power. We may believe that what happened to us was some sick punishment that we received for an unknown reason. We may ponder: 'I must have done something HORRIBLE in a previous life to deserve this!' Maybe we believe that God has forsaken us or that we are cursed, or that something we have done means we deserved this terrible fate.

In stark contrast, the Thriver Way to Heal means accepting that what happened was for the purpose of our personal evolution – that it was 'for' us and not 'to' us, and that by working with it from the perspective of the bigger picture, we will be able to get the release we crave and gain the blessings. If we don't, we may remain stuck in the breakdown experience of narcissistic abuse, rather than gloriously reach the breakthrough stage.

It's not just our community that is adopting this aspect of the Thriver Way to heal, which acknowledges the growth that can come from traumatic experiences. For the *Scientific American* blog, psychologist Scott Barry Kaufman, who is known for his work on redefining intelligence, writes: 'In recent years, psychologists have become increasingly interested in the positive life changes that accompany highly stressful life events, such as being diagnosed with a chronic or terminal illness, losing a loved one, or sexual assault. This phenomenon has been referred to as post-traumatic growth, and researchers have discovered five particular areas of growth that often spring from adversity: interpersonal relationships, the identification of new possibilities for one's life, personal strength, spirituality and appreciation of life.'[3]

Regarding narcissistic abuse, at a deep level I truly believe that our souls design it this way – to create this 'make or break' experience that takes away all those props that were supporting our false identity, and to bring us face to face finally with our inner being, leaving us with nowhere else to go. Personally, I know life had previously supplied me with many signposts to help me to get this: to understand that a life lived from the 'outside in' was precarious at best and not my true life, and that the only life that would ever truly fulfil me would have to be lived from the 'inside out'; that is, from my soul. Yet it took a whopping great billboard falling on top of me – narcissistic abuse – before I made that shift.

Working through Step 3 helps move us on from feeling victimised, stuck, traumatised and struggling to assimilate everything that has happened to us. By working on any traumas around feeling cursed and punished by God and Life, we make peace with the flow of Life both within and outside ourselves. I have discovered, both by working on myself and with so many others, that we feel closer to a Higher Power as a result of the healing work in this Step than we ever did before it (including pre-abuse), even if we have always been spiritual people or religiously inclined.

Step 3 brings about an empowering soul realisation that what has happened is in fact in perfect and divine order. Our experience with the narcissist has stopped us in our tracks along the path of the false self, down which we were previously travelling, by knocking us squarely on to our behinds in order to grant us the opportunity to realign ourselves with the path of our true self.

The shift that you can experience through Step 3 is the knowing, acceptance and peace that *you purposefully co-created at a soul level exactly what you needed to heal.* The highest level of forgiveness knows *there is nothing to forgive* – and there is only the gift of your healing, resurrection and evolution to take forward.

Through working on Step 3 and healing the regret and pain of what you did to yourself and of what life has delivered to you, something powerful happens: you start opening up to the wellbeing and abundance of Life. You start moving away from the chaos of your past and into the promise of your future.

Not only will you heal and release yourself from the regretful patterns of what occurred with the narcissist, you will clean up the pain of your previous shameful experiences – the ones that unconsciously contributed to your becoming involved with a narcissist in the first place. And this means you will no longer continue to attract and maintain abusive and painful relationships.

Take a deep breath and know I'm right by your side, because I understand that forgiveness is a biggie! It's the hardest thing to do, but I promise you the relief and Life Force that will enter you afterwards is epic! Also by letting go, you let Life, Source or Creation take care of the narcissist rather than you taking all that bad energy on from them (which is what happens when we are still reeling in the injustice of it all). As I said in one of my recent *Thriver TV* episodes, it is like the karma bus was sent to the wrong address!

Okay, now it's time to work with your healing in Step 3.

EXERCISE: STEP 3 – LETTING GO AND FORGIVING YOURSELF, LIFE AND OTHERS

1. To prepare for this exercise, find some time and privacy so you won't be disturbed. Set the clear intention that you are granting yourself permission to devote this time and space to yourself. Then close your eyes for a few minutes and focus on breathing in and out with long, full, slow breaths. If your mind wanders, don't pay the thoughts any attention; just ignore them and come back to your breath.

2. Take your attention inside yourself, and ask your inner being lovingly, 'What are the things I'm hanging on to that I can't forgive?' They could be things about yourself, the narcissist, people in the narcissist's life, God, Life itself – anything at all. Don't hold back: open your eyes and write them all down.

3. Then, with all the love you can muster, talk to your inner being/inner child the way you would talk to someone you adore, and ask him or her, '[Endearing name] what is this inability to forgive about?' Write any answers that arise in your journal. When you are ready, move on to this question: 'What are you trying to protect us against?' Again, record the answers you receive. Next, ask your inner being: 'What is the terror of forgiving and letting go of this trauma?' Record the answers you are given. If you sense any blockages or resistance, say to yourself: 'Inner Child [or Inner Being], I give you my full permission to share with me how you feel – and in no way will I judge you for this. I am here to love you unconditionally and help you heal.' Record any additional information you feel or receive.

4. Now tell your inner being/inner child: 'I grant you permission to set yourself free and to hand this energy of trauma, all the incidents that have hurt you, all of the blockages and fears and hanging on around not letting this go – all of it – back to Life/Source/Creation to set yourself free.' Then perform the following visualisation: imagine all these traumas wrapped up in a parcel – you can have separate parcels or one big package – which you then hand back to your Higher Power (in whatever form you want to imagine this Higher Consciousness), who absolutely knows what to do with this energy. If a Higher Power visualisation doesn't work for you, then just imagine sending the parcel(s) off into the distance where it dissolves or disintegrates into 'nothingness' for recycling. Now the energy is no longer stuck inside you; and it was never your toxic energy in the first place! You get to go free now. Imagine and really feel space opening up inside you where all that toxic pain used to be.

5. Visualise bringing down Light (or whatever your understanding of a Higher Power is) via a pipeline that connects from the top of your head to a big ball of white Light above your head. Feel Light entering the space where the trauma previously was. Allow the feelings of relief, warmth and healing to wash through you, and feel these in your body as strongly as possible.

6. Record in your journal how this feels. Do you feel lighter and freer? Do you feel like you can forgive or have forgiven now? Do you feel like you

> have closure and you can move on? If there is still any resistance to forgiving, repeat this exercise.

Forgiveness can be a major Step to process and one that might need to be repeated many times during your journey. From the NARP Community, I know that Module Three of the Narcissistic Abuse Recovery Program is a stage that is often revisited because forgiveness – particularly when we feel like we are trying to forgive the unforgivable – can be very hard to achieve. Especially forgiving ourselves for what we've continually put ourselves through with narcissistic abuse. However, when people break through into a complete letting go of all toxic feelings towards an abuser, as well as themselves, they reach levels of unprecedented freedom where this person has absolutely no power over them anymore. It's so worth the journey to get there!

Letting Go

After working through Step 3, which of course may take some time to complete (forgiveness can have a great deal of resistance stacked up against it!), you will have a solid platform in place that will allow you to start seriously detoxing yourself of the traumas caused by the very personal and terrible things that have happened to you.

As mentioned earlier in this book, compared to the experiences of some people in traditional recovery, the Thriver Way to Heal is about releasing and shifting out the trauma from deep within our being on a cellular level – which is the only place real recovery can take place. I can't wait to get you started on this specific release work, so let's move on now to Chapter 10!

10

RELEASE AND HEAL THE PAIN OF INJUSTICE AND BETRAYAL

After working on forgiving yourself and Life for what you have been through, you will discover that you start to feel much more peaceful. If you are doing healing work with NARP, as a result of releasing tons of trauma and reprogramming your beliefs from a victimisation to a Thriver orientation, you will have the ability to be *in the present* without the agonising regret of your past. Very likely, your energy is no longer tied up in beating yourself up about the mistakes you made, and you have a greater acceptance regarding healing and empowering yourself – knowing this process is *meant to be.*

You may have also noticed that doors have started opening for you, doors that represent your new 'nourished by Life' future, and you feel you are able to direct more energy and even enthusiasm towards creating your new way of living. You may also feel a greater strength and warmth inside yourself, knowing that you are starting to feel what it is really like *to love and accept yourself.*

Now, it's time to consider the next Step of your healing journey. Step 4 is about releasing and healing the pain of injustice and betrayal. This is another very powerful Step, because it breaks you free from the belief and the illusion that your identity, life and the creation of yourself are controlled by what other people do or don't do to you.

Attempting to Reconcile the Irreconcilable

Releasing and healing any feelings of injustice and betrayal is a crucial process. This is where much of our obsession loop, triggered by traumas in our body, can be stuck on repeat – because truly the things that narcissists do are unfathomable, and, from a logical perspective, it can be virtually impossible to get our heads and our hearts around their actions, however hard we try. At a basic human level, it is inconceivable how anybody could even think of doing the things they do, let alone carry them out – and to be on the receiving end of their narcissistic abuse feels like a soul violation that is incomprehensible.

This is what Joan told me about her obsessive thoughts of Craig: 'I just can't stop going over particular scenes. There's not a day goes by where I don't replay the scenes of him looking me in the eye and telling me how I am his one true love and how much he has missed me, after returning home from a supposed "golf trip" with his mates – when he was really shacked up with his affair for five days in Thailand. My head goes over and over other times when he was away, or when he walked outside to take a phone call, and I rack my brains trying to work out what he was really up to. It sickens me to my stomach and I can't stop thinking about it. It's been three years now; why can't I stop hurting and get on with my life and meet someone else?'

I truly believe that one of the major reasons why narcissistic abuse victims don't traditionally heal from their inner wounds and fractures is because we just don't have the cognitive abilities to facilitate a resolution. Logically, there is no way out of the highly activated trauma in our bodies. This keeps psychologists in business, because week after week people continue to talk about the same old traumas and to look outwards at what somebody else did to them – yet after each session the temporary relief fades and the pain returns. And the hurt isn't relieved, even if they never hear from the narcissist again. Nothing changes because the trauma has never been truly dealt with *inside.*

Step 4 validates the fact that we took the trauma of what the narcissistic person did to us and placed it *inside ourselves* – where it festers in an incredibly damaging way until we can release it. Negative emotions that remain painfully stuck in our being don't allow us to evolve; instead, they break us down emotionally, mentally, physically, spiritually and financially. All of our energy becomes tied up in trying to survive the devastation inside ourselves and we don't have any energy available for forward movement, solution and the creation of a new life. Toxic emotions cause us to 'dissolve' rather than 'evolve' – because if we are not growing, we are dying.

Additionally, the fact that you are reeling in the pain of the injustice and the betrayals you have experienced is one of the deadliest hooks the narcissist has in their arsenal against you. Narcissists can only win if someone else is losing, and they can only attack when we feed them the pain and fear that energise them to do so. Your suffering and obsession ensure that your attention is *firmly planted* on what the narcissist is or is not up to. And that is what narcissistic supply *is all about.*

Breaking the Ties by Releasing the Injustices

Step 4 of the recovery process is about purging yourself of the pain caused by the narcissist's behaviour, which previously kept you in anger, resentment and despair. This means you can break even further away from the narcissist's antics, games and punishment of you. After working through Step 4, whenever the narcissist next behaves immorally, lies, fabricates stories to discredit you, projects on to you and gaslights you (i.e. twists information to try to confuse you about what is real and what isn't), you will have reclaimed enough inner solidity and security that you will not be triggered into further despair, powerlessness, grief or rage.

Additionally, you won't be looking for accountability, acknowledgement or validation concerning what you are going through, and you won't be interested in getting even or reaping revenge. You won't try to prescribe to the narcissist or attempt to make him or her understand you are 'right' and he or she is 'wrong'. So what will you do instead? You will *detach.*

After working through Step 4 with Quanta Freedom Healing in NARP, Roger reported, 'Of course she kept trying to get to me, but I stopped responding to her threats, her attempts to bully me for more money, or to bring my business down or to go for full custody. In the past, I was always trying to placate her and keep her happy to minimalise the damage she could do to me and the kids, but it never worked anyway. After doing this inner work, I realised I didn't fear anything she would try to do. My attitude became "whatever – if you try, I'll deal with it", and I started to get on with my life. To my absolute delight, I found the rubbish that was previously unrelenting suddenly stopped. It was like someone flicked a switch.'

When you achieve the inner shifts afforded by this Step, it is much easier to stop allowing the narcissist's injustices and betrayals to derail you emotionally. The gift is that you graduate to a state of mind where the narcissist's behaviour no longer affects you, and where you accept that he or she behaves in this way purely because he or she is a narcissist – and that's just the way it is. It is the indisputable truth that when what someone does is able to affect you emotionally *they still have power over you.* Understanding this is of paramount importance.

As Nelson Mandela wrote in his autobiography, *The Long Walk to Freedom:* 'As I walked out the door toward my freedom, I knew if I did not leave all the anger, resentment and bitterness behind that I would still be in prison.' That's it in a nutshell: by working on Step 4, we are detoxing ourselves of much that keeps us chained to narcissists.

Narcissists cannot keep doing what they do when you no longer hand over attention or emotional energy to them. This healing Step is about *disconnecting* the energy supply that has been feeding the narcissist. Once you do this, the narcissist will stop receiving narcissistic supply from you and be forced to move on to another person onto whom they can offload their inner turmoil and from whom they can drain energy and resources.

Cleaning Up Patterns of a Victimised Past

What you will discover by dedicating yourself to this Step of your healing process, is that not only will you release the pain of the injustice and the betrayals caused by the acts of the narcissist, but also the pain of other injustices and betrayals in your past; the ones that were still energetically playing out and unconsciously generating more of the same – the continuation of the pattern of abuse and pain in your life.

You will feel a freedom within yourself once you release and transform these emotions, and you will know in a profound way that *you are no longer emotionally compatible for this pattern of injustice and betrayal.* This is where we start to understand that people and their behaviours cease to have power over us when we become responsible for our own wellbeing and the creation of our life, which is now unfolding from within us.

You may have believed that hanging on to the pain was keeping you safe, because it kept you on the lookout and warned you about what the narcissist was up to. However, after working on this Step of your recovery and making the shift out of the pain, you will experience a level of peace and safety that far surpasses anything you have previously known. Because you now know you can observe inappropriate behaviour, honour yourself, create boundaries and say 'no', without fear and pain, to what is no longer your truth.

Jeanette admitted the following after working through Step 4: 'The narcissist took my money, savings, property, car and possessions away. Originally I thought this was all just about him being a disgraceful person. After doing the deeper inner healing work, I realised this was a pattern of trauma that started when I was very young. My narcissistic mother used to take my toys away and throw them out to punish me. I was so terrified of her that when she asked for them, I would hand my prized possessions over without a fight to try to avoid her screaming and hitting me. I realise now I gave the narcissist everything when he demanded it to try to avoid being hurt, yet of course I got hurt all over again. After healing what happened when I was little – the devastation of losing my things – I know there is no way I am repeating this pattern again. From now on if I say "no" and people don't like it, then they don't deserve to be in my life.'

I have found that for many people, myself included, injustices and betrayals can be very difficult to release by any means other than the deep, inner shift work that takes place directly in the subconscious, because these events tend to become superglued to our inner being. This is completely understandable: these are the extremely painful, highly charged traumas of being 'wronged' that we naturally tend to hang on to very determinedly, in order to retain our position of being 'right' and 'victimised', and in an attempt to protect ourselves from those sorts of experiences ever happening to us again.

There are those people who, like Nelson Mandela, can let go of this sort of trauma using means other than Quantum Tools such as Quanta Freedom Healing, yet the majority of mere mortals such as myself (and virtually everyone else I have met in narcissistic abuse recovery) simply can't achieve this.

If you too have been struggling to let go of obscene injustices and betrayals, I'd love you (if you haven't already) to join me in my free workshop to experience just how powerful healing is when we apply the Quantum Tools directly to the trauma and shift it out of our cellular being. For the free step-by-step workshop and to receive lots of other Thriver resources, you can join me here: www.youcanthriveprogram.com.

At this next stage of your journey, it is time to claim, release and replace the terrible injustices and betrayals you have experienced. So let's get started with the exercise.

EXERCISE: STEP 4 – RELEASING BETRAYAL AND INJUSTICE

1. To prepare for this exercise, grant yourself the space and time where you will not be disturbed. Have your journal with you and start by taking deep, long breaths with your eyes closed. Imagine opening up your body and releasing stress – just letting it go. If any thoughts pop up, don't give them energy; just refocus on breathing in and out.

2. Now connect to your inner being/inner child. Connect to the awful injustices that you experienced and that you continue to carry with you in the form of a continual thought loop. Open your eyes and write down what those incidents were, in no particular order, just however they arise.

3. Then, while connecting with your inner being/inner child, say, '[Endearing term], I love you unconditionally and I am here to love and hold you. I am never leaving you again. Please share with me, how did those bad incidents make you feel?' Write down the emotions you have in your body about them, while remaining present with these feelings with love, acceptance and compassion. The incidents that you recorded at stage 2 above may have caused you painful feelings of being unlovable, unworthy, unimportant, abandoned or devastated, for example. Honour absolutely anything that arises while remaining unconditionally present with your inner being. Allow your inner being/inner child to share with you all that he/she needs to. Record these feelings.

4. Next, tell your inner being/inner child, 'I want to hear you, understand and help you. When in the past, [endearing term], have you felt like this as well? Where did this start for you?' Trust what arises (this could be information from your childhood or a past life) and record it. If no information is forthcoming, that is perfectly okay; just move on to the next stage of the exercise.

5. Now go back to your injustices and betrayals that you recorded at stage 2 and, one at a time, connect to the painful emotional charges in your body about it. Rate these out of 10, with 0/10 being the lowest rating and 10/10 being the most intense emotional charge. Number these incidences from their highest to lowest emotional charge.

6. Starting with the highest-rated trauma, tell your inner being/inner child: '[Endearing term], I grant you permission to release this trauma and send it back to native nothingness so that you go free from it.' Perform the following visualisation: imagine the trauma's negative energy inside you (however you see it in your mind's eye), then imagine pushing it out to the sides of yourself with whatever visualisation tool you want to use. For example, you might imagine steel plates pushing it out, a vacuum sucking it up, a hose washing it out, magnets drawing it out or a Higher Power removing it for you. Whatever visualisation tool you use, imagine that when the trauma leaves your body, it dissolves or disintegrates into nothing. You get to go free now. Imagine and feel space opening up inside you where all that toxic pain used to be.

7. Then bring down Light via the pipeline into yourself and the space where the trauma previously was. 'See' yourself fill up – in every cell of your body – with this white Light. Allow sensations of relief, warmth and healing to flow through you.

8. Write about how you feel now. Does it feel like 'that thing' which was terrorising you has shifted considerably? Do you feel free of it? Does it feel like it happened to someone else now? Keep working, over time, at your own pace with Step 4 until it does.

9. Now repeat the process with the next highest-rated trauma on your list.

Releasing Ourselves from Obsessional Trauma

Once we start identifying ourselves less and less as a victim and become more detached from other people's bad behaviour, we can begin to release any dense energy that is tying us to a narcissist at an even deeper level. The Step that we will explore in the next chapter involves another powerful and necessary soul shift that will change your life from the inside out beyond description. I really can't wait to share with you the incredible impact and release this next Step will grant you – and how it makes it so much more difficult for the narcissist to affect your life.

11

LET GO OF THE FIGHT TO WIN AND YOUR NEED FOR JUSTICE

After letting go of the pain of the injustice and the betrayal that you have suffered, you will discover that what used to hurt you profoundly, and in all-consuming ways, doesn't matter to you nearly as much as it once did. At this stage of your recovery, if you are committed to self-partnering and diligently tackling the obsessional loops of those inhumane things you couldn't previous process, and if you also practise the NARP healings, you will have discovered that you are going hours or even days without thinking about those things the narcissist did to you. Other issues may still come up – and that's okay; just keep addressing them and releasing them too.

You may also find that your outer life is opening up more and more with opportunities, good feelings and fortuitous events, and you start feeling a connection with, and a gratitude to, Life. You are no longer stuck in obsessively focusing on and unconsciously manifesting more injustice and betrayal in your life. Rather, you have started aligning yourself with the good stuff, regardless of what the narcissist is or isn't doing.

Additionally, the narcissist's attempts to derail you and hook you in are not working as powerfully as they once used to. This is because you are disconnecting from being a source of narcissistic supply for the narcissist, which means that he or she will soon realise there is no more energy to be gained from you. Without you handing over emotional energy, there is nothing left for the narcissist to feed from and none of *your energy is available to be used against you.*

Now it is time to consider the next Step of your healing journey. Step 5 is about letting go of the fight to 'win' and the need for justice. This Step tackles the trauma of what happened to us at a deeper level.

Trying to force the narcissist to do anything to help you feel better means you are playing straight into the narcissist's hands. The urge to 'win' is enormous for most of us, and it truly can destroy us. This is why every time you walk into the ring with the narcissist and you try to gain the upper hand, you will simply be knocked down again. The narcissist just ups the ante and delivers endless blows without compunction, in a way that you simply are not capable of matching.

It is incredibly disempowering to live according to the belief '*I am in limbo and can never be happy until justice is done.'* Truly, that is a waste of the life you are meant to live, and which you *can* live.

So much of our human conditioning and programming encourages us to be incensed about wrongdoing and to try to combat it in order to make the wrongdoer accountable. But this always sets you up for failure with a narcissist. If you are honest with yourself, you know this to be true; you will have experienced how every time you try to expose the narcissist, or try to make others aware of what he or she is, or try to corner him or her into taking responsibility, showing remorse or making amends, your efforts backfire. These episodes are fraught with pain, frustration and even more twists and turns, which end up with you feeling even more abused – and *you being the one who is discredited.*

Janet was set up by Mike. Once, when he was maliciously abusing her, she sent him texts in total despair and anguish, which included the statement: 'I may as well end my life.' Mike used this information to smear her to her family, boss and friends – behaving like the nice guy, claiming he was frightened for her mental state, and saying how hard it was for him living with her. Naturally, the concerned people in Janet's life approached her about her text. In horror, shame and unspeakable anger at this twisted deception and betrayal, Janet went into overdrive, trying to show what Mike had been doing to her and that he was the abuser who was responsible for this state of affairs. The more she tried to prove her point, the more Mike could sit back calmly, effectively letting her dig herself into a deeper hole. Janet's despair worsened as all her attempts to bring Mike to accountability failed miserably. As a result, her depression, obsession and anxiety intensified.

Fortunately, once Janet started working with NARP, she discovered the real reason why she was stuck in the powerlessness of trying to exonerate herself and expose Mike. In her family of origin, Janet was scapegoated by a father and sister who took no responsibility for their poor behaviour. Once these traumas where cleared and healed, she felt no urge to replay them with Mike – and relief and her recovery began.

Trying to 'win' against the narcissist and to force him or her to accept accountability is one of the biggest mistakes people who have been narcissistically abused can make, and it is one of the major hooks that keeps us handing over narcissistic supply, allowing the narcissist to carry on abusing us. When we consider the Quantum Law – *so within, so without* – we can understand the energetic reason why trying to force someone else to reveal their true colours and be accountable doesn't work. The reason is that as soon as we think we need a certain set of conditions or circumstances to exist outside ourselves in order for us to feel whole inside – and we try to force those conditions into existence in order to feel better – all we receive is more of not feeling whole within ourselves. The only real solution is to create the resolution, the wholeness *inside* ourselves, and then the outside world will, and does, follow suit. As Gautama Buddha famously said: 'Peace comes from within. Do not seek it without.'

One of the most important realisations we can have about co-dependent behaviour and our enmeshment with narcissists is that if we remain hooked into them and simply can't let go until they apologise, repent or whatever else it is that we 'need' from them, then we simply can't stay away from them and begin to heal. We remain dangerously attached to them and vulnerable to abuse, and we also give them tons of ammunition with which to discredit us, as well as high-grade narcissistic supply in direct proportion to how adversely they are affecting us.

Dean was hell-bent on holding Renee accountable for syphoning his money into a separate bank account and then running off with another man with his funds. Yet, because he had trustingly granted her access to his accounts, he couldn't prosecute. Renee took all his calls and emails – and threw back in his face everything she had ever done for him over the years, saying how badly he had treated her, as well as how happy she was in her new relationship by comparison. Renee was revelling in the drama; not only was she energised by the narcissistic supply she got from Dean, his behaviour gave her all sorts of material to share with other people, enabling her to gain even more attention and support in relation to how terrible

Dean was now being. Dean, in stark contrast, was becoming even more panicked and deranged.

Dean finally understood that the harder he pushed for accountability and justice, the sicker he was becoming. When he had reached the point of (as he expressed it) 'driving myself into a tree', he knew he needed help. It took him a long time to accept the need to take personal responsibility for healing himself, which entailed letting go of the injuries to his ego, working on no longer being over-trusting and setting healthy boundaries for himself, as well as healing previous traumas from his narcissistic mother. However, after he dedicated himself wholeheartedly to NARP, within eighteen months he no longer felt any concern or pain relating to what had happened with Renee. He had also started a new relationship and was now taking his time to get to know his new partner before moving her in and allowing her full access to his finances. And he was well on his way to rebuilding his lost assets.

My own story is a great example of the profound shifts we can make around our own sense of righteousness and judgement. Righteousness was a massive issue for me. I firmly believed bad people should be brought to justice and be forced to suffer the consequences of their actions. When I suffered narcissist abuse I was smeared horrifically, his story being that I was constantly having affairs, and that I was crazy and abusing him. Virtually everyone in my life believed his stories, including the police who didn't grant me any protection against his stalking and threats, and I was manically terrorised, disturbed and vilified, while trying to clear my name and hold him accountable.

It wasn't until I stopped trying to change anyone else's mind and worked on changing my own – by releasing the associated traumas out of my being with Quanta Freedom Healing – that I discovered the deep fear of persecution that I had inside me. I held within me a literal white hot terror of being accused of doing something wrong, and because of this I was highly invested in what people thought of me. When I released those traumas, I came home naturally to a deep inner calm brought about by knowing that what was important was what *I* thought of *me.* It was no longer important to me to try to convince other people that I wasn't adulterous or crazy. It wasn't even important to try to make people realise who he was anymore. I simply started feeling at peace, even though there was no evidence of any physical change outside me.

And that is when it always happens – things shift and start to flow differently, in alignment with who we have now become on an inner level. People started approaching me, telling me how sorry they were for what they'd said about me. Key people in my life saw the truth about him and what he was doing. The police caught him out. All sorts of things changed without me 'doing' anything. I was starting to understand powerfully and deeply that things were changing because I was 'being' someone different.

Katie's narcissistic sister, who had power of attorney over their parents' estate, had coerced their dying father into signing nearly everything over to her and her children, leaving the other siblings robbed of their inheritance. Katie was completely devastated that her sister had done this, and, despite trying to bring her to justice, she was powerless to right the wrongs. Katie said, 'I literally burnt in hell about this. I started to have terrible thyroid problems, my fibromyalgia became unbearable and I was so consumed by my hatred for my sister that I had no energy at all to enjoy my life.' That was until Kate started shifting that trauma out of her body with Module Five of NARP. The relationship with her sister was always going to be destroyed, yet Katie became clear and clean enough within her own emotions to start getting on with her life. 'It was amazing,' Katie said, 'how after really focusing on this work, I woke up one morning and my resentment was all gone. I was free.'

Of course, before we shift our traumas out, the painful feelings of injustice can make us hungry for accountability and retribution. Jay, for example, was seething. His narcissistic ex-wife, with whom he shared four children, took him to court regularly for more child support and to try to get her hands on his superannuation payments. Every time he tried to make any headway in his life, she would force him back into court.

Eventually this broke Jay down completely. He was forced to sell his home in order to pay her more money; and because Jay was actively involved with his children and was already paying expensive school fees, he was incensed. He hated the fact that she had 'won' and achieved what she wanted, which was to stop him moving on and being happy and successful. He couldn't let go of attempting to have her tried and prosecuted as a vexatious litigant. But all his efforts to do so fell flat and ended up costing him even more money. What Jay didn't realise, until he started releasing his traumas, was that no amount of 'doing' can compensate for a traumatised 'being'. Until we begin to release our pain and unhelpful attachments, it is the inner trauma and more of that trauma being generated which will win out every time.

The incredible soul-evolution phenomenon that is the steep and necessary learning curve offered by narcissistic abuse is this: the necessity of claiming back your true self and detaching from any people and experiences that aren't in harmony with that true self. This is the greatest win you can achieve. And it is the only way you *can* win – because when you reach this level, the narcissist, and what he or she represents, will be far from your reality.

We have to learn to let the narcissist win this stage of the game and to take ourselves out of it. This is, moreover, not a part of the game you want to win, because it is merely a false, ego-driven charade. As Cyrus Stuart Ching, head of the US Federal Mediation and Conciliation Service, put it in a speech back in 1948: 'I learned long ago never to wrestle with a pig. You get dirty, and besides, the pig loves it.'

When you do the necessary work to bring about the shift offered by this Step, you will experience great relief, and achieve a greater sense of closure than you could ever have gained from the narcissist being held accountable. And you will know in the depths of your heart that Life will deal with the narcissist; for somehow, somewhere, Life holds everyone accountable. A false life, which is not built upon a foundation of integrity and truth, is a house of cards that cannot stand the test of time – and always eventually crumbles. However, *this is the narcissist's life and business; it's not yours.*

One of the most powerful ironies of life is that when you no longer need someone to be held accountable, that is when it generally happens; I can't tell you how many times I have seen this happen over the years. The 'how' or 'when' this accountability is forced upon the narcissist is not something that needs to concern you, though, because your emotions, identity and creation of the truth of your life are NOT dependent on it happening. The healing process of Step 5 allows you to break free from this deadly hook and will eradicate a huge amount of the toxicity in your emotions and your mind, releasing you to an even higher level of freedom and relief.

For years Henry had been terrorising Fiona with bullying and abuse, even though he had supposedly moved on with a new life and family. Feeling totally traumatised by him, Fiona tried fruitlessly to bring him to justice. The authorities didn't take her seriously and deemed her to be an unstable, mad person. Fiona was tormented by the fact she couldn't expose what he was doing or get support from anyone.

When she changed focus and worked instead on healing the deep trauma within her body that came from being made the family scapegoat as a child – which had led to her continuing to be the emotional dumping ground for her narcissist ex-husband now – she felt different. She no longer cared about his attempts to beat her up emotionally. She didn't hook in, feed the situation or fight back. She detached and ignored him. As it turned out, Henry then turned on his new wife, leaving Fiona alone, and his wife left him and started divorce proceedings. The karma bus struck.

Was this coincidental? I believe not.

This next exercise is another one that you will need to breathe deeply into while remaining firmly committed to the process – because it goes against all our previous conditioning not to blame or hold somebody else accountable for the hurts and injustices we have experienced. This is especially true when we have been affected by the narcissist doing something terrible to those we love, as well as to ourselves.

Now it's time to start letting go of your need to defeat the narcissist, thwart them and get back on top. By doing so, you will find a deeper, truer and much more powerful way to win.

There is such a relief within our inner being to be gained from this Step – as well as the ability to let our Higher Power work through us more effectively. When we try to control our life, we block so much of the richness and power of infinite wisdom and energy moving through us. Letting go of the toxic trauma at this stage of the journey is all about this – and I can't wait for you to experience it!

EXERCISE: STEP 5 – RELEASING THE NEED FOR ACCOUNTABILITY

1. To do this exercise, create space and time for yourself so that you won't be disturbed. Have your journal with you. It's very important to commit to being present lovingly with yourself, and to treat yourself and your inner being (which is the real you) as a top priority. We all want other people to show us that type of devotion, but, as the Quantum Law teaches us, *so within, so without:* if we don't grant ourselves self-partnering, no one else will meet us lovingly either!

To prepare for this exercise close your eyes, breathe deeply and open up your body. Still your mind by coming back to your breath if your thoughts wander.

Do this for a few minutes until you feel relaxed and centred.

2. Check in with your inner being. What things do you want to force the narcissist to be held accountable for? Or maybe it's the legal system as well? Or is it somebody else? Feel the traumas light up in your body and connect to what these are about. Open your eyes and write them down in whatever order they arise.

3. With your list of things that hurt regarding a lack of accountability, connect to the painful emotional charge in your body. Rate the incidents out of 10, with 0/10 being the lowest rating and 10/10 carrying the most intense charge. Then number these incidents from highest to lowest emotional charge.

4. Starting with the highest rating emotional charge, whilst holding your attention deeply on the trauma you are processing, ask your inner being/inner child how it feels not to have received accountability for this trauma. Be lovingly present as you give your inner being/inner child full permission to share with you these emotions – and reassure him or her that in no way will you judge these feelings, because they are all valid. The emotions that are likely to surface could be things such as feeling let down, unsupported, invalidated, brutalised, discarded, etc. Record whatever comes up.

5. Now, ask your inner being/inner child this question with complete openness, love and dedication: '[Endearing term], what is it that you didn't receive from [the name of the person or institution] that feels like emotions you have suffered in the past?' Then ask: 'Where did this start for you?' Pay attention as you connect with any feelings and thoughts that emerge from your inner child. (Note that information about past lives as well as your childhood may surface.) Trust and record whatever you are given.

If no information comes, just remain accepting, loving and present – and move on to the next stage of the exercise.

6. Now say to your inner being/inner child: '[Endearing term], you now have permission to let go of the need for accountability so that you can receive perfect resolution and freedom for yourself.' Then perform the following visualisation: imagine the part of your inner being who has taken on this trauma (however he or she appears – possibly as a child or a past-life self) standing in front of you. Then see divine beings (such as angels or any other energy that resonates with you) surrounding your inner being, reaching inside him or her and taking a big ball containing that trauma out from within. The trauma is then taken up and away, where it dissolves back to nothingness. As a result your inner being gets to go free now. Imagine and feel space opening up inside you where all that toxic pain used to be.

7. Now bring down Light and Power (or whatever your understanding of a Higher Power is) via the pipeline that connects you to the ball of Light above. 'See' yourself fill up – in every cell of your body – with this white Light. Allow the feelings of relief, warmth and healing to wash through you, and know this to be so. Experience these feelings somatically as much as you can.

8. Write in your journal about your experience in this exercise. How do you feel in your body now? Do you still feel like you need accountability concerning the trauma you were processing? Do you feel resolved, whole and at peace about it? If not, continue working with the Step 5 processes until you do.

9. Now repeat the process with the next highest-rated trauma on your list.

Going Free from Needing Accountability

Once we have released our need for accountability, which of course may take some time to unravel and heal (we're only human after all!), the next part of our journey is about a further breaking of any ties we have with abusers and abuse. At our next level of healing, Step 6, we move through releasing the need for accountability to letting go of taking responsibility for the narcissist. This next Step affects virtually anyone who has been abused by a narcissist. In fact, this next Step is so impactful that it can be the very trauma that people become stuck on, even when the love and the need to gain anything (such as approval, affection, attention or validation) from the narcissist has gone. Often this trauma can be the last remnants of the glue that holds a toxic relationship together.

So let's dive head first together into Step 6!

12

RELEASE AND HEAL THE NEED TO TAKE RESPONSIBILITY FOR THE NARCISSIST

When we have made the considerable effort required to release ourselves from needing to hold other people accountable, and let go of our own need to 'win', our recovery begins to feel much more solid. Many people, when they are halfway through these healing Steps, report that they already feel freer and more relieved of the pain of narcissistic abuse than they could have ever possibly imagined.

People who dedicate their efforts diligently to the Steps can, and often do, feel quite liberated (sometimes even more so than they ever previously felt) within timeframes that they wouldn't have believed possible. Sometimes after only weeks or a few months, they look back in amazement at how far they have come. And this is true even for those individuals who are still embroiled in property settlements, custody deals and other unresolved business with a narcissist. However, it is so important at this stage not to think

'I feel better now, so that's enough', and then rest on your laurels – *because there is still more crucial rewiring and healing of your subconscious to achieve.*

In order to experience your own true Thriver Recovery – and not just a survivor recovery – it is really important that you keep moving forward, and keep working on all the Steps. As mentioned, this next one, Step 6, is about releasing and healing the need to take responsibility for the narcissist.

People Who Are Abused by Narcissists Are Nice People

As we saw in Part One, most people who have been narcissistically abused are empathetic by nature. This makes sense because narcissists are in it for the business of taking – and nice people are the ones who are most likely to give. People who like to please others may struggle to say 'no' and are likely to do their best to help those close to them in times of need. A significant part of handing away our power and enabling abuse to continue in our lives comes from our taking responsibility for those who refuse to take responsibility for themselves, thereby inadvertently allowing damaged people like narcissists to keep doing it.

Angela was forever looking out for George. She played the peacemaker constantly between him and his family. She covered for him and lied to clients when

George didn't turn up to jobs, or when he didn't follow through on what he promised. She paid his speeding fines for him, did his tax and looked after his bills. She was in constant overdrive, trying to keep a check on his life and to offset the disasters caused by his loose and irresponsible behaviour so that her own life wouldn't be destroyed. However, the more she did this, the more drained and emptied out she was of time and resources, all of which was severely impacting on the energy available to her for leading her own life; and meanwhile George just kept doing whatever he wanted.

This was a role that was very familiar to Angela. Her mother had been addicted to prescription medication and from a young age Angela, as the oldest child, ran the household and brought up her siblings. Caretaking sick irresponsible people was her love trajectory; hence why she was so habituated to it. It wasn't until Angela discovered George's affair with his secretary that she decided she wanted a divorce. Angela was shocked (as we all were!) to discover that her decision to leave George didn't guarantee she would feel better. In fact, she was stunned at how frightfully anxious and depressed she was.

Thankfully, Angela worked on NARP for a solid six months to release her original traumas, which related to trying to receive love in her dysfunctional family of origin. After reclaiming these lost and damaged parts of herself, all of her abuse symptoms left her and she started to glow, honour herself and Thrive in her life. George tried to hook her in again with the guilt that used to derail her, but now she was emotionally unaffected, said 'no' and enforced No Contact.

Guilt is a trigger that can play havoc with our boundaries. Rhonda's mother had her daughter at her beck and call. She would ring Rhonda any time of the day to demand that she take her shopping, or to the doctors, or to get whatever it was that she needed, including picking up certain pastries weekly from a shop miles away. She also enlisted Rhonda to clean her house and do her garden. However, there was no gratitude forthcoming from her mother – only entitlement, criticism and abuse.

Rhonda was single and believed there was no energy nor time for anyone else while her mother was still alive. Her mother certainly had lots of time for herself, though. Sometimes, when Rhonda was cleaning or gardening for her, her mother drove herself to dances or to meet men that she was dating. Despite Rhonda's best friend telling her over and over to stop letting her mother treat her like garbage, Rhonda said, 'I can't stop helping her. I couldn't live with the guilt if I stopped looking after her.'

As with Rhonda's story, over the years I have heard so many people ask themselves, 'How can I detach when it makes me feel so guilty? How can I say no and leave him (or her) without my help?' Those abused by narcissists can agonise over these sorts of questions in relation to their parents, siblings or children and, of course, romantic partners.

Feeling Obligated and Bonded to Narcissists

In the time that I have been working with narcissistic abuse, I have observed many women (and some men) stay attached to narcissistic ex-spouses, parents, friends and children, granting them whatever they need, regardless of how badly they are treated or even, in the case of an ex-partner, whether the narcissist is in a relationship with a new person. It's eerie, the hold that narcissists can have over people in this way.

Max had been in love with Annie for forty-five years. He had never moved on despite her having had three different husbands after him. Max was a hermit and drank too much; he only lived for the times when Annie called and wanted to see him. She had asked him for many favours over the years – money, references, an ear to listen to her dramas, and a shoulder to cry on when things weren't working out with her other husbands. Yet everything was on Annie's terms; she was never there for Max unless there was something in it for her. Despite this, Max felt like she still needed him, and couldn't let go.

Often, people who are attached to narcissists feel like they are on a crusade to save the narcissist from themselves. They firmly believe that they are the person who can bring the narcissist to the light and heal them. I too used to feel like this, but at a deep subconscious level it is really about the belief that 'if I can heal you and you are no longer sick – you will be able to love me'. The truth is that in these instances we are still trying to get from others what we have not as yet healed within ourselves.

Naturally, if we are trying to save our child from themselves, there are many other powerful emotions and forces compelling us to try to help them. Yet the truth still remains – we are not helping them by attempting to fix their life for them.

If you have reflected on your tendency to take responsibility for people who won't be responsible for themselves, you probably already realise how much of your life has been sacrificed in order to take care of others. You also know how painful that pattern is – of being attached to others and trying to help them grow and heal, while this severely impacts on your own needs and emotional health.

As we have seen, these sorts of behaviours were all learned at any early age. We may have had a sick, unpredictable or emotionally volatile parent whom we had to tune into and monitor in order to keep ourselves safe; we learned that pre-empting and catering to this person might minimalise the abuse or neglect. Or we discovered that when this person demanded something, if we didn't give in to their demands we suffered painful consequences. We may have been trained with the use of guilt and deeply damaging comments, such as we were a terrible person or selfish if we didn't fulfil their needs.

That was exactly Rhonda's plight. Because Rhonda was a tender, gentle soul, her mother had been able to groom her, using guilt as her weapon, and turn her into the family scapegoat and her personal slave from a very early age.

The experience of narcissistic abuse brings home a powerful message, which is: *we are NOT here to take responsibility for those who are refusing to take responsibility for themselves.*

The narcissist is the epitome of someone who is unwilling to take responsibility for him-or herself. He or she is defensive, uses many avoidance tactics to shirk responsibility and then projects all of his or her inner damaged parts and flaws on to others. The narcissist is never truly accountable for his or her own faults, weaknesses, mistakes or bad behaviour, and instead shifts the blame on to others relentlessly. By staying attached to the narcissist and feeling responsible for them, we allow the abuser to continue blaming and maiming us over behaviour for which we were never responsible.

When trying to help the narcissist, or trying to force him or her to take responsibility, you will very likely have experienced that instead of the narcissist accepting and embracing any flaws, you simply got attacked instead. You felt like you were going mad, trying to explain basic human decency to an angry five-year-old trapped in an adult's body. This is *exactly* what happens in every dynamic of 'trying to help someone who refuses to help themselves'. It's lose–lose all the way.

Margaret wrote this to me: 'My daughter is the narcissist in my life. I have supported her from the day she was born and been emptied out emotionally, mentally, physically and financially for forty years. There is never any thanks, only abuse. Again, I've received a scathing letter from her, threatening to cut me off from my grandchildren whom I adore.'

Margaret quickly learned that to help herself and her grandchildren she had to heal herself first. She did the hardest thing a mother or grandmother could ever do: let go and focus on just herself for a while. After eight months of NARP work, she was able to say 'no' to her daughter's unreasonable demands, and create a boundary whereby she refused to stay and listen if her daughter was abusive to her. Her daughter soon gave up this kind of behaviour towards her, because Margaret simply wouldn't accept it. After three more months, her daughter, much to Margaret's delight, asked if she could drop her children off with Margaret while she went on a short break away. Regular contact with her beloved grandchildren followed.

People who take responsibility for those who refuse to take responsibility for themselves don't receive love, support and integrity in return from them. They struggle to maintain healthy boundaries and to speak up honestly about their own needs, and consequently don't have those needs met. Individuals who are empathetic and who don't have healthy boundaries tend to take on other people's problems and make these 'their' problems, and those of us with co-dependent tendencies tend to focus on fixing and helping others rather than fixing and helping ourselves. This only *enables and promotes the narcissist's bad behaviour.*

The irony is, in our attempt to help a narcissist (even with the best of intentions), we don't actually help them at all because we don't empower them to take responsibility for themselves. And we certainly don't help ourselves by assuming responsibility for their irresponsibility.

Creating Genuine Relationships with Others by Being True to Ourselves

The healing gift from this Step is the release from all the traumas that are keeping you trapped in taking responsibility for others. This not only frees you up to focus on your own needs and self-growth, it allows you to help support and nurture the growth in those people who *are* willing to take responsibility for themselves. Truly, this is one of the most wonderful feelings that life can present: serving others who are willing to help and improve themselves brings a joy that is *indescribable.*

When Rhonda suffered a particularly terrible episode with her mother, Rhonda's friend came over and made her watch my video about empaths. Rhonda decided enough was enough – and become a member of the NARP Community. After several weeks spent releasing the childhood traumas inflicted on her by her mother, she found the courage to say 'no' to her mother at last. Her mother threw a terrible tantrum, smeared her to other family members and even staged a robbery at her own house, claiming that Rhonda was the culprit and enlisted the police to call at Rhonda's home to question her.

Rhonda nevertheless kept diligently working with NARP, releasing every trauma that her mother triggered within her, and she stayed strong and firm. Rhonda is now No Contact with her mother and has an intervention order in place against her. She says, 'I can love her from a distance. The mother I want to love is in there somewhere, but being around her only allows me to get damaged by her demons. I can't help her anymore and I need to help myself. Thank goodness that terrible guilt is gone. I feel free finally to have my own life.'

Step 6 is such a necessary stage if caretaking other people at your own expense has been an issue for you. After working through this Step, you will have the ability to create healthy relationships with other emotionally mature individuals, which will lead to win–win outcomes. Additionally, the deep shift within your subconscious from a state of guilt to self-love opens you up to receiving *genuine* support and kindness from others.

Interdependency is the ability to enjoy a healthy sense of self and to connect with other people who also have a healthy sense of self, and who are willing to be self-aware and grow with you. This creates relationships that are not co-dependent or narcissistic in nature. After completing Step 6, you will be on your way to interdependency. You can then begin to experience positive relationships that generate mutually rewarding outcomes.

After doing the specific inner work of this Step you will be able to say goodbye to co-dependent/narcissistic relationships that only bring you pain and sadness. And you can continue to provide healthy support and love for others without neglecting and potentially destroying yourself.

It's now time to let go of your over-responsibility for others, which has been causing you to hand your power away and allowing people to drain you of your life force, resources and wellbeing. By doing so, you will then have the available energy and self-dedication needed to fill yourself with Light and love first, before giving to others in appropriate and healthy ways.

EXERCISE: STEP 6 – BECOMING RESPONSIBLE FOR YOURSELF

1. Make sure that you are in a place where you will not be disturbed with your journal. This means not checking your phone or any notifications on your computer. This time has to be exclusively for you. Close your eyes, relax your shoulders and take long, deep breaths. Each time you exhale, imagine breathing out stress, while relaxing your body just that little bit more. If any thoughts pop in to disturb you, don't give them any energy but just come back to your breathing.

2. Feel deeply into your emotions about handing your power away to others, such as by doing too much for them, caretaking them in order to be loved and saying 'yes' when you know you should say 'no', etc. What do you do that you know is enabling people to take advantage of you, to refuse to take responsibility for themselves and to drain your energy?

What do you do that does not represent healthy giving? Open your eyes and list these occurrences in your journal as they arise for you.

3. Now go back into these occurrences and connect to the painful emotional charge in your body about them. Rate them out of 10, with 0/10 being the lowest rating and 10/10 being the most intense emotional charge. Then number them from highest to lowest according to their emotional charge.

4. Starting with the highest-rated incident, tune into your feelings when you imagine stopping doing these things for others. What fears come up? They might be beliefs such as: 'I have to serve others or they will leave me', 'if I don't do what they ask, I will be punished/annihilated', 'my worth is only how much I give to others' or 'if I am not the responsible one, everything will fall apart', etc. Record the feelings that come up for you.

5. Say the following to your inner being/inner child: '[Endearing term], I am here to support and love you, and to help you do things differently. I want you to know that you have done an incredible job of surviving up to this point, and now I give you permission to transform and make space for a new way.'

6. Next say to your inner being/inner child: '[Endearing term], you now have permission to let go of being over-responsible for others.' Perform the following visualisation: imagine the trauma connected to this issue. What does it look like and where is it in your body? Trust your answers. Then, with whatever visualisation tool you would like to use (see box entitled "EXERCISE STEP 4 – RELEASING BETRAYAL AND INJUSTICE" for suggestions), send it out of your body in whatever way feels right for you. See and feel it dissolve when it leaves your body, back to nothingness.

7. Now bring down Light through the pipeline to fill up where that trauma previously was. Feel the expansion and warmth inside you. Be open to receiving and connecting to this feeling as much as you can.

8. How did this exercise go for you? Write about your experience. Now tune in to the emotional pangs you had when you were over-responsible for others and handing power away. Are they still there? Really test this out by imagining a familiar scenario in which you used to give away your power. Does this feel like you anymore? Write about how you would behave now in the same situation. Would you do things differently? Do you naturally know how to deal with this in a healthy way now? If you do – you have had your transformational shift. If you still don't, keep clearing the trauma that is causing you to feel blocked, frightened or confused, because then your true self (who exists under all the layers of trauma) will absolutely know what to do! If you're not there yet, continue working with the Step 6 processes.

9. Now repeat the process with the next highest-rated trauma on your list.

Putting the Responsibility Back Where It Needs to Be

Once you have moved through Step 6, taking responsibility for your own life while healing the need to take responsibility for others, you can honour your right to focus on your personal wellbeing by working with the next level of healing – which is all about expanding your self-awareness and stepping into your true self. As you will discover, by being true to ourselves we also become the most authentic, empowered and loving beings we could possibly be.

The next chapter marks a lovely Step on our journey. It is one of my favourite levels of healing, because it is about experiencing the spiritual boost that leads to a major shift out of survival mode and into the creation of your true life.

13

CONNECT TO THE GIFT OF YOUR OWN SPIRITUAL EMPOWERMENT

After letting go of any responsibility to fix the narcissist, it is usual to feel an even greater detachment from him or her, and there is the added bonus of starting to interact with other people in your life in a much healthier way. You are able to give more to yourself, speak up for what you need and set better boundaries with people. You will feel that you deserve more of the good stuff in life, and you will no longer believe you have to fix other people in order to feel okay within yourself.

It is such a relief when we are able to stand back and allow people to take responsibility for themselves, and to get involved in helping others *only* when it is appropriate – and in much healthier ways. Now that your unhealthy attachments to guilt, responsibility for others and trying to fix other people instead of focusing on taking responsibility for yourself have dropped away, you have created the space in which to *really* create your life healthily.

Which brings us to the next Step. This is a beautiful Step. It brings us home to a greater level of acceptance on the journey that began with Step 3.

This Step is a little difficult to explain in concrete ways, because it is an intensely energetic spiritual process, not just in the way in which we bring about the shift, but also in terms of the actual shift that we are reaching for. Here you are going for an expanded state – a freer, more empowered, visionary way of being – where you can open up to your new life and start powerfully and organically generating it, no matter what you experienced in your past.

Our Evolutionary Leap into 'Who We Are' From 'Who We Were Being'

At this stage of our journey we are taking an exciting, soul-evolutionary leap into higher consciousness. We are purposefully seeking out and releasing the dense energy in our being that is attached to holding on to judgement and which resists the experience of being truly conscious and expanded – so that we can open up the space in our cells to let in Life/Source/Creation. Yet while we may think we want to make this leap, there are often many parts of ourselves that resist this sort of radical change.

As Marianne Williamson so eloquently expressed it in her book, *A Return to Love:*

Our deepest fear is not that we are inadequate. Our deepest fear is that we are powerful beyond measure. It is our light, not our darkness, that most frightens us. We ask ourselves, Who am I to be brilliant, gorgeous, talented, fabulous?

Actually, who are you not to be? You are a child of God. Your playing small does not serve the world. There's nothing enlightened about shrinking so that other people will not feel insecure around you. We are all meant to shine, as children do. We were born to make manifest the glory of God that is within us. It is not just in some of us; it is in everyone and as we let our own light shine, we unconsciously give other people permission to do the same. As we are liberated from our own fear, our presence automatically liberates others.[1]

In this Step, we purposefully seek out those parts of us which are subconsciously invested in remaining a victim, and which refuse to permit us to be our highest and best selves.

This is what Andrew said about his experience when he started working with Module Seven of NARP: 'I thought this Module work was going to be something really easy and simple. I was astounded at how I spent a month solid on these shifts. So much was revealed to me regarding what was blocking me from true joy and glory in my life. Even before I started making these shifts I had barely any change left on my ex at all, yet I realised right here, in these specific shifts, that even with her completely out of my life, I still had so many limiting beliefs and traumas about my deservedness and that Life would not support me moving forward, and that I would be annihilated if I became my true self. There is no way I would ever have lived without these inner barriers, had it not been for this work. I felt like a completely different person. There's no doubt I'm not the old me anymore.'

This shift takes you from all that has been holding you back – the limitations, fears, guilt, lack of deservedness, lack of belief and low confidence, etc. – into the knowledge that you are on a wonderful journey towards the creation of the real life you desire and deserve.

Emma said this about her Module Seven experience: 'One of the biggest things I noticed was this incredible space inside me. Where I used to be so caught up in the pain of what my life had become and regretting what had happened, I now had feelings of inspiration and joy constantly coming up from within. And there was no reason for these feelings other than just feeling happy to be alive. My thoughts were no longer about loss and regret, they were about creating new things and going after my dreams that I had never previously had the confidence to pursue.'

This is the alchemy of transformational healing, the shift that occurs when our subconscious programmes and the wiring of our brain synapses switch from 'survival' to 'creation', and the energy that was previously tied up in surviving our wounds is now released as a pure, positive force that can be harnessed in the generating of our true life.

Knowing We Are Nourished and Loved By Existence

Often, by the time we get to Step 7, many of us are already feeling great relief and emotional freedom; yet there will also be those who feel like something just won't budge until they work with this Step. If we have any painful and fractured beliefs about a Higher Power and can't yet connect to a consciousness that is working for us and not against us, things may not align in our Thriver Recovery until we do the deep work at this stage.

This was very true for me. I had so many defunct beliefs about my connection to a Higher Power. I believed I had been abandoned by God, was unworthy of Light, and that I was being punished and must be a bad person of whom God did not approve. I have seen so many people who are also subconsciously suffering from the same inner traumas – feeling a deep, dark shame and defectiveness inside themselves. Many people are unaware of this until they start doing the inner work in Module 7.

Sophie's story was about exactly this issue. She had made her way to the Thriver Community as a result of becoming dreadfully depressed after leaving Joe, an abusive narcissist. Sophie felt like she still loved him, and she was employed in the same workplace as him, where his new lover worked as well. For Sophie, it was like living in a private hell, seeing them together every day and being unable to move on. She wanted to leave her job but every time she went for a new position, she was unsuccessful. Sophie's health was declining and she was in no position to try to date someone new. Because her depression and body pain with fibromyalgia were so extreme, she had no energy to do anything other than go to work, go home and cry herself to sleep most nights. That had been her plight for three long years.

After being prompted by many Community members to start NARP, Sophie finally did so. Each Module helped her find some relief from her depression, her longing for the narcissist and her body pain, but it was when she worked with Module Seven that an enormous shift took place.

This is what she wrote about it: 'In this Module work I let go of so much dark, black energy inside me, which had been thoroughly invested in blaming, being a victim and angrily resisting accepting the opportunity to take on my own growth. The angry child inside me was stamping her feet and saying, "Why should I have to do this work when all these other people have been so mean and terrible to me? It's their fault, and they should fix this!" It was then that I realised that he had done exactly to me what my mother had. Promised to love me, let me down, left without a backward glance and taken up with a new family as if I didn't exist. Then, when I went even deeper, I discovered I believed God had forsaken me, just as my mother had and all my lovers had. I believed I was unworthy of love from anyone, beginning with God. Suddenly I felt a connection to something, a force of love so much greater than myself and I was filled with more joy and love than I could ever remember feeling. Now I saw it all so clearly – all that dense energy of believing I was forsaken and that I would never be able to experience love had blocked my own life force. It had made me sick and stuck and literally dying. By letting it go, I felt the Life Force enter and I knew, for the first time, even since I was a small child, that finally I had the right energy inside me for my real life to begin. He and her didn't matter anymore, and neither did my mother. I just felt an overwhelming gratitude to all of them for this gift that ultimately gave me back to myself.'

Evolutionary gifts do come about at this stage of our conscious shift. We have, at this point, cleared enough of the trauma to take this spiritual leap – to embrace and actualise our true self without our traumas. This brings about an embodiment of a new way of being that far surpasses mere learning. It is virtually impossible to assimilate higher spiritual concepts from a logical perspective; instead we have to become them.

This stuff gets addictive – in such a good way! When we let the Light into where the darkness once was, we feel energised, we feel alive; this inspires us to want to work with NARP as an ongoing lifestyle. At this stage of our healing journey, we start to understand that, rather than being a necessary chore in order to survive, this type of healing work becomes an incredible way to use every single opportunity to set ourselves free, expand our lives and enjoy incredible experiences that we couldn't have accessed if we hadn't applied Quantum Tools to ourselves.

It is usual after this Step for more doors to swing open, and for experiences that you *do* desire in your life to start coming towards you. In this new empowered state, which I call our 'true self', you will leave the toxic energy and the false and painful reality of the narcissist far, far behind. By connecting to the gift of your own spiritual and personal development, you graduate to a much higher vibration, one where the narcissist is *no longer your reality.*

This means that your focus is firmly on you. You want to grow, you want to heal and you want to expand, and you are excited about this personal journey! This feels like quenching your thirst in a wonderful lagoon after being stranded in a barren desert for so long.

You now deeply feel that your soul is delivering you *all the right messages* – the right people, prompts, cues and 'ways' for you to move forward into the claiming of who you really want to be – and you are open and receptive to these signals. Life has started opening up to become a source of wonderment and day-to-day happy synchronicities which fill you with gratitude and joy.

Processing Step 7 makes it much more difficult for the narcissist to latch on to you, manipulate you or extract narcissistic supply from you. This is because you feel complete and healthy, and your focus is on creating your own freedom, truth and progress. You can now manifest what you want to experience in ways that serve the collective good, living your purpose and bringing joy, love and peace into your life.

So let's start getting this really important work done!

EXERCISE: STEP 7 – RELEASING VICTIMISATION AND EMBRACING YOUR TRUE SELF

1. Go to a quiet space with your journal where you will not be disturbed. Set your intention that you will be connecting with your inner being for a healing process. Then close your eyes for a few minutes and focus on breathing in and out with long, full, slow breaths. Simply ignore any thoughts that pop in and come back to your breath.

2. Take your attention deep inside yourself. With presence, love and kindness, ask your inner being/inner child to share with you the parts of him or her which are locked in resistance. What are these parts that don't want to let go of feeling victimised or to grow and heal? Reassure him or her that you are here to listen and in no way will you judge these feelings. Open your eyes and record all the information that comes up for you. If you don't receive any information, that is okay; just be aware of any dense energy you feel inside yourself.

3. If you did receive information that concerns any issues, go back into these one at a time and connect to the painful emotional charge your body has about them. Rate these out of 10, with 0/10 being the lowest rating and 10/10 being the most intense emotional charge. Number these painful issues from their highest to lowest emotional charge.

4. Then say to your inner being: '[Endearing term], I now grant you permission to let go of this wound, this fracture which has been keeping us separated from Love, Creation and Life.' Imagine opening up a space at the top of your head and seeing the trauma sucked out from above by a giant tube, or vacuum-like tool. See huge chunks of toxic stuff leaving your body, all of it being sucked up and out, and dissolving back to native nothingness as it leaves. Feel the sensation of your inner being going free from these traumas.

5. Now imagine the big ball of Light above you, which represents your personal understanding of a Higher Power, and bring it down into you through the pipeline. Allow it to fill you where the trauma previously was. Feel your cells expand with Light as it enters. Open up as you fill up and take note of that feeling of expansion.

6. Check in with how you feel. Do you feel different? With all your might, try to check whether you still feel any major resistance inside you. Is that block still there? Do you feel as though you deserve evolution, expansion and your own personal growth now? If you still feel resistance then repeat the Step 7 processes to keep shifting trauma out of your body until you do feel expanded, joyous and free.

7. Now repeat the process with the next highest-rated trauma on your list.

8. When you feel like you are in the expansiveness of your true self, write on the 'My True Self Declarations' page in your journal: 'I now go free from those false ideas and beliefs that keep me separated from my true self. My true self is who I am without my trauma. It is safe to be my true self. My true self is adored and supported beyond measure by Source and Life, because it is Source and Life.' (If you want a manifestation boost, write out this intention eleven times!)

Being Released Into Your True Self

I hope with all my heart that by now you are feeling pretty darn amazing! But there is more to come. If you have been fortunate enough to experience a profound shift into expanded consciousness at Step 7 (as many people do), you may think at this point you are home and dry – yet I promise that for most of you this is not the case!

The evolutionary lesson – the profound make-or-break experience of narcissistic abuse – is a powerful soul opportunity to release all that is not our true self, so that we can unpack whatever else has been holding us back in our spiritual evolution. It is very common to reach a crescendo of emotional relief and release – and then for the curve ball to come. People think they have 'arrived', and nothing can touch them, but this higher vibrational existence can't be sustained when the last vestiges of whatever it is that we need to release – any deep programmes of fear, pain, victimisation or low self-belief, etc. – are still lurking within us.

This is what the next chapter is all about: it explains what these damaging programmes are, how they appear in our lives and how to release ourselves from them so that we can step even further into our true self and connect with Life itself.

14

RELEASE AND HEAL THE FEAR OF THE NARCISSIST – AND WHATEVER HE OR SHE MAY DO NEXT

After connecting with the gift of your own personal and spiritual development, you will start to become much more aligned with the creation of your own truth. The feeling that you *know* that you *can and will* create the life that you want to live, grows stronger.

However, when we start healing and moving into a more solid of way of feeling and being, life has a way of testing us. It comes along and says, 'Have you really got the message? Do you truly know your own power? Let's just challenge this to really make sure.'

We are tested by the erupting of our deepest, primal fears into vivid consciousness, usually brought on by events that trigger our terrors of persecution, fears of authority or abandonment, or our anxieties about being replaced or deemed obsolete; the list goes on and on.

Why does this happen? Haven't we already cleared so much trauma that life should become easy from this point forward?

The surfacing of these traumas is absolutely a perfect blessing. It is all to do with the interconnectedness of Life – of your soul and its quest for evolution, and the narcissist being the vehicle to help you attain this.

When our major primal terrors emerge for us to release, they are not a simple or a light matter, and they may demand a lot of inner work from us in order to process them to completion. One thing is for sure, we are not emancipated from fear and distress until we have released and reprogrammed these traumas. This stage of our healing journey – when yet more difficulties arise in spite of all the work we have done – is totally to the point, because we are being called on to live completely free of these traumas. When our deepest, darkest fears are triggered, not only is the terror extreme, but we suffer the anxiety of the unknown. This may feel crippling, like our very survival – emotional or literal – is at stake. As the American horror writer H.P. Lovecraft wrote in his essay 'Supernatural Horror in Literature': 'The oldest and strongest emotion of mankind is fear, and the oldest and strongest kind of fear is fear of the unknown.'

This is where we need to assimilate a higher spiritual lesson if we wish to find lasting relief from our fears and to claim our real power. Ironically, none of us was ever taught to turn inwards to transform our emotions from painful to liberated. As a result, when life or our emotions don't grant us what we'd like, our default reaction is usually to feel stressed, and, depending on the level of disappointment, even to feel powerless.

The evolutionary goal here is: *My state of being can be mastered regardless of what is or isn't happening outside me, and then all of life will follow my inner state.*

Has All of My Good Work Been to No Avail?

I have often seen people find incredible relief and reach a platform of empowerment quickly, and then, just when they think everything is going along swimmingly, their deeper layers of survival programmes are triggered (often by some horrible thing the narcissist does or as a trauma emerging simply from within) – massively and painfully.

Naturally, when this happens it's a shock after feeling so good. So many people initially feel powerless and exclaim, 'All my good work is down the drain; I'm right back where I started!' or 'I never thought I'd be feeling these crippling emotions again.'

Louise was one of those people. She had been working with NARP for two months solid, was successfully maintaining No Contact and had experienced glorious relief and emotional freedom as a result of clearing her childhood terrors of abandonment. Louise was no longer trapped in the cycles of emotional panic and powerlessness that had caused her in the past to chase after and cling to her narcissistic lover, Claudia, no matter how many other people Claudia was seeing and despite how badly she treated her. Louise had been thrilled at how great she felt, and had regularly reported the marvel of simply not thinking about Claudia anymore.

Then a friend of Louise's called her to report that Claudia was going to pursue a lawsuit for a share of Louise's business. Bang! Louise felt the old powerlessness and terror resurface like a white-hot energy inside her. She shared what was happening with the NARP Community and admitted that she felt she had slipped into 'stinking thinking'. She was so emotionally paralysed that she didn't apply NARP to the trauma she was feeling right now and she fell right back into the bowels of hell, not being able to sleep, eat or function.

Even though Louise had only worked with NARP up to Module Three, given her exceptional circumstances her fellow Thrivers suggested that she go straight to Module Eight and start doing those specific shifts – to find and release all of the terrors and fears about what the narcissist *might* do, which were still causing her to feel powerless and terrified. Louise did this and unearthed deep-seated survival programmes concerning a fear of persecution and annihilation, which sprang from generational (epigenetic) and past-life as well as childhood traumas. Once these were released from her inner being, she felt fearless and solid again. Right on cue, not long after this, she learned that Claudia had seen a solicitor and had been told it would be impossible to claim a legal stake in Louise's business.

Of course this wasn't a coincidence, or even a miracle. It was Life responding to the Quantum Law – *so within, so without.*

When the Narcissist Attacks

As a vital Step for releasing our fear about what the narcissist may do next, Module Eight is one of the most worked and revisited Modules of NARP. The surface reason why people need to use this Module a lot, is because narcissists don't like losing. They don't like people pulling away and not caring. It irks them profoundly, because their false self is not being appeased by that person any more. They are also intensely paranoid, imagining everyone is out to get them, discredit them and expose them. Narcissists, quite frankly, are all about revenge, punishing people and eliminating the competition: *if I get you first then you can't hurt me.*

As we have seen, narcissists hit you wherever your deepest fears and insecurities lie, and they go after whatever matters to you the most – be that your children, your loved ones, property, security, your future dreams and your reputation in the world. Unless we heal ourselves in Quantum ways, the narcissist ensures that he or she receives A-grade narcissistic supply through targeting with deadly accuracy whatever matters the most to us. By punishing you and compromising your life in this way, they ensure they receive the retribution they feel they deserve. As we have seen, the end justifies the means for narcissists, and can be brought about in underhand, vicious and conscienceless ways.

It's very important to understand that no healing will come from simply understanding why narcissists behave in atrocious ways. Fortunately, when we 'go Quantum', we seek the bigger-picture truths that grant us access to evolutionary healing, which surface-level information just doesn't provide. The true reason this is happening to you – why the narcissist is attacking you with the things that hurt you and traumatise you the most – is to make you conscious of those inner traumas, so that you can release them and live free of them. I really believe Life/Source/Creation and our soul doesn't get it wrong. There is a purpose to all of it.

By the time I met him, Daniel had experienced two years of utter heartbreak as a result of being left by April. Even though April had remarried, she turned extra nasty when, after a year of inner work, Daniel healed significantly and decided to start dating again. It was then that Daniel was investigated by the Taxation Office and his business was put through a full audit. He was also interrogated by the police about bathing his five-year-old daughter. Even though the authorities concluded there was nothing in his behaviour that was at all threatening to his daughter, Daniel was shocked to his very core. April had smeared him at his daughter's school, and now he was viewed with suspicion, and other parents were no longer letting their children come over to play with his little girl when she stayed with him. Additionally, April was continually taking him to court to claim more money and demand business and pay reviews in order to try to increase his child-maintenance payments to her.

After going No Contact (or in Daniel's case Modified Contact), doing the necessary inner work and thinking that you are out the other side, it is very possible that things really are a little too good to be true. Daniel had reached this level; he truly thought he was in the clear, yet here he was – dealing with deep and terrifying traumas about persecution, as well as the threat of his reputation being ruined. To add insult to injury, he also began to suffer financial fears. Fortunately, Daniel realised there was more work to do, rolled up his sleeves, stopped trying to fight back against April and instead addressed the huge wounds that had surfaced within his inner being during his Module Eight work in NARP.

The trauma subsided; peace came. Things started to fall into place. The audit that had dragged on for months concluded in his favour and the Taxation Office now owed him money. And, true to the Quantum Law – *so within, so without* – when April no longer had any of the energy generated by his past traumas or wounds with which to attack him, all her attempts fell flat. People at the school came to Daniel to apologise, and they were flabbergasted at how April could involve her own daughter in such a false allegation.

The Soul War

Your surfacing fears concerning what the narcissist is capable of don't have to be as vicious and obvious as in Louise and Daniel's example. The following examples are subtler yet equally revealing about the various ways in which we can be triggered into obsessing about what the narcissist might do next, causing us to feel emotionally crippled and powerless again.

Caroline's situation was the perfect example of this. She was serious about No Contact, blocked her narcissistic ex-girlfriend on all her devices and told anyone whom she begged to pass on messages to Caroline, not to respond. Then one day everything went silent. After a period of time it became clear that Caroline's narcissistic girlfriend had stopped trying to contact her.

Caroline started obsessing about *why* she had stopped trying. Was she plotting something in the background? Was there a smear campaign taking place? Was it a ploy to try to get Caroline to contact her? No matter how hard she tried not to, her thoughts kept ticking away relentlessly.

Many people didn't understand Caroline's obsession, but what was really happening for Caroline was that her unhealed childhood wounds had surfaced. When she stopped beating herself up for taking a dive back into trauma, and instead met and healed her childhood wounds about feeling unworthy of attention, and being made the scapegoat, she achieved an even higher level of freedom, empowerment and disconnection. This is the inevitable benefit we receive when we intentionally go towards our deepest traumas in order to heal them, instead of shaming and blaming them and trying to run away from them.

Many people suffer from triggers such as the fear of the narcissist making contact and 'hoovering', and not being strong enough to resist them. Another common anxiety is finding out that the narcissist has replaced you with someone else. When this happens it is usual to start obsessing along lines of: 'Maybe the narcissist will be different with this person and their relationship may work.'

At this point in our journey, fears arising from within and without are pretty much inevitable. The danger is that if we forget the process of meeting the traumas in our body and shifting them out, one at a time, we get caught up in 'stinking thinking' instead. And if we do this, we could be in for a very hard time. Yet this happens to people regularly, because after the initial empowerment and relief they have acquired from diligently working on themselves, they might have dropped the practice of making internal shifts. After all, life has returned to 'normal', hasn't it?

I've fallen for this too, over the years – returning to that old chestnut, the illusion that when trauma strikes we can change how we feel with our thinking, despite experience teaching us time and time again how futile this is.

As Bessel van der Kolk writes in his book *The Body Keeps the Score,* 'Most of our conscious brain is dedicated to focusing on the outside world. However, that does not help us manage ourselves. Neuroscience research shows that the only way we can change how we feel is by becoming aware of our *inner experience* and learning to befriend what is going on inside ourselves.'[1]

This is especially true of narcissistic abuse, which underscores the necessity of understanding Quantum Law. You can't beat narcissists by combating them directly. This is an energetic war, it's a soul war, and you are fighting not just to *evolve* your soul but to *save* it. If you stay trapped in fearful inner programmes, the narcissist strikes a claim on your soul to feed off it and drain it dry. I know that sounds terribly macabre and even sci-fi, but I promise you it's true.

And, no matter how kooky it may seem, this fear does not have to be personally expressed to a narcissist for him or her to hook into you and start emptying you out. Even if you are No Contact, if the trauma is raging within you at the subconscious level – where all of life is connected – he or she is absolutely getting a feed, and is receiving your fear as the fuel to continue residency in your life and to carry on their campaign of terror inside of you.

The Bright Light That Dissolves All Darkness

We can never defeat narcissists by trying to beat them at their own game – by trying to hurt them, expose them or take revenge on them. And we certainly can't reason or make deals with them to get them to stop what they are doing. All of this only embeds you in the abuse further and hands the narcissist the bullets with which to shoot you.

In stark contrast, when you shift and release all the pain and the fear, and come back to your inner detachment and peace, incredible things start to happen. The narcissist loses his or her power. The lies, the manipulations against you, and the actions intended to hurt you and cause you grief, start to be exposed. The deceptive tactics fall flat and the narcissist gets caught out.

This happens as a result of you ceasing to combat the narcissist and instead tending to your own inner being first. Many people initially mistake this for complacency, but this does not mean you won't stand up for yourself. Rather, you will be defending yourself from a place of solidity, calm, knowing and truth. No longer are you trying to expose the narcissist and to undo him or her as a condition for being your true self; instead you are walking your truth in *your own integrity.* This is powerful beyond measure.

Premi, a guest on one of my Thriver radio shows, had been through a highly abusive narcissistic marriage that eventually had her fleeing, fearful for her life. He had threatened that if she ever left him, he would kill her. He had also threatened her with one the biggest traumas a parent can imagine: taking her children away from her. As a result of diligently working with NARP, Premi regained herself, her emotions and her life. Module Eight was especially vital for her recovery, and after multiple sessions of Module Eight work, Premi was awarded full legal custody of her two daughters. This occurred despite her initially being terrified that he would charm the courts and no one would believe her.

This is what Premi wrote about the experience: 'I'll never forget it. One morning in July 2015, I woke up and I could feel I was different – that something had changed. The fear was gone! The heavy weight that was my connection to the narc was gone. My buying into the fear and anxiety was gone. It didn't control me anymore. It was as if a cord was cut and I knew I was free. After that, I had no fear of seeing him in court. I felt solid, like a rock, and I knew everything was going to be okay or that I would be able to handle whatever happened.

'Then I got into court, and he wasn't there! It was just me. We went through the whole proceedings and the judge said, "I'm granting you everything that you asked for and you don't even have to pick up the phone."

'It turned out that he had called the court, saying he'd got a ticket to come, and then the plane was delayed in Chicago and for whatever reason he couldn't get on the flight. He couldn't come. And it wouldn't have mattered anyway because it turned out that even the paperwork that he had sent in to the court didn't arrive! It was like an energy force field around me and the kids, preventing him from being able to do anything to us. It was a miracle!'

Like Premi's example, I have witnessed countless examples of narcissists losing out in custody cases, property settlements and joint business dealings. They display just how powerless they really are when their previous victim stops handing over energy to them. This is when the almighty mechanics of Life starts backing real, aligned energy, which is anything other than what the narcissist represents. I have even seen narcissists capitulate and hand over whatever was asked of them, because a narcissist recoils in the face of an authentic person in their power as much as a vampire does in the beam of a bright light. They have to do whatever it takes to get away.

Truly, you may have to experience this phenomenon to really believe me, but I can assure you with every ounce of my being what I am saying is true.

What you can expect, if you work hard on this Step, and repeat it whenever you feel the fear starting to take a grip on you again, is an incredible freedom of living your life without fear. You will discover that *if* something does happen that would normally frighten you and send you into panic, once you have cleared all the associated trauma from inside you, you will instead respond calmly and effectively. You will be able to stand up, walk your truth and absolutely know and believe it is all working out in perfect and divine order.

This Step not only allows you to break free from the narcissist's actions, it also provides you with some of the greatest breakthroughs of your entire life. It's only after our evolution beyond the terrors of persecution, abandonment, annihilation and the unknown that we can look back and see how so many areas of our life were previously affected.

Can you imagine how powerful it is when you achieve this? You will finally be free to be your authentic self, without being paralysed by these primal fears. Your actions will no longer be dictated by what you fear, and will instead be directed towards creating your happiness, success and spiritual expansion from the truth of your soul.

When we are experiencing deep, triggered trauma, it can be very difficult for us to focus on the processes needed to release, shift and reprogramme it. Sometimes, it is necessary just to *experience* the terrorised energy in our body and not to search for information about it – so as to feel it, then release it and start healing from it – before our mind can shift a little in order to access information calmly about it. Until we do this, our highly traumatised thought patterns can send us into loops of distraction and thinking that spirals down into the trauma, simply cementing us deeper into it.

Processing Step 8 will encourage you to self-partner, meet and release those traumas that have been immobilising you with fear. By doing so you will start to regain vital control of your emotions and your life.

This can be extremely difficult work, because it is the self-healing we LEAST feel like doing (when triggered significantly) yet it the work we MOST need to do when we are. (If you know you need extra help in facing these terrors and shifting beyond their grip, the 'You Can Thrive Program' will help you significantly with this Step. You can register for free here: www. youcanthriveprogram.com.) Okay, so let's get down to the exercise for Step 8!

EXERCISE: STEP 8 – RELEASING THE FEAR

1. Go to a quiet place with your journal where you won't be disturbed. Resist the temptation to check any messages that may come through to you, or the urge to continue any arguments that you are having with the narcissist, even if you feel like you are in the middle of a crisis. (Or a warzone.) Set the intention that you are no longer going to obsess about what is happening, but rather that you are ready to address it, heal whatever requires healing and claim the next level of your glorious evolution.

Spend a few minutes with your eyes closed, breathing deeply in and out, and focus on opening up your body. You may discover that you feel like crying or screaming as you start to relax physically. Go with this, giving yourself permission to express whatever it is that you need to. Know that doing so offers a healthy release of pent-up emotions.

Keep breathing deeply and slowly. Even though your thoughts might be running wild, ignore them to the best of your ability, and keep bringing your focus back to your breath.

2. Take your focus deep inside yourself and visualise your terrified inner being/inner child. Accept whatever image of this wounded part of yourself that arises. It might be yourself as a small child or it could relate to a past-life self. Trust it. What is he or she doing? What does he or she look like? Imagine observing this little person/past-life self and then hug him or her close and pour love from your heart into your inner being/inner child.

He or she may snuggle in with relief, or squirm or fight back. Stay unconditionally loving, no matter what. Even if your inner being/inner child tries to get away from you, keep pouring love towards him or her, and say: 'I am here [endearing term] to be present with your pain; I am not judging you at all. I know your trauma and your feelings are real and important and I love you as you are. I am not leaving you ever again, no matter how traumatised you are. I am here to hold you, love you and help you.' It may take some time until your inner being/inner child starts to settle down and connect with you.

3. Then tell your inner being/inner child, '[Endearing term], I know this trauma is terrible and big, but I promise you that when we heal it – no matter how awful it feels – you will go free from this and not have to suffer this fear or its consequences again. I am here with you to help you, and together we can and will do this.'

4. Ask your inner being/inner child to tell you what these fears are. Really feel and connect inside of yourself to get your information. Don't censor or judge the information; just allow it to surface and, when you are ready, open your eyes and record it in your journal.

5. Now, check in with your body and rate, one at a time, the emotional intensity of each trauma that you have identified, with 0/10 being the lowest rating and 10/10 being the most intense emotional charge. Number these painful issues from their highest to lowest emotional charge.

Starting with the highest-rated trauma on your list, ask your inner being/inner child to connect to the feelings this brings up for him or her, and then record them. These are likely to include emotions such as being scared, powerless, defenceless and unable to survive, and feeling as if he or she is threatened with annihilation or with losing loved ones.

6. Now make this declaration: 'Inner Being/Inner Child, I now grant you permission to let go of this wound, this fracture which has been keeping us separated from safety and the power of all of Life to partner us.' Then imagine packaging up the trauma in whichever way you choose, before calling on Higher Beings (of your choice) to come and take it away for you – back to Life/Source/Creation for recycling back to love and truth. Feel the sensation of your inner being going free from all the trauma.

7. Now bring down Light through the pipeline that connects to the ball of white Light above your head, to fill up the space where that trauma previously was. Feel the expansion and warmth inside you. Be as open as possible to receiving and connecting to this feeling. It is likely that you will feel a sensation of relief as a result of being freed from that fear.

8. Write about how that felt for you. Go back to the trauma you are working on and try to bring up the emotion of it again. Is it still there? Has it diminished? Is it gone all together? Even if there is only a tiny bit left, I thoroughly recommend digging into it and releasing every last bit of it in the best way you can using the Step 8 processes, to truly change what has been happening to you.

9. Now repeat the process with the next highest-rated trauma on your list.

The Power We Have Without Our Wounds

Through working with this Step, you will develop your ability to accept, bless and deal directly with any trigger that appears. This is immensely powerful in a very real sense, in that it makes you impervious to the destruction that the narcissist tries to force on you, and it liberates you, enabling you to expand into a life without fear. This creates a huge evolutionary leap, enabling you to be your authentic self and to know that Source and Life truly has your back when you are living, unwounded, from within.

We come now to Step 9 – our penultimate Step. It is here that we achieve disconnection from the narcissist at a radical level, fully reclaiming our soul.

Because of the other work we have done in preparation, we are ready to do this now...

15

RELEASE AND HEAL THE CONNECTION TO THE NARCISSIST

Once you have experienced Step 8, released the fear and cleared the deep trauma that relates to your primal survival programmes, you will have reached yet another milestone on your journey towards greater personal freedom. 'Fear' becomes something that simply doesn't affect you like it used to. You have started to connect to a deeper power within you, which affords you the Quantum understanding that something greater has your back; you now have the key to handling situations that used to be terrifying – simply by releasing your fear and allowing a powerful *knowing* to enter you.

Yet the healing journey continues, because with narcissistic abuse comes intense interpersonal entanglement, or enmeshment. Salvador Minuchin, the world-renowned Argentinian family therapist who developed structural family therapy, described enmeshment as: 'Relationships with loose boundaries, little separateness, and a hyper concern for others in the relationship that leads to diminished self-autonomy.'[1]

The enmeshment that comes with narcissistic abuse is a heightened experience of toxic ties. It is a parasitical entanglement that represents no less than a psychic takeover. Many people have likened the process of freeing their inner being from a narcissist to an exorcism. Without agreeing with any particular religion, or even myths about demons, I have to say I concur. We have to release ourselves from this intense darkness to be able to fill ourselves with Light – with Life itself, wellbeing, the possibility of a new future and with the creative expansion to enter it. We need to purge the narcissist totally from our being, which means cutting the cords and releasing all the associated belief systems that unconsciously ensnared us in the first place, so that we will no longer be on an energetic level whereby they can keep their hooks in us, sucking dry our energy, self-worth and resources.

If we don't, not only will the mental, emotional and psychic bonds that tie us to the narcissist endure, we will miss the incredible opportunity to heal those parts of ourselves that unconsciously called forth and allowed us to endure a narcissistic abuse experience. At our deepest soul level, the purpose of this was to allow us to be emancipated, one step at a time, into the highest and most expanded version of ourselves possible.

Taking the Power Back Within Ourselves

Many people who have worked on their spiritual and personal development understand the principles of tie-cutting. Tiecutting means tuning in to the unhealthy, unsavoury ties we have with people and, through a visualisation or meditative process, imagining removing those ties in some way. This may be performed by visualising them being burned or dissolving, or by asking Higher Beings to remove them, or by some other process of ritualistic healing.

Quantum Law addresses this at a deeper level and states *so within, so without,* meaning that if we don't heal the original traumas that allowed those ties to form in the first place and then remain, even if we do a tie-cutting ceremony, the ties will simply reform again – just like a cancer can regrow if the root cause of the illness is not addressed.

The evolutionary leap I believe we need to take when recovering from severe trauma (or indeed anything significant in our life) is to acknowledge that the real power to change lies only in changing ourselves.

I know, in relation to tie-cutting, how true this is. When I remained focused on trying to sever the narcissist's connection to me (before I worked with Quanta Freedom Healing), I tried every tie-cutting, energy-protection and blocking method I had ever heard of. I was desperately trying to get rid of the insidious feeling that the narcissist was continually feeding off my life force. Some of these processes and tools gave me temporary relief, yet the feeling came back time and time again.

At this stage, I had not yet released what was really taking place. As Mateo Sol says in *Awakened Empath: The Ultimate Guide to Emotional, Psychological and Spiritual Healing:* 'An energy vampire can never "steal" energy from us unless we consciously or unconsciously permit them to.'[2] Trying to stop the narcissist being energetically connected to me was not the answer. The real answer lay in healing those parts of me that *were allowing this to take place.*

Therefore, I'd like to suggest to you that practices such as cleansing your energy field and protecting your aura are not the true healing. I talk about processes like these, as supplements only, in my eBook *Self Care When Recovering from Narcissistic Abuse* (which accompanies NARP), and it is important to know that we may end up re-visiting those processes indefinitely if we think they represent the core work. The deep reprogramming of ourselves in order to purge and replace every part of our being that creates the unconscious match for the narcissist – i.e. through tackling our as-yet unhealed trauma – is the only real way that our energy field will remain clear forever from narcissistic attachment and free from the possibility of other narcissists latching on to us in the future.

The work in Step 9 is intense, deep and powerful. We are only fully ready to address the work entailed in cutting all our energetic attachments to the narcissist after going through the specific inner reprogramming work in the earlier eight Steps. A NARP member, Jane, pleaded with me to allow her to start working with Module Nine of NARP early because her terrible feelings of emotional and psychic takeover felt so crippling. I told her she was free to do as she liked, yet Step 9 would not work at this stage. I explained: 'All these ties will simply reform and you will need to do the essential foundational work anyway. You will simply be taking a wrong turn off the track. Would you really want to miss out on all the incredible evolutionary growth and expansion these earlier Steps grant you, even if you could cut your ties from him now?' Jayne understood and continued with her earlier Steps, and discovered as she did so that not only was he being exorcised from her being organically, but she was growing solidly and continuously in her own inner courage, joy and hope.

By the time we reach Step 9, we are ready to reclaim our essential nature, which is not a match for a narcissist. During this Step, you will also let go of any residual grief, loss or pain. This allows you to move forward freely in your new life without harmful past memories and old wounds re-surfacing. After graduating from this Step, you will feel absolutely indifferent towards the narcissist. He or she just won't matter in the way he or she used to. It will be like this person is *a memory of a memory.* The level of relief that follows is, naturally, *indescribable!*

The Parts of Us We Don't Realise We're Still Hanging on to

Following Step 9, many people experience the huge revelation that there was a part of them that was still consciously or unconsciously invested in hanging on to the narcissist. They may not have realised this until facing this stage of the journey. Without exception, all of us who have been enmeshed have unconsciously assigned a narcissist to be our source of love, approval, security or survival. Either we were born into a narcissistic family, or, as an adult, we carried with us unhealed childhood or generational trauma that caused us to seek a parent figure who would do things differently this time round.

Dana said this after her NARP Module Nine work: 'When I confronted the stuck place inside my heart that didn't want to let go of my emotional tie to the narcissist, I found my four-year-old inner child crying because Daddy left her and didn't want anything to do with her. The feelings she had were, "If I let go of loving Daddy, I know he will never love me, and then I'll have no love with him."' Dana then did the releasing work on this trauma, letting go of her emotional ties to her father, and consequently found that she could easily let go of the ones that had been binding her to her narcissistic ex-husband.

Dana had no idea that this trauma had been operating inside her; all she had known was that she was continually having dreams about the narcissistic ex – about her and him being happy together. This was haunting her at a time when her reality was not this at all. After clearing the trauma of 'hanging on', the dreams stopped.

Often people unconsciously keep connected to the narcissist 'just in case'. When Christopher probed deeply into those dense parts within him that were resisting letting go of his ex, Margie, he discovered that there was a part of him that was still living in hope of her returning and healing and being the wife he wished she was. He said, 'Logically, I would have thought that was usual; however, after becoming a NARPer, I love that wisdom emerges where unconsciousness once was. Now I know hanging on was only going to keep matching me up for more narcissistic, disappointing relationships in my life. And now I am just happy for her to be free and me to be free to create our lives in whatever way is the truth for us. My happiness and future are not dependent anymore on her healing.'

Other reasons we can have hidden attachments are that maybe on some level we don't want the narcissist to move on, to forget us, or replace us. Maybe we believe 'the devil we know' is better. Or perhaps, again on an unconscious level, we stoically want to hang on to our energy exchange with them so that other people we love don't suffer the brunt of their behaviour.

When we did Quanta Freedom Healing work together, Tammy and I unearthed this particular reason: she didn't want to break energetic ties with her narcissistic mother because of her guilt about healing and moving on when her mother was powerless to heal. She had unconsciously taken a vow to remain connected and drained by her mother to help try to sustain her mother's life force. (I know that may sound crazy – but it's true!) Until doing the Step 9 work, Tammy had no conscious knowledge of having made this inner vow emotionally at a very young age. However, when we found it, it resonated with her 100 per cent: it made so much sense in relation to how she felt! After it was cleared from Tammy's energy field, she was able to let go of her mother's ties, which were threatening to drain her all the way to her own demise.

When the Narcissist Keeps Reappearing or Coming at You

Naturally, one of the greatest indications that we still have toxic ties with a narcissist is that they keep reappearing in our life. My own personal experience of this was profound. I lived in a neighbouring suburb to the one where the narcissist lived, with a major social and shopping hub being the central point for both areas. Before working with Step 9, I was still bumping into the narcissist randomly. This had decreased significantly due to all of the other Steps detoxing him from my system, yet, on occasion, it still happened. However, after Step 9 work, it never happened again. It was like we both lived in two completely different vibrational universes, and I never even thought about the possibility of it happening – and quite frankly couldn't have cared less if it did!

One of the NARP Forum Senior Moderators, Lisa, recalled in her recovery how, after nine months of going No Contact, a third party got in touch with her about a piece of art work that supposedly belonged to the narcissist and which was allegedly in her possession. Lisa had no knowledge of this, yet then the narcissist emailed her, threatening her with police action if she didn't produce it. Lisa worked with Step 8, tackling a terror of persecution which arose, and then intuitively worked on Step 9 to clear all last vestiges of any connection with the narcissist out of her body.

This is how she describes her shift when it clicked into place after Step 9: 'The major trauma that I found and released, which had been responsible for the last bits of this connection, was: *I don't deserve to be free.* I was standing in my kitchen and a calm came over me. I instantly knew what to do. I wrote a brief message to the third party, explaining I had no interest in, nor any wish, to be involved in the narcissist's business, and told him to refrain from contacting me, with respect. Then I deleted all correspondence and blocked the third person. It was an innate knowingness that this was "all about boundaries". I was not obliged to cooperate with such nonsense. And in that moment, every single trace of fear and doubt dissolved. I graduated. That to me was the day when I knew I had transcended the narcissistic experience once and for all. All fear left and I was left feeling total peace.'

Reclaiming Yourself Without the Narcissist's Energy

When we work towards a complete release from our ties with the narcissist, we are purposefully targeting those dense, painful or clingy parts of ourselves that aren't ready to let go of that connection, even if we didn't previously know these existed.

When we get to this advanced stage of our journey, we can't kid ourselves – we need to be really serious and not skirt around this Step. Personal evolution isn't handed out to all and sundry on a silver platter; it is for those who are earnest about becoming self-actualised and giving up their dependency props. Narcissists are major dependency props, because when they steal your energy, they make you dependent on them – and if we are involved with them, we stay that way, even though they are destroying us. It is like someone has stolen your soul and you are continually clinging on to them in an attempt not only to get it back, but also to try to force them to be those parts of yourself that never properly developed or grew up. Little do we realise that the narcissist doesn't have those parts of him or herself shored up and healed either; the narcissist is only pretending that this is the case in order to drain you of whatever energy you have.

So in this toxic-energy entanglement, we have to give up all connections of desire and any hopes that the narcissist will one day become the person they professed to be. But it's even more than this – we have to feel into what it would be like to be our own energy source without them, and heal whatever is preventing us from being that.

This is now a deeper, more intense stage than Step 2, which was about becoming a source to ourselves. This is 'Custer's last stand', where we tackle all those parts of ourselves that are still hanging on and stopping us from becoming a fully actualised, independent, whole being supported by our own energy. We may have addressed some fears before – and you certainly will have done so if you've come this far – yet it is here that we discover symbiotic energetic ties, vows and cords that we may never have dreamed of.

In the process of finding them and clearing them, it becomes very apparent why some people never move on, forget or heal from narcissists. Many people can literally feel an empty chasm inside and an accompanying terror when they do the deep inner work that is entailed in letting go of those last ties with the narcissist and becoming their own power source.

This is what Rebecca reported about her Step 9 experience: 'I tracked my trauma through to a deep black hole inside me. When I connected to it and asked it what it was about, the answer I got was, "Without you I am nothing. I have no life force of my own. I need you to exist." At first I was terrified by the realisation: *I am no different from the narcissist! I need other people's energy to exist!* Then I remembered that no matter the trauma, all we need to do is load it up and release it. When I applied Quanta Freedom Healing to it, I felt my life force return *on its own.* I don't know how or why I didn't have my own life force before, but now I do, independently of the narcissist. In no way do I feel that I need or want that connection again.'

For this exercise, it is vital to be true to yourself. This means you need to stand up to any of those parts of yourself that would like to retain the symbiotic toxic connection with the narcissist. It is parasitical because it grants the narcissist an energy feed from you, and there is also some unconscious form of payoff for you – that is costing you dearly.

Therefore, to break free, our intention is to find those parts of ourselves that are hanging on. And they may be very determined; so much so, that you may feel like you will literally die when you let them go. Oh gosh, I remember this myself – wailing out those ties and feeling like a part of me was being ripped out, but knowing I would not survive if I held on. When we get to that stage, truly, there is nothing to lose. I promise you, once I had this Step completed I felt SO free – freer than I ever had. Many other people have reported this too. However, if you really don't feel like you can face this stage of the journey yet, it could mean that you haven't processed the other Steps to the degree that is necessary to be ready for Step 9 – and that's okay. Just simply revisit those Steps where you know you have more clearing work to do.

You can use the Step 9 exercise, coupled with Quanta Freedom Healing, to shift the trauma from deep within your DNA and set yourself free. If you haven't already begun to use them, I thoroughly recommend the powerful Quantum processes to help rid yourself of the deep soul virus of narcissistic infiltration. As mentioned, the 'You Can Thrive Program' teaches you exactly how to apply Quanta Freedom Healing to your healing journey. Access it for free here: www.youcan thriveprogram.com.

EXERCISE: STEP 9 – RELEASING THE TIES

1. Make sure you can dedicate the time and space to yourself so you will not be disturbed. Have your journal with you. When you are ready, set the intention that you are going to release yourself and the narcissist from each other. Know that this is the highest act of unconditional love, which states: *I love myself and you enough to set us both free to pursue life in any way that we individually choose.*

As you set that intention, open up your body and breathe and take your attention inside yourself. Gently observe any feelings that this statement brings up for you. You may already be feeling tightness, sadness, resistance, fear or a host of other emotions. Quite possibly you don't feel a calm space within which to unpack those sorts of feelings.

Even though lots of thoughts and memories or distractions might be trying to race through your mind, don't pick them up or give them any energy. Don't go into the 'story'; just stay present with your body, observing the emotions and the sensations, without hooking into the logical information about what exactly they might relate to.

2. Keeping your attention inside yourself, ask your inner being/inner child lovingly what this fear and hanging on is about. Make sure your energy is open, inviting, interested and supportive – and without judgement. Don't get caught up in fearing what the answer might be; simply know that energy is energy and in no way does Life/Source/Creation sentence you to a doom of deadly and painful energetic connections. Any energy that is not the true you can be let go; the choice is always yours. Remember there is nothing to fear but fear itself, and whenever we walk up to our fear fearlessly, we always find it is simply a part of ourselves which needs our love and healing back to wholeness. When you are ready, record your answers.

3. Now check in with your body and rate the emotional intensity of each reason for hanging on. Feel the intensity of these charges, with 0/10 being the lowest rating and 10/10 being the most intense emotional charge. Number these painful issues from their highest to lowest emotional charge.

4. Starting with the most intense reason, ask your body to show you the 'tie' that represents it. Then inwardly scan your body and feel into where this energy lies and what form it takes. What does it look like? Is it thick and heavy like chains, or is it rope? It might not even take the form of a tie; trust yourself as to what you 'see'.

5. Then talk lovingly to the part of yourself where the attachment lies, saying, 'It's okay, [endearing term], I understand that you are hanging on, and that's perfectly understandable. I am here to help support you and heal you so that you can safely let go.' Make this statement sincere and heartfelt, until you feel something 'allowing' you to work with this part of you.

6. Now say to your inner being/inner child, '[Endearing term], I love you and I can help you release this and replace it with the real love and connection to what you truly need and want.' Then imagine the tie (or energy) being cut, taken away, dissolved or undone in whatever way, with whichever tool comes intuitively to you; simply trust and go with this process. Make sure you see it dissolve back to native nothingness (i.e. Life/Source/Creation) for recycling. Do you feel the release in your body? Stay open and willing. If you do feel it, know you absolutely are letting go.

7. Write down what you experienced in this exercise. Do you still feel the connection to the narcissist, or is there space and relief where it previously was? If you sense anything left at all, keep processing Step 9 until you feel relief and freedom.

8. Next, repeat the process on the next attachment that you find in your body.

9. After clearing all the toxic attachments that you can find, write on the page in your journal headed 'My True Self Declarations': 'For the highest expression of love, I set you and myself free to be our own energy source. I release myself from power struggles and symbiotic relationships. I thank you for the gifts and the lessons, and I willingly and lovingly take on my development to know the glory of me to be free.' Write out this powerful intention eleven times to assist its manifestation into your life.

The Release into Your True Energy

After this Step, many people tell me that they feel filled with energy, joy and purpose, and motivated to take exciting new steps in their lives. The energy that was previously being sucked out of them has returned. Another wonderful thing is how some people, who have suffered from narcissistic ex-partners, say that after Step 9 work, they know they're ready to start dating again!

Consistently, the reports are that people feel a distinct disconnect from the narcissist after Step 9, as well as a whole new level of release and freedom from the pain, regret and resentment in relation to their experiences with them.

We come now to Step 10 – our last healing Step. It is here that everything comes together, where we graduate from 'Who We Were Being' into 'Who We Really Are', thereby releasing trauma and making space for incredible Life Force to flow freely through us.

16

REALISE YOUR LIBERATION, FREEDOM AND TRUTH

All of the previous nine Steps were designed to deliver you here. You have been working on taking back your power, releasing the hooks, pain and fear of the narcissist, and coming home to healing, recovering and claiming your true self.

Narcissistic energy is not the true force of Life, which consists of love, integrity, peace, honesty and joy. Rather, narcissism is a false existence born from illusions, masks, deception, pain and fear. As children, we absolutely had no rational choice (even though subconsciously there were deeper forces at play, which I will explain in Part Three) as to the family we were born into and how we were raised, but as adults continuing painful and abusive relationships, we know the trauma of remaining connected to false selves and trying to force them to come to the party of a 'happy healthy life'.

Through our brutal experience of narcissistic abuse, and then beginning our Thriver Recovery work, we have learned that if we're not aligned with an authentic life, we can pay a terrible price. We also discover that the only way to reverse and release ourselves from our suffering is to let go of victimhood and to stop handing away our power by focusing on the abuser, and instead to self-partner and commit fully to finding and doing the necessary healing work on our inner being.

The true goal of the Thriver journey, after survival, is to claim the gift of becoming the only version of ourselves that could have ever completed us – and that is the person who is aligned with and integrated with our soul truth, the living embodiment of our real potential and truest desires.

This is what Step 10 work is all about! So let's get started.

What Does Loving and Accepting Ourselves Really Mean?

Step 10 is where we really click into loving and accepting ourselves. The following two questions are possibly the most asked among those who are searching for self-development, spirituality, enlightenment and inner peace: 'How *do* I learn to love and accept myself?' and 'What does loving and accepting myself *really* mean?'

The confusion surrounding this area can be over whelming! It drove me crazy for years, wondering what self-love and acceptance actually was. I used to think, 'If I hear one more person telling me I need to LOVE myself more, I'll throttle them!' I tried so many different processes in a bid to work out how to love and accept myself at last, but I was coming at it from totally the wrong angle. Before I took the Quantum path to healing, I had no inkling (let alone the deep cellular understanding which I have had now for some years and which has never left me) that self-love and acceptance are fundamental parts of my true nature and therefore require no extra effort on my part. Within the very coding of my natural DNA is the innate ability to see and accept myself exactly as my Higher Self and Creation recognise me: as a being worthy of love beyond measure, *simply because I exist.*

This is in stark contrast to how I used to view and treat myself, which was much more akin to self-criticism, self-abandonment, self-destruction and self-loathing. Why was I doing this? The answer is simple: because the unhealed traumas inside me were driving me to treat myself in this way.

Many NARP members come to understand the night-and-day difference between conditional and unconditional self-love and acceptance, and realise it's impossible to shame and blame ourselves into shape. Josephine said this: 'My love was so conditional. I could only like myself (maybe) if I achieved some incredible task I had set myself. Any deviation from total excellence was never good enough. It wasn't until my NARP journey that I found true unconditional love for myself. My previous shame and pain shifted to support, tenderness and beautiful self-encouragement. From then on, the times I stumbled, rather than beat myself up mercilessly, I gave myself even more love.'

I love this quote from 'The Philosophical Tree', an essay by the psychologist C.G. Jung: 'One does not become enlightened by imagining figures of light, but by making the darkness conscious. The latter procedure, however, is disagreeable and therefore not popular.' Jung was so right: it is only by bringing light into our dark inner places and thereby healing them that we become well (or 'enlightened'), yet this is the very thing we are mostly brought up to avoid doing!

And, even after we've realised that acknowledging our inner dark places is necessary for healing, we may nevertheless still become caught up in trying to do all sorts of things to rid ourselves of them in an attempt to love and accept ourselves at last. That is still a symptom of 'conditional love', whereby we subconsciously believe that we are unacceptable and defective as we are (especially when carrying the wounds of narcissistic abuse) and that, until all these wounds are gone, we cannot be loved and accepted as ourselves by a Higher Power or by others.

At this stage we haven't as yet anchored ourselves in the cellular *knowing* of loving and accepting ourselves unconditionally; we are not *being* it yet.

At Step 10, we target precisely the trauma that is keeping us disconnected from truly loving and accepting ourselves – from knowing our true nature and how this connects us to the sacred ecology of our soul and all of Life. It is our separation from this knowing that keeps us in judgement and pain, suspending us in a conditional way of being that means we cannot accept and love ourselves until we have this or do that, or feel this or become that.

Step 10 is a beautiful transition to knowing right here, right now (no matter where we are in the journey), that everything we experience and everything we feel – without exception – is in perfect and divine order. All roads lead home. Our soul doesn't make mistakes. Everything we are creating is in perfect unison with our soul's choices and purpose, and we can't get it wrong. It is all happening 'for us' and all we need to do for the pain to stop and the glorious conscious creation of our life to start, is to awaken to this truth and to start intentionally working with it.

The Thriver Way teaches us that to be a divine creator, it is important to tend to emotion first – to feel whole inwardly regardless of what our outer world looks like. It is then that we can make the shift to loving and accepting ourselves as exactly as we are, regardless of how we are feeling and what we are going through, and even who we are being.

The Trauma in Regard to 'Loving Ourselves'

This is what Aaron shared after his Step 10 work: 'I knew I carried shame and that I didn't love myself or feel deserving of my own love. Even though I had come so far with NARP healing, I was excited about tackling the Step 10 shifts. Astoundingly the belief "I don't deserve to exist" came up for me, and I felt like some force of life had punished me, which of course meant I was still incredibly hard on myself. When I cleared that trauma and felt Light fill me, I cried with relief and joy.'

Our human conditioning can be incredibly hard on our belief systems when it comes to loving ourselves. We are taught it is 'narcissistic' to do so and that loving ourselves means we won't care about others. (I hope now, as a result of reading this book, you absolutely understand that narcissism is the *exact opposite* of self-love!) We are infused with so many primal beliefs about our carnal nature being sinful, soiled and attracted to evil, rather than believing we are children of God. And, of course, how do people behave who believe they are shameful, defective and undeserving of love? They behave in ways which reflect that inner trauma; they play out what it is to be abused or an abuser or both. This is the damaging cycle that the Thriver Way overturns by bringing us back to our organic, essential, true nature – which is love, and which means being unconditionally connected to ourselves, life and others in wholesome, authentic and joyous ways.

A Different Vibrational Attraction Point

At this stage, Step 10, we are leaving the trauma and the effects of the narcissist further and further behind us. In Step 9, we disconnected ourselves at a deep level from the narcissist in order to become the source of our own authentic self. Now, in Step 10, we become organic, connected, true love – which is in no way a pushover or a target for abuse.

In fact, it's quite the opposite, because when we are true love, we are truthful. We know how to have difficult conversations, how to honour ourselves and speak up, and we know this to be an expression of love and truth. As a result of showing up as whole, truthful, self-loving people, we are inoculated against narcissists. We are also impervious to them as the result of looking after ourselves healthily rather than diminishing or hurting ourselves in an attempt to win approval and love from outside sources.

We only reach this level of no longer being susceptible to abusers if we love and accept ourselves unconditionally, as well as the results of the life that we generate. Our motto becomes: 'I will be REAL – regardless – and then all of life will follow.' We are totally prepared to lose it all (the version of life we thought should have been ours) in order to get it all (the true Life that awaits us when we honour our inner being).

Another wonderful by-product of finally coming home to love and accepting ourselves unconditionally is that we start becoming attractive and attracted to people who represent true love. We also find that those people who might have been a good match for those parts of ourselves that weren't self-loving become unattractive to us. I remember a distinct experience that highlighted this shift to me. I met a man who was intelligent, attractive and successful, and who seemed really lovely. On my third date with him, when I was still assessing him as a potential romantic partner, I realised, as he got more familiar with me, that he talked about other people in very judgemental and disparaging ways. At one point, he asked me how I thought the date was going. I told him the truth about my reservations – calmly and matter of fact. He exploded into a narcissistic rage, and the date was called off easily and respectfully. I was so excited and elated about how my loving myself and showing up authentically now flushed people out who were not capable of healthy love.

Kate said this about her shift with Step 10: 'I woke up one morning, and instead of automatically reaching out in bed to where Jake used to sleep next to me, I actually felt a repulsion that he used to be there. Not anger or disgust; more like, why on earth was I even with him? Relief surged through me and I felt totally free. I knew I really truly loved myself, and I could feel love surging through my veins. For the first time in my life, I felt what feelings of true love are for others, including my children, and what they could be for a future partner. I had no doubt real love would happen to me – because it already *was* me. Two months later, the man who now unconditionally adores me, supports me and has my back – even when I am not being my best or most loving – came effortlessly into my life.'

The Full Circle

Our Thriver Healing journey from narcissistic abuse started with our intense disconnection from ourselves, others and from life itself as a result of our unhealed traumas, and brings us to the personal mission of closing all the gaps and finally becoming an integrated being.

At this stage we have woken up from our previous trance knowing how vital it is to be the generator of our own wellbeing in order to create life authentically and interact truthfully with others. When we connect to our true self, this state of being sets us free; it feels solid and real, and the neediness and the pain of trying to get outside forces to fill us and fulfil us drops away.

What Does It Mean to Feel 'Whole'?

Step 10 is where we get to discover and experience a higher level of 'wholeness'. However, before you get all excited and think 'Yippee, this is when I'll never have to do any work on myself again!' (as I once believed!), it is important to understand that our healing journey is not just about processing these ten Steps sequentially. We will have to revisit the Steps at different times in the future whenever our deeper traumas are triggered. I realised long ago that our inner being has many layers to it, and it ingeniously sheds trauma in an order which supports the multidimensional being that we are. As we grow and evolve, we are then ready for the deeper layers of our trauma to be revealed and healed. So please don't think that Step 10 is the end of your Thriver Healing, because it isn't. We will never stop experiencing opportunities to free ourselves from our false beliefs and traumas in order to make even more space inside ourselves for the expansion, joy, love and success that are our true birthright.

Because we are working on the specific wounds that are blocking us, we can start to align ourselves with the knowing that finally we 'get' what life is about at Step 10. What I am about to share with you is impossible to digest logically, and I therefore ask you to *feel* these words I am about to express, because some part of your cellular knowing recognises these words to be true: when we start figuring out life, it is because we have become 'life'. No longer do we agonise and wonder or hope that life is somehow going to turn out right, because we ourselves have become the centre nucleus of *knowing* and *being* our truth.

Truly Thriving means we can be fulfilled and whole even before what we want turns up as the physical manifestation of our desires, and we can embody joy and expansiveness as we are now. Feeling great is no longer reliant on the 'outer'. Resentment, pain and regret from the past, and fear of the future, are all replaced by peace and fulfilment. We experience the deep resonation that love, truth, growth and happiness are already present in our lives, and that life will unfold for us simply by virtue of our acting as the caretakers of the health of our inner being.

In this true self state, we know and believe that we can trust ourselves, and that we will no longer accept 'less than' ever again. We understand that we are unlimited and can align with, and create exactly, what we truly want in our life; and that we can easily and without pain or regret say 'no' to whoever and whatever isn't right for us – and hang out successfully in all the grey areas of uncertainty in between. We know that, regardless of what our life looks like now, or how many practical losses we may have suffered, our soul and our life are ripe with potential; yet we don't *need* any of that potential to be realised in order to be happy – although, ironically, it generally is easily realised as a result of us just being ourselves.

Of course, we still slip up and regress back to being 'human beings' rather than 'Quantum beings', but we are learning (hopefully) to give up the stinking thinking and self-condemnation much more quickly than we once did, and to replace this with inner love and healing instead. In certain respects, we even get to enjoy these times of 'slipping' (of being emotionally triggered within or without when things don't seem to be going right for us), because we get to release yet another stuck part of our inner being that was not allowing us to evolve on to the next highest and more glorious version of ourselves.

The nature of our true self *is* love and acceptance; it knows there are no mistakes, that everything happens for a higher reason, and there is nothing to regret and only liberation, freedom, joy and truth to create. It knows that, without exception, every breakdown heralds a breakthrough of equal magnitude.

After working with and aligning yourself to Step 10, you will have the potential to free yourself from the shackles of our programmed human experience, whereby living life from the outside in results in the pain of conditions, expectations, disappointments and our trying to find love and fulfilment in all the wrong places (goodness gracious, haven't narcissists smashed us over the head with THAT lesson!). Step 10 helps bring about incredible spiritual growth that enables you to start truly living life from the inside out, generating the manifestation of more goals and dreams than you ever thought possible from a place of not needing them to happen in order to feel whole – because you already are anyway.

The impact Step 10 has on you generally depends on how diligently you have worked on the previous Steps. If you are feeling disconnected from the narcissist, and have started to feel and know that your personal power is expanding, this final Step will be incredibly liberating for you. You certainly can perform this Step in sequence even if you do still feel some hooks and pain. It will give you a boost and it will definitely help, although please make sure you commit to yourself by revisiting the other Steps diligently in order to heal any other unhealed parts as necessary. And, of course, when you feel drawn to work with Step 10 again, there will always be more to release and claim for yourself.

The individuals who dig deep and do the work usually experience profound liberation, freedom and truth – coming out on the other side as empowered, whole and integrated beings. Life then starts reflecting this transformation unconditionally back to you, as your outer circumstances start to match your inner being as part of the knock-on effect.

Anki, a beautiful member of our Thriver Community, shared this about her journey, culminating at Step 10: 'I am a totally different person. I was told at fifty years of age that I had chronic, untreatable diseases, leaving me with no ability to function or work, yet after only three months of going through NARP, I am now working and exercising again. I am almost completely free from fifteen years of medication. I feel beautiful and strong and the greatest gift is I

LOVE myself finally. After losing everything in my life to the narcissist, I had no idea how on earth I could provide accommodation for myself and my son. Now I have my own place near my work, in the nature with forests and a lake outside my door! The shift in my son's as well as my other children's emotional and health states have been nothing short of miraculous as well.'

It is such a self-nurturing and beautiful experience to clear the beliefs and trauma that are not allowing us to love and accept ourselves, and I know you are really going to enjoy the following exercises which can help you to achieve this! Yet know that these parts of ourselves can feel quite painful, because they are often to do with deep shame and the primal traumas that the entire human race has carried of feeling defective, unlovable and even 'dark' and 'evil'. I honestly have not met one narcissistic abuse client who I have done healing sessions on with Quanta Freedom Healing, who has not been infected by beliefs like this.

One of the most important things that we need to know as Thrivers is that energy is only energy; trauma energy is not who you are, and, as we begin to embody the Thriver Way to Heal, there is nothing to fear other than fear itself – as we saw in Chapter 15. There is no mysterious force that can take you out; there is only the illusion that these things are real. They're not – they have just been having their way with you for some time! So when you get in contact with these challenging parts of yourself, no matter how painful they are, just remember that emotional pain can be approached like a physical trauma. A flesh wound hurts somatically but it is not your whole and true self; likewise, when you experience emotional pain, don't get drawn into believing what your ego (the internal narcissist) would have you believe – that what the trauma stands for is real. It's not – it's simply another wounded part to release from yourself so that you can set yourself free.

So, with that in mind ... let's get started!

EXERCISE: STEP 10 – COMING HOME TO YOURSELF

1. Have your journal with you and make sure that all of your devices are switched off so you won't be disturbed. Now close your eyes and spend a few minutes relaxing your body and focusing on your breathing. Ignore any thoughts that come in; just return to your breath. Tell yourself you deserve this time and space just to 'be', in preparation for this exercise.

2. Be really open and honest as you feel into the ways in which you don't unconditionally love yourself. Open your eyes and write these down. How are you hard on yourself? What is it that you deeply feel in your body about yourself with regard to being lovable, acceptable and worthy of love? List your beliefs about this, stating them as: 'I am...' or 'I am not...'.

After you have listed them, turn your attention towards whether you feel that Life/Source/Creation loves you. Do you feel loved and accepted by a Higher Power? Do you feel comforted, held and loved, or do you feel like you have been turned away and you're on your own? List your beliefs about this stating them as: 'I am...' or 'I am not...'. Record your answers in your journal. (This can take some time. Don't rush it!)

3. Have a look at the two lists you have written in your journal, and one at a time, check in with your body and rate the emotional intensity of each trauma that you have identified, with 0/10 being the lowest rating and 10/10 being the most intense emotional charge. Number these painful issues from their highest to lowest emotional charge.

4. Starting with your beliefs about Life/Source/Creation and the highest-rated trauma, feel it in your body and breathe deeply into it. Say to your inner being/inner child: 'I bless and accept this trauma in order to transform it and set us free.' While staying fully present and accepting of the inner wound, say to your inner being/inner child, '[Endearing term], we are going to hold this energy together, knowing that it came from another time and other beings who were also told that they were unlovable and unacceptable. By liberating you from this and by transforming it, we are helping to liberate all others as well.'

5. Now say out loud, 'I now know I am not my trauma, and I am not anything that holds me separated from my true self, which is Oneness and Love. I release and allow all illusions to go back to the native nothingness from whence they came, and I go free.' Imagine in any way that feels right for you (this may be your favourite method from previous exercises) the releasing of the false energy and your inner being going free. Really feel that happen.

6. See yourself filled with Light, which comes from above and down into where the trauma previously was. It fills your cells until your very outline disappears and you are just one magnificent ball of Light. Let the Light expand further out until it fills up your auric field (the energy field around the physical body). Then expand the Light right out to meet all of life, so it connects up with the Light that IS Life. Now breathe and open your body and become aware that you and the Light are one. Say this to yourself: 'I am the Light, the Light I am. There is nothing else, it just is.' And then, with your body open and relaxed breathing, *just be the Light* without thought.

7. After completing this exercise, record how you feel. Did you feel a sense of space, warmth and love deep inside? When you go back and try, can you still pick up on the trauma of disconnection from love in your body? If you can still do this, keep working with Step 10 until you have cleared it out.

8. Now repeat the process with the next highest-rated trauma on your list, and then repeat again, working through the list of traumas related to not loving yourself unconditionally.

The Full Circle Keeps Turning

After processing Step 10, remember that you might need to revisit any or all of the Steps again at some time in the future – and it is normal to do so, because our evolution is an ongoing process of expansion that has no destination, other than to clean out fear and bring in Light – which is our true self, allowing us to *get better and do better.*

From this point forward, as a result of working with these Steps and being committed to honouring our inner being when in need, we are moving away from the illusions and traumas that once trapped us unconsciously in narcissistic abuse – and we are ready to emerge, as a butterfly does from a cocoon, spreading our winds fearlessly and soaring in life as an authentic being.

PART THREE

HEALING THIS GENERATION, OUR CHILDREN AND FUTURE GENERATIONS

'*The wound is the place where the Light enters you.*'

attrib. Rumi (1207–1273)

Part Three is all about how we go forward as Thrivers in the understanding that although we need to make healing all about ourselves – taking our focus off the narcissist and what happened to us in order to self-partner and release and free ourselves from our inner trauma – this journey is absolutely not just about us alone. It is about all of us: our children, our world and our future generations.

*

As mentioned in Part One, a parent's trauma and the ways in which this affects their relationship with their offspring (nature and nurture both being responsible) is significant, and can cause biological and cellular changes in their child. Abuse, victimhood, power struggles, non-accountability, addictions and learned helplessness, such as handing power away in an attempt to stay safe, are all part of the damaging dynamics of those families who carry trauma. As adults, we continue the patterns of those skewed love trajectories: they are the only ones we know.

Yet something spectacular happens when one person frees themselves from their own inner wounds and starts to become self-actualised and whole on the inside. There is in virtually every case a profound ripple effect passed on to others around them, including their children. As a mother and a woman who feels deeply for the struggles that our children go through (heaven forbid they have it as hard as we did!) and being passionate about doing my bit to help raise consciousness for all humans who have suffered, I am so excited about the far-reaching effect we create *when we heal ourselves.*

One NARP member, Pippa, wrote this: 'I started healing five years ago, and went No Contact with the narcissistic relative who nearly destroyed our family. Today, our family is closer than ever. No more secrets or triangulation. As time goes on, not only have I healed myself, but I've included many other family members in my healing sessions too. The ripple effect has increased. My son, who suffered so much, including parental alienation because of his narcissistic ex-wife, is now finally reunited with all his children after twelve heart-breaking years of separation. So am I as their grandparent, and my mother as their great-grandparent. We are all now connected with my son's son's children – my own great-grandchildren! This is five generations of family, gloriously and lovingly reunited! I truly believe that NONE of this would have happened unless I'd led the way for myself and others to heal the terrible traumas our family were enmeshed in.'

This section, Part Three, is about how to take Thriving forward, absolutely for ourselves yet also for everything and everyone we touch; because as authentic, real people, who are connected firmly to the ecology of our soul, life and Higher Power, and who show up as love and a force for good, we are powerful entities who contribute to life positively, rather than becoming part of the abuse/abused cycle, which certainly doesn't.

Even if you aren't a parent, the very fact that you are growing up by healing your inner child and creating a healthy, Thriving inner adulthood, means that you will have an extraordinary impact on the world – not only for children, but as an example to other people's inner wounded children as well. Also, at the Quantum level, every time you experience an inner shift and release of trauma energy, allowing you to become a creative force for wellbeing, you help others with identical human wounding to loosen up and shift their trauma too.

The truth is we are all in this together and, through one person at a time, we are freeing the whole. So, please know that regardless of whether or not you are a parent, Part Three will hold some very powerful keys for you – because it applies to every one of us.

17

THE PERSONAL AND COLLECTIVE THRIVER SHIFT

Right now, I believe that many of us are being rocked to our core in order to heal. Time is flying by and many of us find ourselves wondering what is becoming of our lives. This is especially true if we are enmeshed in painful or abusive relationships, or if we haven't yet been able to forge healthy relationships or see our dreams and aspirations come to fruition.

I truly think that I and my peers belong to the 'era changeover' generation. The lives of our forebears were defined by gender and by fixed relationship roles, which were in many ways symbiotic and mutually reliant. Similarly, many of us today who are in our forties and older have come from backgrounds characterised by traditional male and female relationships, in which 'power over' and 'power relinquished' formed the dynamic. The man usually wore the pants – and if he didn't, the woman almost certainly did! However, these days power tends to be shared in relationships. I observe that my son and his age group, although they might have struggles with other things, seem to model equality, joint-decision taking, shared responsibility and duty sharing *naturally.* As for my generation, who form a large part of the Thriver Community, we are stuck in the middle, battling away as we try to work out who is who and where we really fit in. This is while the older generations are left wondering whether anyone their age, themselves included, can really change co-dependent patterns even if they do the necessary inner work. And, of course, narcissistic abuse issues are still rampant among younger generations too.

Things are so different now; for the first time in thousands of years, women have been able to survive, even thrive, without a man. Modern-day romantic relationships are no longer thought healthy when based on defined gender roles for their structure and survival; they require a deeper mutuality and bond now to stand the test of time. I believe we are midwifing a fundamental shift that is unprecedented in human history and totally necessary for our evolving world. This is the changeover from the era of Power to that of Co-creative Consciousness – of choosing cooperation instead of domination; interdependence instead of co-dependence; love instead of fear; oneness instead of separation.

The arena of relationships is not all that is going through radical, rapid transformation. Technology and medicine are evolving at lightning speed; in the West, we now have unprecedented access to information and freedom of choice. Yet, despite these developments, many people are realising that their happiness and the health of their relationships are not defined or granted by these sorts of advances. Emotional, mental, physical, sexual and substance abuse, depression and suicides still exist in epidemic proportions, and place incredible strain on personal lives, families, businesses and the entire collective. I believe that at the core of this lies trapped trauma, which, like an abscess that has not yet been lanced, means our society simply can't heal until it is released – regardless of how much technological or medical advancement we have experienced.

Through my healing work on myself and with so many others, I have observed that it is *now* that we are being forced to come face to face with our deepest fears and insecurities, and with exactly those unhealed traumas that have been passed on to us from our forebears and our childhoods. Relationships offer the greatest way to mirror back to us our unhealed parts, especially those relationships which are meaningful to us: they supply all the triggers for our deepest fears to come to the surface. As we have seen, narcissists work out what these fears of ours are and they then use them mercilessly to hurt, control or even purposefully destroy us. Maybe like myself, you have had to live through the holocaust of your deepest fears becoming reality, and losing what you formerly believed gave you your identity, in order to turn inwards and finally know the necessity of creating peace, wholeness and happiness within yourself. In hindsight, I knew I would never have experienced my liberation into my true self other than by being stripped bare, left without props and having no choice other than to come face to face with only myself.

We are in times where a great shift in consciousness is required if we are to heal individually and collectively. I really do believe that in terms of our heart, spirit and soul – those precious inner commodities – we have veered off course. Our values have shifted away from community, sharing and kindness, toward individualism, consumerism and instant personal gratification. This has come at great cost to our inner being, as well as to others and our environment, because when we try to fill ourselves up with 'stuff' in order to be whole, we will always come away empty.

This is exactly the model where narcissism flourishes the most: 'The more power, significance and acquisitions I have – the more superiority I gain.' With all false power, more supplies are needed if it is to be sustained. Enough is never enough, because it can't support durable, lasting, embodied wholeness. Do inner peace, happiness and love come from outer stuff? The answer is 'No'. When it comes to true personal fulfilment, you can't 'get' it; you can only 'be' it. No amount of *doingness* can make up for defunct *beingness* (i.e. an inner being clogged up with trauma).

Please don't think I am anti-stuff or against having nice things! I'm not! I simply know that if we keep trying to restore our inner wholeness through acquiring more possessions, we are in Wrong Town. Acquisitions (as well as people) can only ever be appreciated, enjoyed and loved when they are not a condition of our having a complete sense of self. Things and people are only wholesome in our lives when we are already unconditionally whole, and our selfhood is not dependent on acquiring – or losing – them.

Not only has this collective shift of consciousness – which ironically has been into unconsciousness, away from our inner being and the importance of togetherness to a state of disconnection and worshipping material acquisitions – helped to create narcissism *en masse,* it has encouraged people to assign supposedly powerful individuals (i.e. narcissists) as a source of those things that provide them with a sense of identity and inner wholeness that they think they can't feel and obtain by themselves.

Consciousness and Our Choices

Narcissists only have to *appear* to be the supplier of the resources that we feel are missing – such as wealth, connections, lifestyle, beauty or flattering compliments – for co-dependants (who are not whole within) to get hooked in by them and to fall quickly into their clutches. Hungry people make the worst shoppers: they often buy foods that are innutritious and damaging to them. Identically, we choose false selves when we are emotionally starved and don't know how to fill ourselves up healthily yet.

Our choices always relate to the level of consciousness we are operating from. If we are still carrying our unhealed traumas, we won't feel whole and we will be inclined to choose instant gratification and quick fixes that may grant us temporary relief, but which ultimately take us further away from that which we seek.

As Thrivers, we realise going forward that we are not just here to free ourselves from *this one person;* we are here to free ourselves from the inner traumas that are creating painful patterns in our lives. By doing so, we can start to make choices that result from being self-partnered and loving ourselves. This means that not only do we stop choosing unhealthy people, we also shift away from other detrimental and toxic habits. Our entire life transforms healthily, beyond description. We no longer wish to do the things that hurt ourselves.

Megan wrote this about her Thriver transformation: 'After detoxing myself from the narcissist, I wanted to tackle the other energy leaks in my life – where I was self-medicating other unhealed parts of me. I tracked and healed those parts with NARP and organically, without even trying, I stopped smoking. I simply could not bear the thought of another cigarette in my mouth after suffering a thirty-year, packet-a-day addiction! I also turned away from toxic food like sweets and pastries, and within four months twenty kilos melted off my body. Now I know why everything previously I tried failed. The trauma inside me wanted more of itself: junk!'

Within your recovery journey, this is the growth you can really start to get excited about: releasing the traumas that have been keeping you addicted to things that make you sick – things such as love addiction with toxic individuals, debt, destructive habits, eating non-foods and taking unnecessary medications. All of it shifts with this work, and you become a new person – acquiring a new body, a glowing complexion and energy to die for, to boot!

As Nancy said: 'Since working with NARP for the last six months, everyone I bump into tells me how great I look! I feel the healthiest, happiest and most attractive I ever have done in my life. I have so much energy and joy inside me! This is a universe away from where I was at my lowest point: in hospital on life support, because my levels of trauma and health were so bad.'

The Number One Key Element to Heal

When we move from being an abuse sufferer to being a conscious Thriver, the real key is giving up victimisation. Victimisation is alluring; it gives us a hit of powerful peptides, and it's a popular movement with lots of support. Misery and victimisation like each other's company – and I know how addictive this is! Before my breakdown and aligning with the Thriver Way to Heal, I used to spend hours every night sharing my war stories with other narcissistically abused people. I felt relief in my righteousness in that moment, but then realised over time that I was progressively feeling worse, not better.

This is the Quantum deal: our inner beings are unconditional. They know no difference between past, present and future (every emotion is 'now'); and they know no difference between our blaming and shaming someone else or ourselves (in Quantum Law it is all 'one'). Therefore, the chemicals of judgement, resentment and the resistance to 'what is' – and refusing, through blaming others, to accept the gift of inner transformation (a refusal which represents the greatest travesty of all) – creates inner destruction on a horrific scale.

In this state, we are not *evolving* – we are *dissolving.*

For a long time, I haven't looked at abuse forums on the internet. The last time I did (years ago) was too much for me. My heart broke to read a woman's post about her ongoing issues with her narcissistic ex-husband, as countless others told her that this would go on 'forever' unless he started tormenting a new partner. Then even the creator of this well-known group agreed this was true – that this would be her only hope of salvation!

I have so much compassion for these sorts of people, because I too once used to be a chronic victim, who nearly died as a result and who almost alienated my son from me because I was so toxic. I am passionate about the Thriver Way to Heal because I know that if we stay within the victimisation model, *there is NO hope of healing.* As victims, we keep waiting for the narcissist to fix the situation and to put right everything they've destroyed, or to apologise and makes amends in some way ... or, if that fails, for him or her to be thrown in jail or to suffer some sort of terrible karma that will give us our life back. Well, good luck with ANY of that. It just doesn't happen!

When I first introduced the Thriver Model to communities of abuse survivors, there was a ton of resistance. The contemporary model was all about focusing on the narcissist and not on ourselves. Yet I held firm, because I understood the virus of unconsciousness that all humans can suffer from is this: *I refuse to take responsibility to self-partner and heal myself from my traumas.* What is so wonderful is now we have a Thriver Community where people are no longer denying themselves their own love and healing by being fixated on the narcissist; instead, they are turning inwards and making it their greatest mission to evolve themselves.

I believe the following with all my heart: people with whole inner identities don't hurt others and *they don't allow themselves to be hurt by other people.* This is the only way these terrible cycles of individual and collective damage will end. Isn't it exciting to think, now that we have the way to heal, we can stop this dreadful disease, one person at a time?

I truly love to think so...

18

OUR MOST PRECIOUS RESOURCE – OUR CHILDREN

As I mentioned in the introduction to this part of the book, even if you aren't a parent, this information is still relevant to you! There are many reasons why I wanted to dedicate a full chapter to the subject of our children. As a mother, I am deeply passionate about our children, and I know that what happens at home is what gets released into the world. Those crucial years of emotional development, as a child, create the adult. And they set the scene for the generations to follow.

Besides working with many adult children of narcissistic parents, I have witnessed the absolute anguish experienced by parents with children they share with narcissists. Countless members of the Thriver Community have gone through unspeakable traumas concerning their children.

In this chapter, I will be sharing with you what I needed to learn in order to save not only my life but my son's. I myself have been both versions of parenthood – the victimised parent and the empowered parent – and the effect on my son was like night and day. (More on that later.)

After being narcissistically abused, and before Thriver Recovery, it is usual to be a victimised parent – meaning we are still suffering from the effects of the narcissistic person deeply. It is also usual to believe that we can't take our eyes off what is happening to our children in order to heal ourselves. This frequently translates into: 'I am going to try to fix it for my children before healing myself.'

Of course, it feels totally counterintuitive to let go and focus on healing ourselves when our children are in distress, because our greatest fears for them have been triggered. We may feel terrorised about the narcissist having access to and custody of our kids, or threatening to take our children away from us. Maybe our children are being severely traumatised by the narcissist, or have been turned against us by the narcissist. Or, devastatingly, you may feel that one of your children is being programmed into being a narcissist. Alternatively, as many people in the Thriver Community have reported, you might have an older child who is in a toxic relationship with a narcissist and you feel powerless to get them to leave.

In all of these situations, one of the most powerful analogies comes from aeroplane safety information: 'Put your own oxygen mask on first, before assisting others.' Just as you are no good to others if you are suffocating as a plane descends, you are totally ineffectual when you are clogged up with trauma and feeling intensely victimised. The more we jump up and down about what the narcissist is or isn't doing, the less energy we have to dedicate to healing our own wounds and the longer we remain horrifically unavailable and emotionally toxic to our children.

Thank goodness the Thriver Way to Heal teaches us *so within, so without:* know that *there is nothing you can affect healthily (including your children) until you address your own emotions first.* When we understand this, we are on the way to becoming an evolved parent and leading the way into a new, solid way of being – teaching our children that they can be whole and healthy regardless of what someone else is or isn't doing. When they organically follow where we have already gone, they absorb and emulate our energy shift and start reaping incredible benefits as well.

Let Your Children See You Be Real

Personal evolution means becoming real, self-partnered and being with our emotional traumas, loving and healing them. The old paradigm of telling our children, 'No, I'm fine, nothing is wrong', while thinking we are protecting them, is one of the most dangerous things we can do to their inner being. The reason is because 1) it teaches them to distrust their gut feelings: 'I thought there was something wrong with Mummy, yet she tells me there isn't – so I must be wrong', and 2) we model to them the process of suppressing our emotions and self-abandonment, rather than meeting our emotions and self-soothing, processing and healing them. Both of these are tragic recipes for sabotaging their self-love and relationship success in the future.

In stark contrast, when I see Thrivers be real with their children about what they are going through, their children feel more at ease – they are not stupid, they knew something was wrong! – and they start to respect and admire this parent naturally.

I am not suggesting that we use our children as counsellors, leaning on them emotionally and engulfing them as our emotional saviours – that isn't healthy either. What I am suggesting is for them to see and know that you are meeting you own trauma in order to heal from it, and that you have stepped up to love yourself enough to do that.

It's also healthy to demonstrate to your children that you are creating boundaries and exercising your right to take time to heal yourself, as well as meeting their needs. Be honest with them about what you are feeling rather than hiding this from them. No matter how scary it may be initially for them to see you cry, or hear you wail out your trauma in a healing session, tell them how wonderful and how much a relief it is to be with your painful emotions and release them now.

With you leading the way, you are teaching them that their emotions are sacred, and that they are lovable and acceptable as they are, just for being themselves. Mostly, they will follow your lead, because they will see the incredible transformation that is taking place within you and feel safe and loved because of it.

Casey said this about her four children: 'One of the most positive things I did for my kids was allow them to see me apply self-love and meet my wounds with total humility and honesty. My children began to respect and trust me more than they ever had. I knew this was all about "so within, so without", because this was exactly what I was granting myself. They also started sharing with me their inner feelings about the things that were going on in their lives. We all became much closer than we had ever been. Everyone mattered more to each other.'

I love the inner freedom we grant our children when we give ourselves permission to be real around them. We gift them this message: *none of us is perfect, and there is no requirement to be.* This gives our children the confidence to be real too.

With respect to your adult relationships, the principle of 'being real' is exactly the same. By being yourself and loving who you are – wounds and all – you will start to attract others who 'get' you and love you truly also. No longer will you repress your true self, thinking he or she is unacceptable. All of that changes when you start showing up as real. You start a revolution that helps others know they too are lovable, acceptable and worthy of love.

Your Child's Soul Growth

As a parent, one of the hardest things to get over is forgiving ourselves for what we have put our children through. However, when we move trauma out of our cells and make way for higher knowing and Quantum Truths (which we are intrinsically experiencing when we have cleared enough trauma from our being for them to emerge), we know there have been no mistakes in this. A spiritual belief shared by many people, myself included, is that at a soul level we 'choose' those connections, lessons and opportunities that will grant us the most fertile environment in which to achieve the soul evolution we aspire towards. Then, when we are born, we suffer the amnesia of forgetting this choice and having to reawaken to get that work done. (All the same, I feel is very important to be clear that in no way am I suggesting anyone would consciously choose trauma, just as I want you to understand that in no way am I inferring that the trauma was in any way 'deserved'.)

When we awaken and realise that this is exactly why, as souls, we chose the parents and environment we did, we similarly understand that what is happening with our children, no matter what it looks like, was their choice too at an unconscious soul level. Like us, our children chose their parents for specific reasons.

They too are dealing with unfinished business in their soul journeys, in order to evolve and awaken back to who they really are.

Once we accept this, we can start working with it rather than condemning what has happened to them. And, as always, this acceptance then creates space and power for everything to unfold and heal, thereby taking everyone concerned to a higher level of energy, joy, love and consciousness.

Just like us, our children didn't come in to this life to have it all handed to them on a silver platter. In fact, those children who have been protected and sheltered often have limited personal resources and a diminished ability to self-partner, self-soothe and actualise their life. Many of these children, as adults, gravitate towards controlling partners because they doubt their own resources and are consequently abused (which is my own and so many others' stories with narcissists, exactly!).

We want our children to be healthy, emotionally whole people so that they can partner other healthy people in the future. We want them to be so capable that they DON'T need us! Just as we were granted the challenge of a narcissist to enable us to come home to our true selves, so our children may go through this experience as well – even earlier in their lives – helping them to evolve beyond narcissistic abuse in their relationships in the future. But this can only happen *if we accept the perfection in this* – and lead the way.

This I will tell you: the children of those Thriver parents who do the work and lead the way – including those children who are being parallel-parented with a narcissist – are some of the most incredibly together, evolved, wise and loving kids you could ever hope to meet.

Theresa wrote this about her and her daughter's journey together:

> Olivia suffered terribly when the relationship was falling to pieces and I was still hooked to him. She stayed in her room for almost a year, only venturing out to attend school or college. When I left him and started working with NARP, I came back to life – and so did she. When I almost returned to him, Olivia was the one whose words stopped me in my tracks. She woke me up from my demented nightmarish slumber and I never met or spoke with the narcissist ever again. Olivia has said to me, 'I won't ever let you make this journey alone. God brought us together for a reason: I chose you and you chose me. I know you have called this your burden, but it's ours because the gift is also ours to share.' For anyone who doubts the existence of angels, I can tell you this: one is alive and thriving and she is called Olivia, and I am privileged to call her my daughter.

At the deepest level, our children will heal and change when we do. They will shift out of old, unhelpful paradigms such as:

- 'If I can fix something outside me, I will feel better on the inside, because my emotional health is reliant on the conditions outside me.'

And instead start living the Thriver Model of:

- 'If my greatest goal is to be my most authentic self on the inside, then regardless of what anyone else is or isn't doing, my life works.'

Even if you are parallel-parenting with a narcissist, there is more than mere hope for your child. Time and time again, I have seen the compelling evidence that it only takes one healthy parent for a child to follow their example.

My definition of a healthy parent can be summed up as being somebody for whom the following statement rings true: *I am not going to try to hold the narcissist responsible anymore* [which is like trying to nail jelly to a wall]. *Instead, I am going to invest in my own Thriver Recovery and become the being who heals and then generates a life far beyond the one I was having – even before abuse – regardless of the narcissist.*

If, as a parent, you detach from the narcissist on emotional, physical, spiritual, financial and mental levels, and become a source of all these things within yourself, then your child has every chance of following in your footsteps and doing this too.

The Awakening from Unconscious to Conscious Parenting

Like so many mothers (and fathers) who are dealing with the trauma of shared parenting with a narcissist, Emma stated, 'I'm very concerned about my kids. He is damaging them so much, and my youngest especially, who is sensitive, has now stated he feels worthless and doesn't want to live. I take them to counselling, which they are resisting, and I feel powerless. I'm trying to get them to understand what their father is, and now they are turning against me and yelling at me.' Sadly, at the time she expressed these concerns about her children Emma had yet to dedicate the necessary time to her healing at the deeper inner subconscious level. She wasn't working with NARP and as a result, despite following my articles and YouTube videos, she kept writing on the NARP Support Forum about the same issues, which were firmly embedded and clearly in repeat in her life. She hadn't embodied the missing key: for our life to change, including the lives of our children, we need to change – period!

I think every parent has experienced this: when we try to make our children do something to alleviate our own traumatised feelings about them, they push back and it usually doesn't work. This is where the

Quantum Law – *so within, so without* – can be hardest to follow, yet is so essential to understand, because what is more important than our precious children? This Law states that when we feel terrible about anything, life will keep materialising and reflecting back to us the exact composition of our inner being at that time. If we are traumatised about our children, until we shift those terrible fears inside us, the 'emotion first' instead of trying to enforce change outside ourselves, we will be powerless to help them.

In the same way, when I held on to unhealed trauma about my son, he got worse. He was on a path of complete self-destruction through substance abuse, and as long as I pictured Zac in this terrible, heart-breaking state, he remained there. The more I tried to force change upon him, the more he rebelled against it. The more I saw him as hopeless, wasting his life and destroying himself, the more evidence I received every day of exactly that. All of my lecturing and prescribing was met with resistance, flat refusal and even near-physical rage.

By telling myself that he was broken, directionless and addicted, I wasn't energetically supporting him. At the Quantum level, I was condemning him – and it wasn't until I *let go* of trying to change him, and made him move out (I would no longer accept his abuse), and used Quanta Freedom Healing on myself determinedly to shift all my trauma and fears about him, and nurtured the belief and inner knowing of his 'coming into his own true self-wisdom', and created boundaries with him that fully honoured myself – then, in the space of three short weeks, he experienced a complete turn-around. He emerged from his trance, and ceased his addictions. Something in him had shifted. Zac had started a profound journey of self-development on his own undertaking – and with no pressure from me whatsoever.

Miraculously, on the very day that I reached complete peace about his soul journey – knowing that his inner being would guide him, and that everything was in perfect and divine order – he contacted me only hours later. Later that week we met and I saw that everything had changed within him. Of course, I was delighted and relieved beyond measure, but I wasn't surprised. I had already 'felt' him like that and I knew the change was imminent; I just didn't know it could happen so quickly after months and months of absolute hopeless heartbreak.

As I am writing this section, I thought I would ask Zac directly what was going on for him to change so dramatically, and I recorded his answer *word for word* because I found it so fascinating. He said, 'Even though I was aware of your work, you were a powerless victim when it came to dealing with me. But then you stopped lecturing and prescribing and telling me what to do. Instead you listened to me, and you had shifted into becoming authentic. That was what inspired me into doing my own self-development and to support your cause by joining the MTE mission. You led by example.'

Today, Zac is passionate about helping abuse sufferers, their families and children – and he is CEO of MTE (the acronym for my organisation, Melanie Tonia Evans). And I know with all of my heart that this transformation from who he was into his true self would never have happened if I hadn't shifted myself – there was no coincidence involved.

The incredible Quantum Truth for our children is this: they came from us. Where our energy goes, theirs follows. We have to stop trying to control, fix and heal them, and master instead healing ourselves with regard to them, and honouring our own wellbeing with solid, clear boundaries – and then they can shift into becoming healthy.

Like many others, Daniel had experienced the devastation of alienation from his children, caused by his narcissistic ex-wife. For eight years, his children had turned their backs on him and refused all contact with him. He was never able to unearth why specifically – other than knowing his ex-wife had poisoned them against him with terrible lies.

When Daniel contacted me, he wanted to know what to do with the Quanta Freedom Healings to get his children back in his life. I empathised with Daniel because I have seen so many parents go through the unspeakable trauma of losing their children to narcissists – and I really wanted to help him – so there was nothing to do but to be completely honest with him. I explained, 'You have to release and heal all the anger, trauma and pain that you have about this, and create the space inside you for them to flow back into your life – but you can't need this to happen for you to feel whole. You have to get to the level where you feel whole and in total acceptance of "what is" regardless of the outcome.'

Daniel knew there were many parents in the Thriver Community who had experienced success with NARP when it came to being reunited with their children, so he got to work on himself diligently. Understandably, the process took several months, but he finally reached the point where he felt at peace. He said, 'I feel nothing but love for the situation. Even if my children don't return, I believe everything is as it is meant to be.' Three days after he reported this, his oldest son contacted him, and he is now reunited with all his children and his new grandchild.

Healing By Proxy

There is an even more powerful and potent method – only after we have healed our own traumatised feelings in regard to our children – which we can use to help those we love. I must add in this disclaimer before I explain any further: under no circumstances is this method to be used on narcissistic people, for if you do connect with their inner being deeply in a healing format, you are inviting terrible consequences. (Suffice to say that the people who have used this method to try to heal narcissists have come off very badly.) So now that I hope I have warned you off considering that as a possibility, I'd like to explain to you what 'healing by proxy' is. It is the ability to set the intention with Quanta Freedom Healing that you are using your own inner being (or body) as the vehicle for someone else's inner being (or body) to clear trauma on their behalf.

It is of vital importance that you receive permission to do a healing on another individual in this way. Permission can be obtained from them in person or by asking their Higher Self for permission and using your intuition as to whether or not you receive a 'yes'. Do not proceed without permission, because that would be acting in accordance with your own will, not Divine Will, and it wouldn't work anyway. All that could happen is that you would receive a higher amplification of the pain you are trying to alleviate by changing the other person.

Many people in the Thriver Community have achieved incredible results for their children with healing by proxy. A dear friend of mine, Ian, does regular healing-by-proxy work with those he loves. Healing by proxy can have powerful results on very young children as well. Beatrice, an incredible, brave lady from the NARP Community, started her NARP work in earnest because she was struggling immensely in a narcissistic co-parenting situation. Both she and her son were deeply traumatised and in a desperate state because the abuse and control were so unbearable. It's important to understand that Beatrice was very much on her own; her mother, another narcissist, had cut her off from her family and turned her friendship support network against her. And it gets worse: Beatrice's mother sided with the narcissist ex-partner and paid for his court cases to attack Beatrice too.

Beatrice did extensive work on herself and her son by proxy with NARP and continues to do so diligently. She is a stand-out example of dedication to creating the best life for herself and her son, from the inside out, *against all odds.* She is SO dedicated to her inner work that when I caught up with her for an update about her and her son (see below) she was busy NARP Modulling at the time! I've included all of her testimony here to inspire you and to show that regardless of how terrible your situation and your experience of parallel-parenting are, like Beatrice, you too can turn it around.

This is what Beatrice reported about her and her son's progress from 'then' to 'now':

> Two years ago I was a wreck; I had severe insomnia and nightmares if I did sleep. At that time my son was given the labels of having ADHD, anxiety, depressive symptoms and much more. He was only twelve months old. Now he no longer has these 'labels', which were due to him being triggered terribly with trauma, and I can proudly say that, at the age of thirty-nine, I've never been in better shape physically, mentally and emotionally myself.

Today my son's brilliance is staggering; his comprehension of the entire situation boggles my mind, and his ability to discern situations and 'vote with his feet' have become so obvious that I have very little concern for him navigating the world and his relationship with the narcissist ... and he's not yet four! As I have emerged, my child has shown strength and fortitude well beyond his years. He is thoughtful and highly empathetic, he's quick to express his emotions (I call him 'emotionally agile'!) and he is able to articulate that emotions are just sensations in his body – and he'd rather let them out! He has many wonderful ways in which he does this. After me doing the work on him by proxy, he organically and intuitively started following my lead! I am awed by him every single day and he's just getting brighter and brighter and more and more gorgeous.

We've also got on top of his massive digestive issues. He had a severe leaky gut and was dealing with malabsorption issues. We've all but cleared it by NARP Modulling and then being open to receiving whichever supplement or dietary change is needed next.

He still struggles to sleep some nights after staying at the narcissist's house and he'll wake with nightmares, but these are fewer and further between. And I am relaxed about it, knowing now beyond a doubt that he is divinely guided and protected, and that everything is unfolding for his highest and best. I also know that he is processing it all in a healthy way and that none of it appears to be getting 'stuck' anymore. It truly is miraculous.

Money has been an issue, as with most narcissistic abuse cases. However, after much up-levelling work, we are about to move into a long-term housesit in a gorgeous palatial home, virtually rent free! So we will be able to recover the financial losses and really leap forward in life. The boundaries with the narcissist are firmly in place; there hasn't been a 'breach' in ... well I can't even remember the last time I was triggered by him, and I don't care to!

I think you will agree that Beatrice's courage, determination and commitment to saving herself and her son have been nothing short of epic. I couldn't help but share this story to the world to help rescue all our children.

I realise it may nevertheless be hard to understand what healing by proxy is, so I would like to offer you an exercise for it. However, the following exercise is only to be performed on your child if you have already been working on yourself to lose your fears concerning them. Step 1 can be used to do that: releasing and shifting 'what hurts the most right now', which in this instance will be the fear for your child. When you can no longer feel it in your body, then you can consider doing proxy work.

The reason you must work on your fear in your body first is this: *so within, so without;* if you try to change someone else so that you feel better, it won't work. You will only create more of what you are feeling for them – and they will resist all of your attempts, even energetically, to make them better if it's primarily to assuage your own inner feelings.

EXERCISE: HEALING BY PROXY

1. Go to a quiet space where you will not be disturbed and take some time to relax and breathe deeply and slowly for a few minutes.

2. Set the intention that you will be using your body as a proxy for [your child's name]. Then ask [your child's] Higher Self for permission to do this healing. Intuitively you will receive a 'yes' or 'no'. Do not proceed if you receive a 'no'.

3. Your body is now your child's body: you have energetically taken on their inner being. Ask for the first wound to appear that can be cleared to help this situation. You will feel it in your body. All you need to do is connect to the feeling of it. You don't need to go into further details.

4. While fully feeling the trauma in the part of the body where it resides, say: 'I bless and accept you, and I now give you permission to go back to the Light.'

5. Release the trauma in the same way that you have been working with your own traumas: sending it up and out through the top of your head, and back to Life/Source/Creation for recycling. See it dissolve to native nothingness.

6. Bring down the ball of Light, which corresponds with Life/Source/Creation, from above your head and fill the space inside you where that trauma once was. Know that this Light is the healing and resolution of this previous trauma. Feel the relief.

7. Check in to see whether the trauma has cleared. Can you still feel it in your body? If you can, go into it and repeat the process in stage 4. Keep clearing until it is gone.

8. Ask for the next trauma which can be cleared to light up in your body. And repeat the process until they are all cleared.

9. State the following: 'This healing is now complete and everyone is now returned to their own consciousness and space.' Imagine and intend that disconnection.

As parents, it is far too tempting for us to start wanting to investigate, meddle and circumnavigate what is happening for our children, whereas the greatest gift we can ever give them is to NOT do that and become the solution inside ourselves so that they can rise up and meet us at that level instead. This happens when we start to perceive them and approach them in the form of their true self.

You will be astounded at the changes that happen for those you love by doing these healings. I often do proxy healing for those I love, and the results startle even me: there are far too many coincidences of people 'getting better' at exactly the same time the healing was being performed. Some of these people have asked me for help, and others don't know (consciously) that I did the healing on them. You can assist those you love with any issue in their life, including health, because once the responsible trauma is released, their inner being starts generating wellbeing.

How We Become Different Parents

Here follows a list of the most significant changes that occur in our parenting and the way in which we manage our relationships, when we take the responsibility for healing our own wounds.

We no longer:

- Hold our children responsible for our emotions.

- Try to fix, lecture or prescribe to our children.

- Compete for or try to win our children's love and affection.

- Require our children to think or be a certain way for us to be healthy.

- Carry guilt and regret about what we did to our children.

- Blame and shame our children's inner identities with the messages such as 'you are wrong'.

Instead, we begin to:

- Accept and bless the growth lessons our children go through and support them with love and space, instead of judgement and control.

- Teach our children by example that their inner state isn't dependent on what others are or aren't doing.

- Model for our children authenticity: vulnerability, honesty and humility.

- Apologise with genuine remorse about any aspects of our previous parenting that may have hurt them; we take full responsibility – admitting and apologising – if we are hurtful to them from here on.

- Allow our children to have a voice and seek to listen and validate them without judgement.

- Uphold healthy boundaries that don't involve lecturing and prescribing, but are enforced with firm, clear and loving actions – which state 'that behaviour was unacceptable' rather than 'you are unacceptable.'

And most of all, we:

- Grant trust and space and 'see' and 'feel' that our children have the inner resources and wisdom to find their way, and

- Empower our children so that they do not need us.

It's up to us, as parents, to break the cycles of abuse/abused for our children and future generations. Then, unlike us, they won't stay enmeshed and attached to others, trying to force people to love and accept them, and wasting years of their lives through resenting those people who don't grant them the commodities they are not yet actualising for themselves.

By becoming self-actualised and empowered, they will be like those HLG (High Licking and Grooming) rats who went on to be the parents of healthy, emotionally secure offspring. In a human sense, this is the ability to self-partner, self-soothe, trust and honour the self, be real, speak up, set boundaries, identify and ask for what we want and need, and leave and carry on as a whole person if something or someone is not a match for us. All of these ingredients, which the Thriver Way promotes, offer the capacity to generate healthy relationships with self, life and others.

Your children and your children's children can and will start embodying this *now* – but only if you lead the way first. If you don't, they will be left with the only option that we had: to crash and burn as adults and do the hard work later.

If there is just one thing I would like you to take from this chapter, if not the whole book, it is this vital message, which is summed up in these three simple words: *Heal Yourself First.*

Because then it can all follow.

19

THE THRIVER MISSION

As a Thriver, I am forever dedicated to my own growth and expansion – to be the most trauma-free, complete person that I can be. Initially, of course, this was a necessity in order to survive: I was not going to be able to continue living unless I followed this path. However, the Thriver lifestyle became for me about so much more than mere (yet absolutely necessary) survival. It became a way of life through which I was able to release myself forever from limitations, fears and confusions, and to surprise myself again and again with just how glorious, free and abundant both my inner and outer life could become.

But, of course, this certainly didn't happen immediately. There was a very consistent dedicated process I took to heal, which was so worth it. And I shudder to think what would have happened if I hadn't! I wouldn't have lived, my son probably wouldn't have either, and, even if he had, our future generations would have been stuck with tons of trauma, and the Thriver Mission – my true soul calling – would never have come about. And we certainly wouldn't be having this conversation now!

Moving Beyond Mere Survival into True Thriving

If you feel like you are only just surviving at any given moment, there is no shame in that whatsoever. I promise there is no judgement from myself or our Community regarding anywhere that you are at. However, I and the MTE team are absolutely passionate about continuing to offer you the tools and ways to get past survival mode into true Thriving – if you choose to accept them.

Moving from 'survival' to 'creation' (i.e. Thriving) is a Quantum concept. As neuroscientist Joe Dispenza describes in his workshop 'Breaking the Habit of Being Yourself', it is when we release the trauma energy that was stuck inside us (which focused us on survival), that this same energy is unleashed and available for Creation.

Many of us get to the point with narcissistic abuse when even our survival no longer seems viable. Jayne explains: 'Things had got so bad for me, survival was no longer an option. I was where many people end up in narcissistic abuse, totally broken and suicidal. I was face to face with the make-or-break choice. I am so relieved I chose to face my wounds and heal them, otherwise they were going to take me out.'

Of course there are those people who can and do continue through life as 'survivors'. (And I take my hat off to you, because, like Jayne, I couldn't have continued living with my wounds either!) But is merely surviving enough? Can we go for more? I totally believe we can, and I hope as a result of reading this book that you now believe you can too.

The orientation of the Thriver Way is to say that 'mere survival', which means living with the ongoing symptoms of narcissistic abuse – such as PTSD, agoraphobia, nervous-system problems and mental and emotional traumas, other probable health issues, as well as a diminished trust in self, others and life – is not the highest expression that we can extract from this experience. And I am certainly not just talking about people stuck with narcissists. The symptoms that I've just described are traditionally – and indefinitely – suffered by those who escape narcissists also.

This Community takes the stand that when we experience a breakdown on the magnitude of those caused by narcissistic abuse (which is off the Richter scale), then the evolution, growth, joy and freedom – the breakthrough – we reach on the other side should be just as impactful. We uphold that we are going through an intense transformation, nothing short of a death–rebirth process which entails transforming the old self and becoming our new true self. In order to achieve this, we have to take the healing journey to a deeper level: beyond 'what' happened to us and into 'why' this happened to us.

As Thrivers, as soon as we turn our attention inwards and give up self-condemnation, replacing it with fascination, inner seeking, self-partnering and healing, we have turned a very big corner. We are on our way to releasing the toxic trauma of our painful life in order to make way for major healing. This is the real shift from merely trying to manage symptoms, to healing deeply at the core so that there are no more symptoms to have to manage.

Facing our painful emotions is challenging at first, because we have been trained to self-avoid at all costs. 'Try not to think about it' and 'focus on something positive' were the messages we received, and of course we have self-medicated with food, alcohol, sex, Facebook, TV and sleeping – anything other than face our traumas and heal them. And the cost has been hefty, because we have not been able to self-soothe, heal and manage our emotions. We assigned other people to do that for us – people who didn't do this and who instead made us irrefutably aware of the trauma we had previously attempted to bury deep in our subconsciousness.

When we do self-partner and seek to rid ourselves of trauma in order to Thrive, we discover some very interesting things; for example, the sorts of judgements, anxieties and depressions that are a part of life when things do not go as intended (irrespective of abuse) start to become exciting catalysts for discovering and releasing more parts of ourselves that are not in alignment with our dreams and the life we wish to lead. Then we see instant shifts. We start making healthier choices about what and who we seek and partner with. We start easily rejecting anything that is not heathy for us – and we punch the air with excitement that we are finally generating our own lives in ways that work and make sense!

That is what Thriving is all about.

I'd love to share with you now the Thriver Principles we start living our life by once we release the traumas that have been preventing us from being our true selves (see overleaf).

So, I hope you can understand that recovering from narcissistic abuse is just the beginning! The Thriver Message is about much more than surviving narcissism. It is a message to help us and our world get well. It is about a bigger picture – a Quantum spiritual perspective that connects us to our true selves and to our birth right, the infinite consciousness and the Life Force of wellbeing which can now flow through us *as we are.*

THRIVER PRINCIPLES

• If trauma is in my body, it is mine to self-partner and heal.

• My relationship with myself is the foundation for all my relationships.

• Whatever people show me as missing and hurtful is representative of what is still missing from, and hurtful between, me and my inner being.

• Anyone who shows up to hurt me is an A.I.D. ('Angel in Disguise') posing as an abuser to help make my unconscious parts conscious, so that I can finally heal them and live as my true self. (And if this person had not come forth, another would have been needed to take their place.)

• When things go wrong in my life, it is perfect, it was all meant to be. Old orders must be let go of, in order to make way for the new order.

• Every time I experience, find and release a trauma in my body – no matter what it is – I graduate to the next highest, most expanded version of myself.

• I have nothing new to learn about how to be an integrated being. When I release my trauma, I simply come home to being what I am – an organically integrated being.

• When I am my authentic self, speaking the truth, having the difficult conversations and honouring the promptings of my inner being (including being willing to lose it all to get it all), I become a powerful light which dissolves and repels all darkness.

• By being radiantly me, without need, expectation or conditions, I am blessed beyond my wildest

> dreams and will flourish and am nourished abundantly.

The Results of the Thriver Mission

I am thrilled beyond measure that this way of life has created a real solution which has allowed me and so many others to free ourselves from inner trauma and toxic people for good, and to enjoy life and relationships at levels that simply were not accessible to us before Thriver Recovery.

After experiencing my own struggle to stay one step ahead of anxiety and depression, and then being faced with a breakdown from which I was told I would never recover, I am passionate about helping people understand *there is another way to heal.* A simpler, much more direct path: namely, when we release the trauma from within, we organically start to get well in ways and timeframes that we may never have believed were possible.

This is where Quanta Freedom Healing comes into play; for myself, it proved to be the super-tool that ended my search for something 'out there' that could help me. It was the only way I was able to break through and unearth the origins of my trauma programmes and release them forever. I am happy to say that today I receive emails from all over the world, reporting the same thing: unprecedented and glorious reversals of agonising emotional, mental, physical, spiritual and financial crises, the effects of which people previously thought they would have to try to survive indefinitely. At the time of writing, over 20,000 people have graduated from NARP and transformed their lives, and many more are discovering and working on the Modules with incredible results. Here are some of these people's stories:

> I was raised by a narcissistic mother but my most recent relationship, where I was engaged to be married, was by far the worst. It nearly killed me. I was suicidal – ruined emotionally and abused financially and sexually. In August 2016, things came to a head and I was hospitalised for seven weeks in a psychiatric clinic, and diagnosed with PTSD and severe depression. It was in hospital that I found your work and joined the NARP Program and started feeling relief and big shifts very quickly. I had told my psychiatrist about NARP and she was very encouraging. We agreed that instead of doing inpatient therapy groups, I could just do NARP Modules in my room and that would be more beneficial for me, because I had been making such good progress. In the last three months I have become a new person: I am completely free of PTSD and I feel no depression. I am consistently, daily, filled with so much joy and gratitude and love for life, I don't recognise myself. After seven months off work, I am back working part-time and I am in training for a

second job, which is perfect for me right now. I dance around and jump for joy every single day at home on my own! I am absolutely a source to myself. I thought I was too broken to ever be fixed. Clearing out the pain of the subconscious was the answer. IS the answer. I am a true believer.

Vanessa

There were days that I thought my pain and suffering were permanent and unsurvivable. I just thought I was crazy and everything was my fault. My life fell apart. I lost my job, my friends, my health, my dignity and gave up on life when I was discarded by my NPD partner. I found myself in the worst situation life could bring. Then I found Melanie and she is literally saving my life. Melanie's programs are nothing short of a miracle. I will be grateful for the rest of my life.

Laura

I started the NARP Program on Sunday – and have been completing two Module One healings a day, and I can feel such a powerful shift and healing unfolding. My love addiction/addiction to narcissists has blighted my life to date and I have tried everything! I am also a trainee psychotherapist and nothing I have come across before works like this does. THANK YOU. I am so looking forward to experiencing the rest of the program and to up-levelling my life.

Sarah

It is so exciting that not only is there a way to reset our inner beings and lives back to wellbeing and love, but we can now be the source, the overflow, the ripple effect which creates profound and dramatic positive changes in our environment and for the people we love. Together, we have the ability to change ourselves, the patterns and the old order that we have come from – including the trauma of abuse and abused – to midwife a more conscious and loving world.

What Can You Do to Be a Part of the Thriver Mission?

So many beautiful Thrivers in the Community ask, 'How can I help others who are stuck to Thrive too?' My answer is always the same: 'Remain dedicated to freeing yourself from trauma and simply become more of your true self.' Because, when we do this, we start living our true life. We impact everything effectively and gracefully; we parent lovingly, we play 'team' cooperatively, we lead inspirationally. One person at a time, we start to change our world. And we connect organically to our highest aspirations and true calling. So many people know there is a mission inside them, yet struggle to find it, trust themselves or connect to it. I can't tell you how many Thrivers in this Community have found their callings and are now presently basking in the joy and success of them – their personal *dharma* (a Sanskrit word which means our essential nature of character, and which I believe means finding our greatest happiness and purpose) started to flow from them when they became their true self; it was simply an extension of who they started *being*.

Deb, a NARP member, wrote this:

> I've been in your community for a while, and I'm thriving beyond my wildest imagination. I am sixty-three years of age and my healing started by my fully focusing on totally disengaging from the narcissist, and healing my unhealed parts up to maturity and health so that I could become the best version of myself possible. I just began a whole new career of life-guarding, teaching people of all ages how to swim and water-aerobics aquatic classes. I love it! This is despite having a myriad of previous health conditions, from a spinal fusion, knee surgery gone wrong, neck and spine ablations, chronic stress complaints, fibromyalgia, osteoarthritis and more. I could barely move or function, but as a result of clearing the horrendous trauma that was trapped inside me, all of it – without exception – has disappeared.

Deb concludes with words of wisdom that really sum up the message here: 'I only hope I can be a shining light to others from your light and heart. Give to self first, then the natural path will lead you to giving to others. It's the Law, Quantum style.'

Without doubt, when we become our true self, everything else unfolds in perfect and divine order: there is space for new opportunities to come to us, and we are free enough from trauma to follow our hearts at last.

Where to Start

Of course, first things first. You may presently be struggling with trauma on a daily basis, which is exhausting and terrifying – and there could be many days when you think it might never end. You might have read this book and thought, 'I'm not better yet.' For most of us, there is no short cut to doing the work of meeting and releasing our inner trauma.

Back when I was completely immersed in the early stages of my journey, there were many times when I thought, 'I just want this to be over', and 'How long will this take before I am well?' It took time to learn unconditional love for myself, which meant accepting and blessing myself and the journey no matter what stage I was at. My level of trauma was such that I spent a good twelve months wailing out the wounds almost daily – letting them go and replacing them with Source Energy – on my sitting-room couch. (It may be less intense for you or even more so. Everyone's layers of trauma reflect their individual experience.) That may seem like an excruciating process, but I promise you that the alternative of trying to 'survive' my wounds was unliveable – as was the prospect of facing them indefinitely. What was twelve months of deep inner work, to be living the life I have now? A blink of an eye – truly. I also discovered the incredible warmth, devotion and love I gained for myself as a result of self-partnering for that period of time. It granted me what I had always wanted: *someone to love me.* No longer would that ever be missing from my life – because I became self-love.

People often ask me if I still do healings on myself. Absolutely I do whenever I feel out of sorts; in fact, on the way to the café today to finish this last chapter, I let go of some inner wounds to do with 'the pressure of deadlines' that was manifesting as anxiety and I felt calm and spacious inside – and my writing is flowing as I finish the first draft of this book. For me, Quanta Freedom Healing is my way of life – and always will be. Long gone are the days when I thought my mind could effectively work out my emotional issues! Nowadays my body, my inner being, is always where my most powerful change takes place.

A burning question you may have is: 'If I do the healings, when will I start finding relief and feeling better?' My personal experience, as well as that of many others, is that we soon start seeing some rapid, positive shifts in our lives. It's Quantum Law: *so within, so without.* When we release trauma and replace it with Source Energy, our outer circumstances (as well as our emotional state) start to match the newly anchored wellbeing inside us. Most people experience startling shifts within months or even just weeks or days – and sometimes even instantly – after working with the NARP healings. Countless people report a profound feeing of relief and hope even after only one session with Step 1.

Yet, even so, there is dedicated work to do and we know this because the trauma will keep coming up until we are free of it. And I promise you this: by the time we have experienced a narcissistic abuse situation – that make-or-break soul deal which brings us to our knees, no longer able to carry on as normal – there is a lot of inner work to be done. Quanta Freedom Healing may be the closest thing to a magic bullet that I have ever known, but we still have to make our healing a very high priority in terms of committing the time and space to work on it.

The great thing is that you don't have to do this alone. You now belong to a tribe, an incredible group of people who understand exactly what you have suffered and what you are going through. As Thrivers, we know it is vital to stay connected to people who can boost, support and inspire us to keep going on our healing journey. In the Thriver Community, there is a unique ethos of forward moving and of sharing supportive and self-loving tools, resources and tips to help you heal the only person you can: yourself. We also provide ongoing support for you, so when the narcissist becomes a distant memory in your life (and it feels like it all happened to someone else and not you), we provide you with the tools to Thrive in every part of your life going forward, so that you can fulfil the dreams that are your personal birth right.

I want you to know, from my heart to yours, that you are now a part of something great: a movement that has gathered incredible momentum and is literally changing the dynamic of abuse/abused for us and for our future generations.

Another beautiful by-product after coming out the other side of narcissistic abuse and Thriving in your abuse-free life is helping others so that they don't have to go through the same hardship you did. Because when you hatch from the cocoon and spread your wings, you will recognise your abundant light and gifts that the world needs and only you can give.

I can't wait for you to Thrive with your Tribe!

NOTES

Part One

[1]   Quoted at: http://bigthink.com/philip-perry/the-bad-newstrauma-can-be-inherited-the-good-news-so-can-resilience.

[2]   See: I.C. Weaver, N. Cervoni, F.A. Champagne, A.C. D'Alessio, S. Sharma, J.R. Seckl, S. Dymov, M. Szyf, M.J. Meaney (August 2004). 'Epigenetic Programming by Maternal Behavior'. In: *Nature Neuroscience* 7(8): 847–54. doi:10.1038/nn1276. PMID 15220929.

Chapter 3. Why We Attract Narcissists

[1]   From the poem 'Shadow and Light Source Both' in *The Essential Rumi* (new expanded edition), HarperCollins, 2004, edited and translated by Coleman Barks.

Chapter 5. What Happens to You When You Are Abused

[1]   Bessel van der Kolk, *The Body Keeps the Score,* Viking, 2014, p.206.

[2]   Quoted in an interview with Fractal Enlightenment: https://fractalenlightenment.com

344

/32650/life/understanding-theconscious-subconscious-mind-with-bruce-lipton.

[3] *The Body Keeps the Score,* p.60.

[4] Quoted at www.brucelipton.com/resource/article/epigenetics.

[5] *What the Bleep Do We Know!?* (US/2004), written by William Arntz, Matthew Hoffman, Betsy Chasse and Mark Vicente.

[6] Candace Pert, *Your Body is Your Subconscious Mind,* Sounds True, 2005 (audiobook). See also: www.azquotes.com/author/24367-Candace_Pert.

[7] From Dr Joe Dispenza, *Breaking the Habit of Being Yourself – How to Lose Your Mind and Create a New One,* Author's Republic, 2016.

[8] Quoted at www.thetahealing.com/about-thetahealing/thetahealing-theta-state.html.

[9] Bruce Lipton, *7 Ways to Reprogram Your Subconscious Mind.* See: www.youtube.com/watch?v=_xz1HrGG8cc.

[10] Candace Pert, *Molecules of Emotion: Why You Feel the Way You Feel,* Simon and Schuster, 2012, p.269.

[11] *The Body Keeps the Score,* p.208.

Part Two

[1] Maya Angelou, 'Still I Rise', in *And Still I Rise,* Virago Press, 1986 (reprinted 2009).

[2] *The Body Keeps the Score,* p.47.

[3] Ibid., p.249.

Chapter 7. Release the Immediate Pain and Feelings of Loss

[1] Amy F.T. Arnsten, 'Stress Signalling Pathways that Impair Prefrontal Cortex Structure and Function'. In *Nature Reviews Neuroscience.* Jun 2009, 10(6): 410–422.

[2] Due Quach, 'What is Brain 3.0 and Why Do We Need More of It?' https://medium.com/@duequ ach/what-isbrain-3-0-and-why-do-we-need-more -of-it-173f95bfbc05, 18 January 2017.

[3] Louise Hay, *Life!: Reflections on Your Journey,* Hay House, 1995, p.179.

Chapter 9. Forgive Yourself and Life for What You Have Been Through

[1] Quoted in Gurmit Singh, *History of Sikh Struggles,* Atlantic, 1989, p.189.

[2]   Quoted at www.louisehay.com/101-best-louise-h
ay-positiveaffirmations.

[3]   Scott Barry Kaufman, 'Turning Adversity into
Creative Growth', 6 May 2013. Published on
blogs. scientificamerican.com/beautiful-minds/tur
ning-adversityinto-creative-growth.

Chapter 13. Connect to the Gift of Your Own Spiritual Empowerment

[1]   Marianne   Williamson,   *A   Return   to   Love,*
HarperCollins, 1992, p.190.

Chapter 14. Release and Heal the Fear of the Narcissist – and Whatever He or She May Do Next

[1]   *The Body Keeps the Score,* p.208.

Chapter 15. Release and Heal the Connection to the Narcissist

[1]   Quoted in Alex Podowski, 'Healthy vs. Unhealthy
Relationships: A Therapeutic Approach'. Published
on https://joinblush.com/healthy-vs-unhealthy-r
elationships.

[2]   Alethia Luna and Mateo Sol, *Awakened Empath: The Ultimate Guide to Emotional, Psychological and Spiritual Healing,* Create Space, 2017, p.00.

GLOSSARY

A.I.D.: an 'Angel in Disguise' posing as an abuser, to help us become aware of those unconscious parts of ourselves such as buried trauma.

beta brainwaves: brainwaves of the alert conscious mind when attention is focused on cognitive tasks such as problem-solving and decision-making.

co-dependency: emotional and/or psychological reliance on another person, often in a one-sided relationship.

conditional love: based on the notion we are only worth loving if our behaviour meets with the expectations of others.

conscious parenting: perceiving and connecting with the true selves of our children, rather than trying to lead their lives for them.

CRAP: the fear of criticism, rejection, abandonment or punishment.

dendrite: a branched extension of a nerve cell that conducts impulses to the cell body.

epigenetic: changes in an organism caused by modification of gene expression rather than alteration of the genetic code.

false self: a façade created as a buffer against the pain of trauma and inner emptiness.

fight-or-flight response: a state of hyperarousal in response to a perceived threat.

grey rock: being as bland and uninteresting as possible so a narcissist won't receive narcissistic supply from you.

healing by proxy: means of using your own inner being as the vehicle for healing someone else's inner being and clearing trauma on their behalf.

Higher Power: an unconditionally loving universal force. **hoovering (narcissistic):** attempts by a narcissist to suck you back into a relationship with them for more narcissistic supply

informational healing: methods of healing which rely on an information exchange at the cognitive level rather than transforming the subconscious.

inner being/inner child: the inner being refers to the inner experience of our body, where our subconscious is operating at a cellular being, while the inner child refers to those young, unhealed and underdeveloped parts of ourselves that lie within our inner being.

journaling: the practice of keeping a diary or journal to explore thoughts and feelings.

karma: the spiritual principle of cause and effect whereby the emotional composition of a person influences that individual's future.

Life/Source/Creation: see 'Higher Power'; other terms referring to the concept of a unconditionally loving universal force.

Modified Contact: detaching emotionally from the narcissist as much as possible in circumstances where practical considerations mean there has to be some contact.

Narcissistic Abuse Recovery Program (NARP): a step-by-step process designed to work at a Quantum level and create liberation from narcissistic abuse.

narcissistic injury: a perceived threat to a narcissist's fragile self-esteem or self-worth.

narcissistic supply: factors such as affection, attention, acclaim, material possessions and wealth, as well as being granted significance including being feared, which are used to bolster the narcissist's fragile false self.

neuropeptide: protein-like molecules used by neurons to communicate with each other.

No Contact: the practice of cutting off all forms of communication with the narcissist.

parallel-parenting: caring for a child while disengaging from the other parent, and having limited direct contact with each other.

past life: an earlier incarnation in which a soul was born into a different body.

post-traumatic stress disorder (PTSD): a condition of persistent mental and emotional stress occurring as a result of injury or severe psychological shock.

prefrontal cortex: a brain region associated with cognitive behaviours, personality expression, decision making and moderating social behaviour.

Quanta Freedom Healing: a unique healing system that creates Thriver Recovery.

Quantum Law: the law of energy that underpins all of creation, which is: *so within, so without.*

self-actualise: the realisation and/or fulfilment of our innate talents and potential.

self-partner: to 'be' with our inner emotions with love and without judgement.

self-soothe: to accept, support and process emotions to a healthy resolution.

shift: a profound inner change, in which we free ourselves from a specific level of trauma.

somatic: relating to the body, as distinct to the mind.

stinking thinking: on-going negative thoughts connected to the painful nature of inner trauma.

symbiotic: interaction between two different organisms living in close physical association.

theta brainwaves: occurring most often in sleep but also in deep meditation, brainwaves that boost learning, memory and intuition.

Thriver: a member of the global Thriver Community who has experienced the life-changing healing offered by NARP.

tie-cutting: using a visualisation or meditative process to undo the unhealthy emotional connections we have with others.

transformational healing: healing that works within our inner being to achieve a major internal shift.

true self: the self we are beyond all the trauma, who expresses our full potential and is in alignment with Life/Source/Creation.

unconditional love: love that is freely given, without expectations or demands.

visualisation: a healing technique based on imagining an image of something.

FURTHER READING

Dr Joe Dispenza, *Breaking The Habit Of Being Yourself – How To Lose Your Mind and Create a New One,* Author's Republic, 2016.

Louise Hay, *Life!: Reflections on Your Journey,* Hay House, 1995.

Alethia Luna and Mateo Sol, *Awakened Empath: The Ultimate Guide to Emotional, Psychological and Spiritual Healing,* Create Space, 2017.

Candace Pert, *Your Body is Your Subconscious Mind,* Sounds True, 2005.

Candace Pert, *Molecules of Emotion: Why You Feel the Way You Feel,* Simon and Schuster, 2012.

Bessel van der Kolk, *The Body Keeps the Score,* Viking, 2014.

Brian Weiss, *Many Lives, Many Masters,* Piatkus, 1994.

Marianne Williamson, *A Return to Love,* HarperCollins, 1992.

ACKNOWLEDGEMENTS

My journey from abused to survivor to Thriver has been one that I feel so blessed to have accomplished, and I know it is one that many Angels have been co-creating with me!

It would be impossible for me to list all the people who played a part in this book being possible, but I will try my best. First of all, Mum and Dad: you provided for me the powerful combination of learning the great values of integrity, wholesomeness and strength, along with all the other gritty bits that were needed for my healing and development. I am so thrilled to have the relationship that I do now with you both as a result of the spectacular journey we took together. I love you both eternally, dearly.

To my son Zac: you are my greatest teacher. In my times of darkness, you were my light. And I was so privileged and humbled to be the same for you in your time of deep despair, and to grant you a way out as you did for me, so that you could shine. I will never forget your words, which pulled me out of the fog: 'Mum, I know this was meant to be and you will be better than you have ever been.' That, my darling son, is *always how I see you.* I can't think of any person as the CEO of MTE who I would rather be sharing the Thriver Mission with; you inspire me and make me proud of you every day.

So much love and thank you's to Susan Goldman, who some years ago reached out to me from Los Angeles, passionately, to help share my work and save more lives. Through Susan I was introduced to some of the most influential global thought leaders in personal development, who then brought my healing system to their communities. Susan was instrumental in my being able to extend my reach to touch even more lives, and to this day is a beautiful, dear friend and fellow Thriver. You were an Angel sent at exactly the right time, Susan!

Likewise, I can't thank Theresa Cheung enough for reaching out to me all the way from the UK, begging me to get someone to publish my book. Theresa then tirelessly set out to help me and Zac find the right publishers and get the process started. Her support, love and guidance have been second to none, and I would go as far as to say, Theresa, sweetheart, you were the absolute Angel needed to bring this book to life and I feel blessed to have you as my dear Thriver sister and friend. Words cannot express the gratitude Zac and I feel for you!

I want to say a special thank you to Katherine Woodward Thomas, Jeanine Staples and Dr Christiane Northrup, who have become dear friends and colleagues, for shining the way forward as they do with this principle I adore: *we can heal our lives from the inside out.* All of you ladies inspired me incredibly before I had the absolute privilege of meeting and working with you. Also to Carol Allen: thank you for determinedly getting behind my work and introducing me to some wonderful soul sisters – including Arielle Ford and Claire Zammit. I am so grateful for your belief and support.

To my Quantum neuroscience heroes Dr Joe Dispenza, Dr Bruce Lipton and the late Dr Candace Pert: thank you for challenging the status quo and for showing us how we human organisms can change our lives, rather then just try to live with our dis-eases. I am thrilled to be living in the times when your information can help wake us up to the truth. Included in this incredible list of thought leaders, changing how we heal from trauma, is Dr Bessel van der Kolk: thank you for your revolutionary work.

Thank you, Jo Lal and the Watkins team, for seeing and feeling my vision and getting behind this book with your expertise. I am so excited to see where this journey will take us!

Sue Lascelles, my editor: your diligence, patience and ability to grasp Quantum principles have made our working together on this book a pleasure! I am so blessed to have had you involved in this project; it's all been perfect!

It's important to me that I also acknowledge my beautiful MTE team, who are not only my work colleagues but my dearest friends. A special thank you to Harry Springford-Williams for your heart, support and belief in this mission, and your hilarious humour which never fails to have us all in stitches!

Also Claire Scott: you astound me with your tireless dedication, belief, soul and application to this mission. I know you love your work and it truly loves you! Sandra Newson: thank you for your incredible vision, duty and how you have brought so much to MTE! We adore having you as a part of our Thriver family.

There are many of you now – extra support staff, moderators, Thrivers and also the incredible members of our Community who regularly contribute and inspire others – it's you that I live and breathe for. I am so proud of us all for taking on the challenge of becoming the change we want to see in our lives, our world and our children, and lovingly, unconditionally holding the space for every one of us, no matter where we are on this path.

We are all in this together.

I am so blessed to have the best job in the world, and I am surrounded by Angels everywhere.

Melanie

Made in the USA
Middletown, DE
08 April 2022

63900112R00216